From the longtime Sonoma County farm family beh
Duck, a comprehensive guide to everything you
cooking duck. With over eighty recipes from the farm kitchen and more than fifty of the country's top chefs and butchers, this indispensable cookbook takes the mystery out of cooking the sometimes-intimidating waterfowl.

It begins with clear, concise instructions on mastering all the basics, from breaking down the bird, the secrets to crispy skin, preparing stock, and making duck leg confit to rendering fat, smoking duck breasts, and more. A collection of must-have charcuterie recipes along with irresistible starters, soups, salads, main courses, and (even) desserts follows, each with a complementary drink pairing. Kick off a cocktail party with Hatcho Miso Duck Liver Pâté, Smokey Black Cardamom Duck Momos, or Duck Carnitas Tacos, or enjoy an alfresco lunch of Crispy Duck, Kumquat, and Date Salad with Pistachios or Tangy Duck Noodle Salad with Herbs and Cucumber. For a weeknight family dinner, sit down to Duck Sugo Cavatelli with Herbs and Orange Zest, Duck Jambalaya, or Granny's Duck Meat Loaf. Pull out all the stops with Duck Confit Basteeya or Roasted Maple-Glazed Duck with Butternut Squash Hash for a special occasion. And no meal is complete without a decadent dessert, such as Duck Egg Custards with Plum Compote or Double Chocolate Duck Fat Cabernet Cake.

With its wealth of recipes celebrating global flavors and its stunning photography of the food, the farm, and Northern California's legendary wine country, *The Whole Duck* provides all the information and inspiration you will need to start cooking duck like a pro.

WELCOME

LIBERTY DUCKS

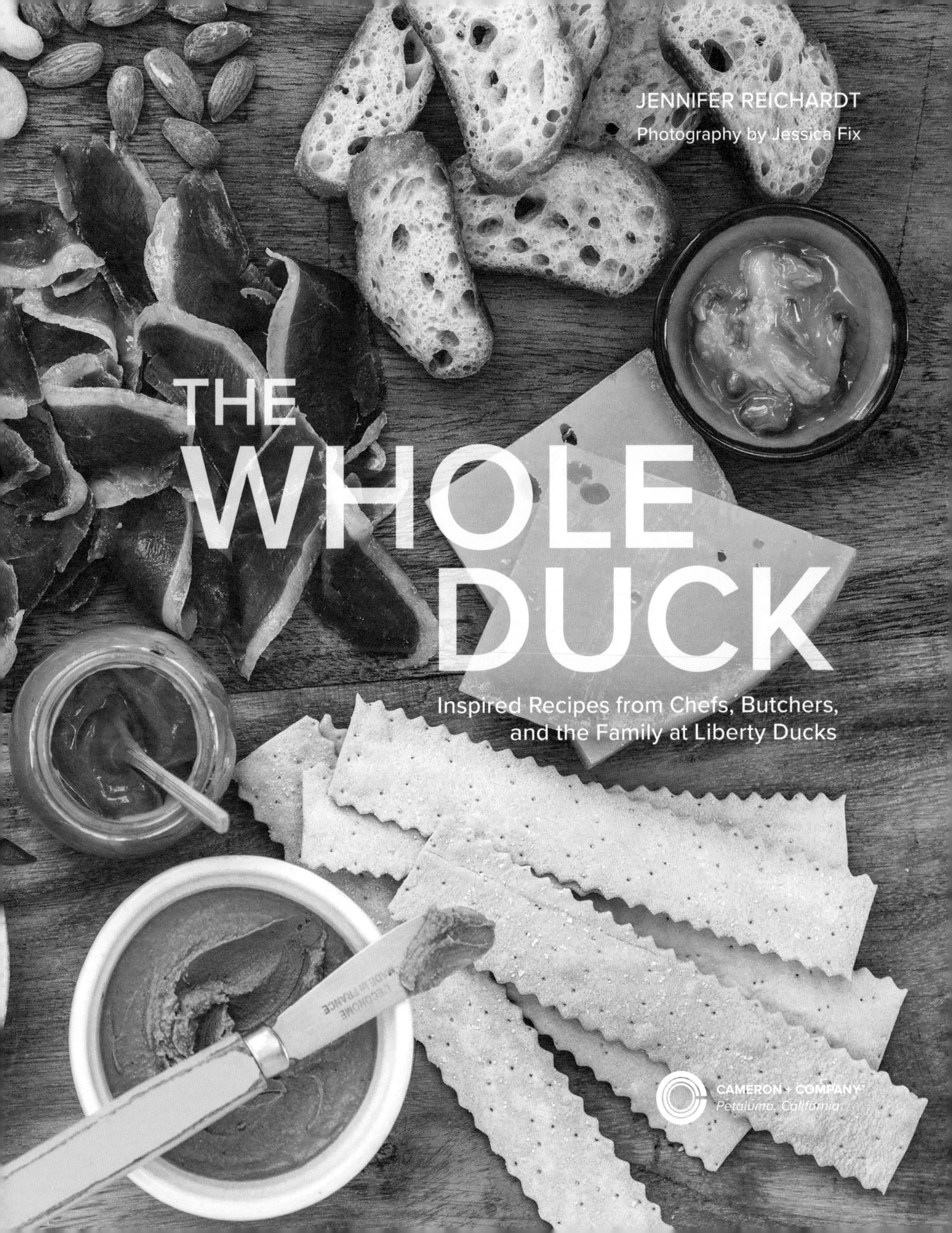

JENNIFER REICHARDT
Photography by Jessica Fix

THE WHOLE DUCK

Inspired Recipes from Chefs, Butchers, and the Family at Liberty Ducks

CAMERON + COMPANY
Petaluma, California

CONTENTS

FOREWORD

When I think of duck, I think of fourth-generation duck farmer Jim Reichardt and his Liberty Ducks. That's just how it's been for me for as long as I can remember. Raised in an open environment on straw bedding in the mild climate of Sonoma County, Jim's ducks are the best in the country.

Let's start with the basics. Duck is an amazing animal that I think of as a flying pig or the unicorn of birds. Perhaps most important, it is almost 100 percent usable: the feathers will keep you warm in jackets and comforters and the meat, fat, skin, offal, and bones all have delicious uses.

But Liberty Ducks—aka Sonoma County Poultry—is more than just its remarkable birds. It's also the wonderful people behind it whom I have come to know and love. I have had many memorable experiences with Jim Reichardt. My favorite time was back in 2006 when we were both in Italy for the biennial conference of Terra Madre, the international network of food communities. Jim and I walked around the tasting pavilion, having a blast, and sampling so many cured meats that, as Jim will tell you, I literally turned green from overindulgence. But Jim is not just my go-to duck farmer. He has been a friend and mentor who has shared a wealth of knowledge with me over the years. He has especially helped me to understand how things work in the world of farming.

As for Jen, I know it makes me sound like an old man to say I watched her grow up in this business, but it's true. And it's been a joy seeing her develop into the incredible leader and accomplished winemaker she is today.

This dynamic duo have given a gift to the culinary world with their incredible ducks. Seriously, their ducks are so good that unless you are a really shitty cook and pay no attention to what you are doing, anyone can make a delicious meal with them. Jim and Jen's ducks have made my job as a chef so much easier. I have to thank them for relenting and fulfilling all those weird requests for specialty items over the years as well as my occasional last-minute "holy shit" orders.

The good news for home cooks is that now you can order direct from Liberty Ducks too. And because there are so many incredible chefs' creations in the following pages, once you begin placing orders, you'll have a treasure trove of recipes to draw on for every cut and bit.

This book will allow you to make the most out of every duck and will change the way you cook this versatile bird forever. So hurry up and figure out which cut you want to use first and dig in.

CHRIS COSENTINO
Chef, author, and co-owner of Acacia House and Rosalie restaurants

INTRODUCTION

In my freshman year of high school, my first book report for my honors English class was on Ruth Reichl's *Garlic and Sapphires*. I can't remember the prompt, I can't tell you what I wrote about, and I can't be sure that I found the book on my dad's bookshelf. But I can tell you I remember this feeling—a passion for food boiling up inside me—as I turned the pages.

It was exciting to read Ruth Reichl's tales of donning elaborate disguises in her role as restaurant critic for the *New York Times* and to find a smattering of recipes—spaghetti carbonara, *aushak*, matzo brei—sprinkled throughout the chapters. It was while reading that book that I first came to understand the importance of two things: the story *behind* a dish and the idea that foods and recipes can establish a sense of place.

My life has always been centered *in* food. From the day I was born, a duck farm has been a part of our home. My dad was raised in the industry as well, and his love for interesting ingredients was evident to me from as early as I can remember. But beyond discovering different types of food, what I recall most about my childhood is that it was very rare that we did not gather as a family around the dinner table. My mom had some classics, among which were the curiously named "more" (a rigatoni casserole), meat loaf, and "trash bag" taco salad. None of them was fancy or difficult to make, but the fact that the four of us always ate dinner together meant a lot.

Over the next eight years, throughout high school and college, I was always aware that I enjoyed food, that I enjoyed learning about food, and that it was important to support food organizations that focused on sustainability, preserving local traditions, and food security. But what I didn't know was how the greater food industry was going to fit into my life. When I headed to college, I was set on a premed undergraduate degree with the intention of going on to medical school and becoming a doctor. But a fateful internship changed my mind, and I was left wondering, "What's next?"

In 2008, I traveled to Turin, Italy, to attend the annual Terra Madre food festival. Organized by Slow Food, it brings together groups of food professionals, farmers, historians, and more from all over the world to celebrate their food cultures and to share them with others. It was the second time that I realized just how much meaning food could bring to one's life. Of course we need food to sustain ourselves. But it was truly a revelation to learn about the many traditions that the participants brought to this remarkable gathering and to see so many small-scale food and wine producers in one place.

It was in Turin that I realized I could have a career in food, even though I was still blissfully unaware that it had been brewing in me for my entire life. I would spend the next eight years traveling and learning more about food and food production. There was a summer in Spain working for free on organic farms, milking goats and harvesting garlic under a blazing afternoon sun. I spent time with Danièle Mazet-Delpeuch, who, as the personal chef to François Mitterrand from 1988 to 1990, was the first female chef for the president of France. She taught me how to break down a duck, specifically one raised for foie gras in the Périgord region. The rest of my time in the Périgord—two months cleaning rooms at a bed-and-breakfast in the hamlet of Castelnaud-la-Chapelle—was where I really started to dive into my own cooking, ingredient sourcing, and storytelling. On a group trek outside Chiang Mai, Thailand, during which we all carried the food we ate, I learned how to make a simple one-pot meal explode with flavor and texture.

Throughout my eight years as a vagabond, I always returned home between adventures and worked on the farm. When I was much younger, my first job had been folding, stamping, and addressing a monthly statement to every one of our customers. My pay was a nickel for every statement. When I turned sixteen and got my driver's license, I made deliveries whenever the farm was shorthanded. I have a vivid memory of coming home for Christmas break one year and heading out to Healdsburg on Christmas Eve with a load of ducks. It was late in the day, incredibly dark, and pouring rain. Even though I was showing up at each restaurant on one of the busiest service nights of the year, and becoming ever more apologetic with each stop, everyone was gracious and jolly. And when I had finished my rounds, I called Dad with a sense of elation and joy.

Each time I returned home, there was a new task to accomplish—and a list of new and exciting restaurants that we had started selling to. I was learning the business from the ground up time and time again—picking up Dad's old tricks and also starting to implement some new ideas of my own.

It was in 2016, when I came back to the farm full-time, that I realized that the business Dad had built was doing what I had been admiring about the food industry all along. He was raising the ducks to establish a true sense of place, what Ruth Reichl was talking about in her book: our ingredient was contributing to a restaurant's sense of place. Our restaurants valued what Dad was raising because of the way that he was doing it and the place it represented. People know us as Liberty Ducks, but the company's actual name is Sonoma County Poultry, and it truly is because of this county that we are who we are—that our ducks reflect the *terroir* of this place. Dad's relationships with *each* of his restaurants made up the story aspect of what we were doing—that he could call up Wolfgang Puck and Thomas Keller to talk about their orders, and that he served even our smallest local neighborhood spot. I watched him drop everything to run orders near and far—San Francisco to Los Angeles. These relationships are what have brought us to where we are today.

And it is something of a miracle that we're still here. Being a 95 percent wholesale direct marketing farm did not work out in our favor in March 2020 when the COVID-19 pandemic hit. We watched overnight as every single restaurant shut down for an unforeseen amount of time. Once take-out programs were allowed, we were humbled by those who fought hard week after week to keep us on their menus, helping us to keep our lights on. We dropped production, and then as restaurants opened up, we raised production. When restaurants were forced to shut down a second time, we dropped production again. We mourned the

restaurants we love that had to close permanently, wishing the chefs the best and hoping to see them in new spaces. It was an intense roller coaster that I sometimes thought we might ride forever.

There were also times that I didn't think we were going to make it, but I could not let Dad's twenty-eight years of work go away without a strong fight. With the introduction of a retail program, we took Liberty Ducks into homes, something we had never done before. If people couldn't go out to eat, they might as well get the same ingredients their favorite restaurants were using. It was time to let the people at home be a part of our story—to put our ducks on their dinner tables, to slow down and eat together again as a family, to create some normalcy where there seemed to be little. It was a return to my childhood when we always had dinner together: cooking, eating, and cleaning up—the seemingly mundane moments that mean the most.

As we rounded into 2021, the twenty-ninth year of business of Liberty Ducks, the idea of a cookbook, which had been discussed several years earlier, reemerged. The light bulb moment glowed brightly: we have these chefs from all over the country cooking fun, imaginative dishes with our product. And we now have these amazing home cooks looking for fun, imaginative ways to cook for their families. We couldn't think of a better way to marry our old world with our new world, to let the chefs continue to tell the stories from their kitchens to an audience that appreciates them and the ingredients they use.

Toward that end, and in recognition of the thirtieth anniversary of Liberty Ducks, we gathered recipes from over fifty chefs and food personalities and then added some of our own and some from our fabulous editor, Kim Laidlaw, to create *The Whole Duck*. In these pages, you'll find not only all the basics, from how to render duck fat to how to make duck leg confit, but also an inspired and varied selection of recipes for charcuterie, starters, soups and salads, mains, and even desserts for every part of the duck. I've also included beverage suggestions with the recipes, such as a chilled Syrah with duck sliders, a rich stout with duck sausages, and a tawny port with duck egg custards and plum compote.

My journey in search of good food and good wine has taken me to many corners of the world, but it's an honor to be here now.

Opposite: Jim and Jennifer discussing food and wine, or maybe what recipe they're going to cook next. Below: Jennifer and her husband, Mike, riding in style at their wedding at Monkey Ranch, June 2019. Who doesn't want to arrive to dinner with a tractor full of beer for their guests?

THE HISTORY OF LIBERTY DUCKS

While 2022 marks the thirtieth anniversary of the founding of Liberty Ducks, our history is linked to a much older story. Five generations of my family have been duck farmers in California, always based here in the San Francisco Bay Area.

In the 1870s, Otto H. Reichardt immigrated to the United States from Bernburg, Germany, and settled in San Francisco, where he found work as a house painter. It was a period in which thousands of Victorian houses were being built and painted in the city, so Otto had no trouble securing employment. But the paint fumes didn't agree with him, and he eventually fell ill. His doctor recommended moving to the country, so in the 1890s, Otto and his wife, Amalia, headed about thirty miles north to Sonoma County, where they bought a chicken farm on McNear Hill, at the edge of the town of Petaluma. At the time, the Petaluma region was starting to become an important player in the California poultry industry, and Otto saw raising chickens as a way to secure a good future.

But country life did not suit Otto and Amalia. They missed the sense of community they had established in San Francisco, and traveling between Sonoma County and San Francisco was a long and tiring journey in those days. So in 1901, they moved back to the city, to Onondaga Avenue in the Excelsior District in the Outer Mission. There they bought a duck farm, where they immediately started supplying ducks to San Francisco's growing Chinatown.

In the early 1920s, the farm moved from the Outer Mission to a location on Mission Road in South San Francisco. For the next thirty years, it provided a steady supply of ducks to San Francisco. Then, in 1958, the property on which the farm stood was purchased under eminent domain to serve as the site for a new high school for South San Francisco's burgeoning population.

The Reichardt family, now with new generations involved, moved the farm to Middle Two Rock Road, just outside of Petaluma, where it remains today. My dad grew up on this farm, and it is where he learned the ins and outs of the poultry business. When he graduated from high school in the mid-1970s, my grandfather encouraged and supported his decision to pursue an education in art and architecture. But there seems to be some inescapable magnetic pull back to the farm, and in the early 1980s, Jim Reichardt (aka my dad) returned to the family farm to manage the processing and promotion of the ducks.

After nearly a decade back, Dad decided to strike out on his own to serve a different market need. Julia Child had brought the cooking of France into households across the United States, and chefs around the country were looking to bring the ingredients she was using into their kitchens. In 1992, the first Liberty Ducks came into our garage, and a new company was born. The original farm was on Todd Road in Santa Rosa, and the first dollar we made was on a sale to Bay Wolf restaurant in Oakland.

Bay Wolf, which opened in 1975, just three years after Chez Panisse, championed locally sourced ingredients, and co-owner Michael Wild would always spend time fostering relationships with his purveyors. It was at Bay Wolf that my Dad had his bachelor party before his marriage to my mom, and it is where he met the late Jim Clendenen, winemaker extraordinaire of Au Bon Climat and a great friend. Every August at Bay Wolf, the two of them would put on the Double Duck Dinner featuring Jim's wines and Jim's ducks. My dad's relationship with Bay Wolf was more than just a

Top right: Ducks from the Reichardt Duck Farm in the mid-1970s. Bottom right: The barns held the laying flock for the Reichardt Duck Farm.

Top left: Dad (Jim Reichardt) with our pet duck Frosty who thought he was a dog and would get in tussles with our Bernese mountain dog, Klaus. Top right: Me at four years old, in our garage in Penngrove with our first ducks, December 1992.

Bottom: Me and friend Benjamin Petrick at our original Liberty Ducks location on Todd Road in Santa Rosa. Opposite: Julia Child toured Sonoma County farms in 1992, making a stop at Reichardt Duck Farm (used with permission from The Press Democrat).

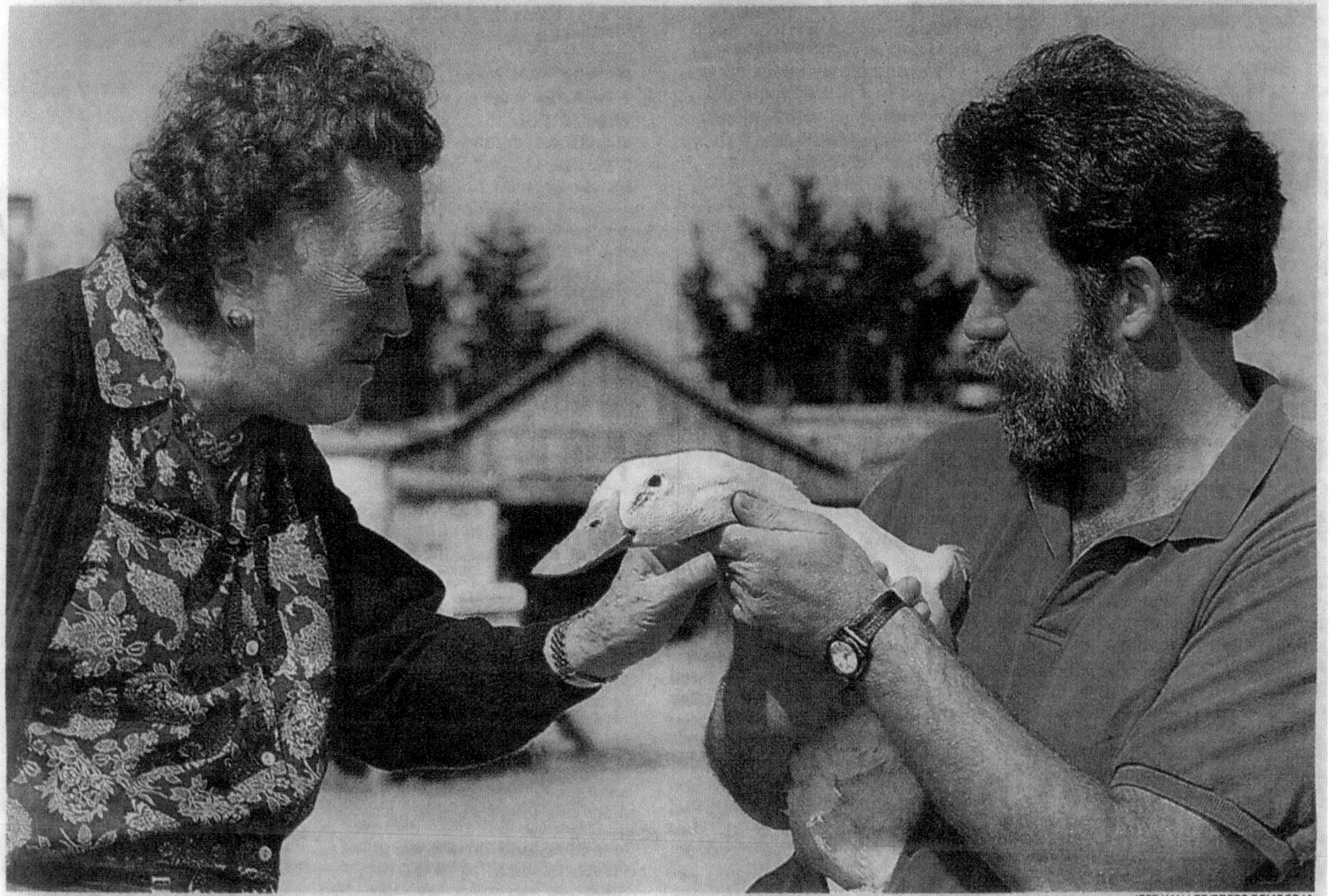

JEFF KAN LEE/PRESS DEMOCRAT

Chef Julia Child examines a duck raised by Jim Reichardt at the Reichardt Duck Farm west of Petaluma.

Julia Child tours Sonoma County

Famous chef tracks food from field to table

By TIM TESCONI
Staff Writer

Julia Child, the grand dame of American gastronomy, on Tuesday completed her cook's tour of Sonoma County agriculture, marveling at the diversity of farms thriving in the urban shadows.

"Let's just hope you can keep developers with their big money from destroying this. It's marvelous to see this kind of agriculture," said Child, 79, whose cookbooks are as famous as her distinctive voice. Her comments came while taking in the sights, sounds and smells at the Reichardt Duck Farm west of Petaluma.

The Reichardt ranch, the second largest duck farm west of the Mississippi, produces 5,000 ducks a day.

Child may be the Queen of the Kitchen, but she is no prima donna. She didn't wince while watching Peking ducks being killed, plucked, waxed and eviscerated. To her it was food for the table.

She didn't hold her nose or become squeamish when the pungent odor from 200,000 ducks wafted to her sensitive nostrils.

On the contrary, it made her mouth water for roast duck breast and a glass of pinot noir.

"I love duck. I would like to have some fresh duck right now," said the famed chef after seeing the operation, which breeds, hatches, feeds and slaughters 1 million ducks each year. Most of the ducks are sold in the Chinatowns of Oakland and San Francisco.

The Reichardt farm was one of the agricultural operations Child visited Monday and Tuesday to learn about the specialty foods produced in Sonoma County. She also toured gourmet mushroom and poultry farms, wineries and vineyards.

"Sonoma County is most unusual because it is both urban and rural. I can't get over the beauty of the countryside," said Child, while gazing at green hills and grazing cattle in Two Rock, west of Petaluma.

Child is intensely interested in food production. She wants to know the source of the meat, vegetables and herbs that land on her chopping block.

During the tour she asked owner Jim Reichardt if the ducks are artificially inseminated to produce the thousands of ducklings on the ranch.

> "Sonoma County is most unusual, because it is both urban and rural. I can't get over the beauty."
>
> JULIA CHILD

See Child, Page B4

place we sold to. It was an integral part of our story, of us as a company, and, most important, of our lives.

In 2015, on its fortieth anniversary, Bay Wolf closed its doors for the last time after the final Double Duck Dinner. I'll never forget the date. It was my twenty-seventh birthday, and I watched a room revel in joy over forty years of wonderful memories. From that very first dollar we made from Bay Wolf, we can trace the next restaurant and the next back to the Bay Wolf kitchen. As sous chefs turned into head chefs, both in-house and in new ventures, Dad watched his product move from kitchen to kitchen, his business growing organically first in the San Francisco Bay Area restaurant world and then to Los Angeles and beyond.

The farm moved from Todd Road to its current home in Two Rock, west of downtown Petaluma, in the mid-1990s. Because of its proximity to the Pacific Ocean, our farm has the perfect climate for keeping ducks—neither too hot nor too cold. The ducks are reared in open-air barns on bedding of straw and shavings and have ample room to run about. They are a strain of Pekin duck that was developed in Denmark and mature best when treated to a slower, less-stressful style of rearing. Because of this, the market age of our ducks is one and half times that of the typical commercial duck. This extra time on the farm yields the bigger, meatier birds that Dad has sought from the very first day of Liberty Ducks.

Above: Three-week-old ducklings at the ranch. Opposite: Me, holding duck eggs at the ranch. While we don't raise ducks commercially for eggs, our employees tend to a small flock for personal use.

FLAVOR PAIRINGS

Arguably, the most important thing you will learn from this book is that you can make almost anything with duck! Sliders, chili, *basteeya*, tacos, meat loaf, even chocolate cake—you'll find recipes for them all.

Ducks were first domesticated in Asia some four thousand years ago, and today, more duck is consumed in China than in any other country, with France a distant second. But you can find duck dishes on the tables of many countries, from Vietnam, Thailand, and India to Poland, Hungary, Germany, and more.

Duck pairs with a wide variety of ingredients and flavors. Fruits, such as cherries, blackberries, grapes, figs, apples, and peaches—both fresh and dried—are popular partners.

Sauces made with such sweet or acidic ingredients as balsamic vinegar, citrus juices and zests, honey, and brandy are common. Some premade sauces, such as Chinese hoisin and plum, are a heady mix of sweet, salty, and acidic in a single jar.

Warm spices, like cardamom, allspice, cumin, and pepper, and spice blends like five-spice powder and garam masala, all complement duck meat. A great example of bringing all of these flavor components together in a single dish is chef Nico Delaroque's duck boudin, which he prepares at his San Francisco restaurant, Maison Nico. In his mixture, he combines apple (sweet), five-spice powder (warm), and Calvados (acidic).

Many of the recipes in this book travel a similar culinary route, creatively mixing two or more of the four basic tastes—sweet, salty, sour, and bitter—in a single dish.

SPICE MIXES

These spice mixes are guaranteed to help you up your duck game. They can be rubbed on duck breasts before pan-searing (page 39), duck legs before roasting (page 36), or even on a whole duck (page 42). These blends are so good that you'll also want to try them in recipes that go beyond duck. All of them will keep in an airtight container at room temperature for up to 1 month.

LOVE RUB

This is a Liberty Ducks classic. It's what we nearly always use to season duck that we take to events. As you cook, be sure to keep an eye on the temperature, as the sugar can burn.

Makes about 1 cup

½ cup firmly packed light brown sugar
2 tablespoons kosher salt
2 tablespoons sweet paprika
1 tablespoon chili powder
1 tablespoon dried thyme
2 teaspoons dried oregano
1½ teaspoons ground coriander
1 teaspoon ground white pepper
1 teaspoon five-spice powder
½ teaspoon freshly ground black pepper
½ teaspoon ground cumin
½ teaspoon cayenne pepper
½ teaspoon ground cinnamon
½ teaspoon freshly grated nutmeg

In a small bowl, combine all the ingredients and mix well.

EVERYTHING SEEDY MIX

Chef Craig Stoll uses this blend on his duck fat–fried latkes on page 85. But if you're a baker, or if you just love an "everything" mix, this is a great staple to keep around.

Makes about ½ cup

⅓ cup sesame seeds
1 tablespoon poppy seeds
1 tablespoon dehydrated chopped garlic
1 tablespoon dehydrated flaked onion
1 tablespoon caraway seeds
1½ teaspoons fennel seeds
¾ teaspoon flaky sea salt, preferably Maldon

In a small bowl, combine all the ingredients and mix well.

RAS EL HANOUT

A traditional North African spice mix, *ras el hanout* has no set formula. Its composition varies from spice shop to spice shop—and sometimes from family to family—and can include more than two dozen ingredients. This more modest blend of a dozen spices will deliver an incredible flavor burst to pan-seared duck breasts (page 39), roasted duck legs (page 36), or the *crépinettes* on page 55. There's no salt in the mixture, so don't forget to add some when preparing duck breasts or legs.

Makes about ⅓ cup

2 teaspoons smoked paprika
2 teaspoons ground cumin
2 teaspoons ground cinnamon
2 teaspoons freshly ground black pepper
2 teaspoons ground allspice
2 teaspoons ground turmeric
1 teaspoon ground nutmeg
1 teaspoon ground cardamom
½ teaspoon ground cloves
½ teaspoon cayenne pepper
½ teaspoon ground ginger
½ teaspoon ground coriander

In a small bowl, combine all the ingredients and mix well.

BELGIAN WITBIER SPICE BLEND

Chef Sean Z. Paxton imitates the warm spice blends of the famous witbier (white beer) from Belgium in this mix. Try it paired with the beer itself to double down on the flavor.

Makes about 1 tablespoon

1 teaspoon coriander seeds, toasted
¾ teaspoon dried thyme
¾ teaspoon kosher salt
½ teaspoon dried bitter or sweet orange peel
½ teaspoon black peppercorns

In a spice blender or clean coffee grinder, combine all the ingredients and grind to a fine powder.

CARAWAY–BLACK PEPPER SPICE MIX

Chef Naomi Pomeroy in Portland, Oregon, uses this spice mix on duck breasts. She suggests seasoning the breasts with this blend, then pan-searing them as directed on page 39 and serving them with a turnip-potato purée. But I think it would go well on all duck parts. The malt vinegar powder packs a punch—think salt and vinegar chips! Used sparingly, it adds a bright pop to the duck. The vinegar powder can also be used in salad dressings or on fish, making it a good addition to your pantry.

Makes about ½ cup

¼ cup fine sea salt
3 tablespoons caraway seeds, toasted
2 tablespoons freshly ground black pepper
1 teaspoon sugar
Dusting of malt vinegar powder

In a small bowl, combine the salt, caraway seeds, pepper, and sugar and mix well. Dust the skin side of the duck piece with the malt vinegar powder, then rub the caraway mixture all over the skin and flesh sides.

QUATRE ÉPICES

This traditional French spice blend adds warmth and depth to a dish. It is commonly used in soups, stews, ragouts, and charcuterie and is called for in the country-style duck pâté recipe on page 56.

Makes 2½ teaspoons

1 teaspoon ground white pepper
½ teaspoon ground ginger
½ teaspoon freshly grated nutmeg
½ teaspoon ground cloves

In a small bowl, combine all the ingredients and mix well.

SIMPLE CARDAMOM RUB

Don't have a lot of time? This simple rub is delicious on duck headed to the stove top, oven, or grill and pairs easily with a lot of beautiful wines—especially a good Sonoma Coast Pinot Noir.

Makes 3 tablespoons

1 tablespoon kosher salt
1 tablespoon cracked black pepper
1 tablespoon ground cardamom

In a small bowl, combine all the ingredients and mix well.

CREOLE SEASONING

Chef Alon Shaya seasons his gumbo (page 128) with this true taste of the Big Easy, but you don't need to make gumbo to enjoy it. I love it on eggs for breakfast or on popcorn for a movie night.

Makes about ¾ cup

7 tablespoons sweet paprika
1 tablespoon celery salt
1 tablespoon garlic powder
1 tablespoon onion powder
2½ teaspoons freshly ground black pepper
1½ teaspoons kosher salt
1 teaspoon cayenne pepper
⅛ teaspoon ground allspice

In a small bowl, combine all the ingredients and mix well.

SICHUAN SPICE MIX

Chef Brandon Jew uses this aromatic mix in his recipe for duck tongues on page 91, but it would be incredible on any duck parts or on a whole duck.

Makes about 2 teaspoons

¼ teaspoon Sichuan peppercorns
¼ teaspoon fennel seeds
¼ teaspoon coriander seeds
2 star anise points
½ teaspoon kosher salt
½ teaspoon ground white pepper

With a mortar and pestle (or with a spice grinder or clean coffee grinder), grind together the Sichuan peppercorns, fennel seeds, coriander seeds, and star anise until finely ground. Stir in the salt and pepper, mixing well.

SPECULOOS SPICE MIX

This fun spice blend from chef Sean Z. Paxton is traditionally used for cookies. But salty and warming flavors make it delicious on duck meat as well.

Makes about 2 tablespoons

1 tablespoon ground cinnamon
1 teaspoon ground ginger
1 teaspoon fine sea salt
½ teaspoon ground cloves
½ teaspoon ground cardamom
½ teaspoon ground white pepper

In a small bowl, combine all the ingredients and mix well.

CASTINGS
NO 12 CAST IRON SKILLET
IRONWARE
COMPANY
US MADE
CHARLESTON SC

CHAPTER ONE

BUTCHERY & BASICS

DUCK BUTCHERY

Breaking down a whole duck will give you a number of meals, plus stock and rendered fat to use for other recipes. You can save and use *everything*. It's a simple kitchen skill that will be valuable for years to come. Start with a sharp knife. It's not only key to butchering duck but will also make any cutting task in the kitchen easier, safer, and more enjoyable. A boning knife is the best choice for breaking down a duck.

1. First, take off the neck skin, cutting all the way around right above the breast and pulling it away in one piece. Save the skin for rendering. Or if the skin is free of holes or other breaks, you can look up how to make a stuffed duck neck sausage. Cut straight down to remove the neck and save it for stock or to make a jus.

2. Find the keel, or center of the breastbone, and cut all the way down along one side and then along the other side of it, keeping as close to the bone as possible.

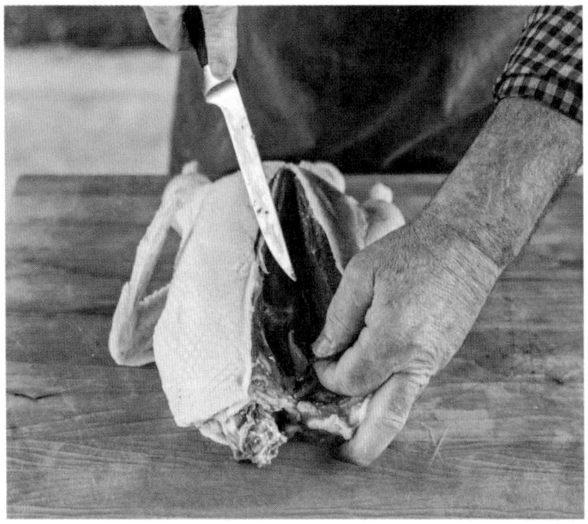

3. Now, starting with one side, tease the meat off the breast plate, cutting right up to the wishbone at the top and trying to remove as much meat as possible.

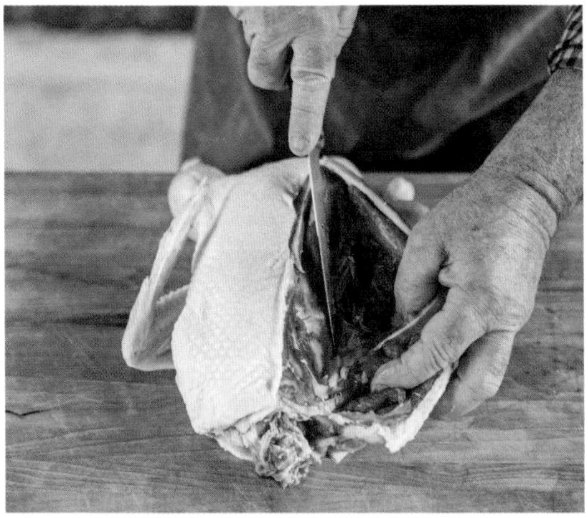

4. The tender, the top of which is near the top of the wishbone, is what connects the breast meat to the breast plate. Make sure you're cutting off the tender as you tease the meat off. Cut the breast all the way up toward the wing joint, leaving more meat and skin on the breast.

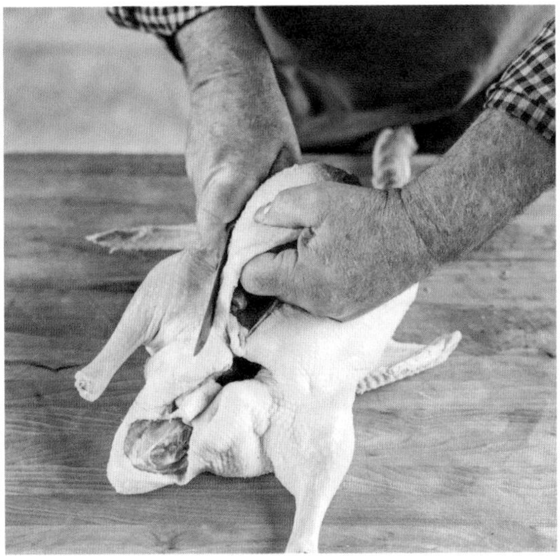

5. As you work, you'll see the breast meat ends at a fatty part that connects to the leg. Cut through the fat to separate the first breast from the whole duck.

6. Lay the breast, skin side down, on the work surface and trim off as much fat as you like. Make sure you keep enough fat, roughly ¼ inch on all sides, available for rendering. As you cook the breast, the skin will pull back, and you don't want to expose the meat to the heat. Leaving the fat intact protects the meat.

7. Taking off the silver skin, a connective tissue setting the muscle boundary, is optional. Leaving it in place won't affect the texture of the meat in the same way it would on a beef tenderloin, for example. To remove it, find a piece of the membrane and cut upward, away from you and the meat. You want to take off just the membrane and not include any chunks of meat with it.

8. Now, remove the tender from the breast, as it will cook differently from the rest of the breast. I like to cook the tender in the rendering duck fat as a little chef's snack!

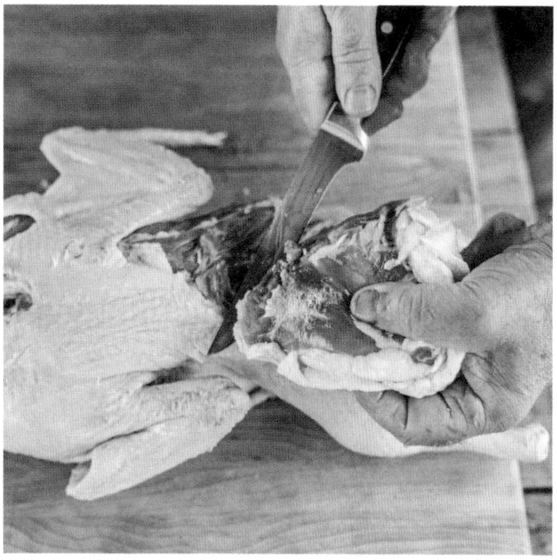

9. Moving to the leg on the same side, cut down along the carcass in the same direction you just sliced the duck breast off, toward the leg. You want to try to include the little oyster of meat above the joint where the leg (drumstick) and thigh meet. Use the weight of the leg to pull back against the joint to create a clean cut.

10. If you're splitting the leg and thigh, the joint is going to be right under the fat piece you see on the muscle side of the leg. Slice through and you'll be able to find the joint to make a clean cut to separate them. Most of the recipes in this book are for the full leg—thigh and drumstick—but knowing how to separate the two parts is a useful skill for the occasional recipe that calls for splitting them.

11. Moving out to the wing, on the exposed side, pull back and you'll see the tendon and the joint. Open up the joint and move the knife through the exposed area to remove the wing. At this point, you can cut off the wing tip, as there's not enough meat on it to use it in a recipe. Using your hands, move the joint back and forth to break it, then cut straight through. Save the tip for stock.

12. At the vent of the carcass is where you find the best—and most—fat for rendering. You can render any skin and fat together. If you don't have enough fat to render, pack it into a ziplock plastic bag, store it in the freezer, and keep adding to the bag until you do have enough.

13. Using the same technique, remove the breast, leg, and wing from the other side of the breastbone. When you find the right spot, the cut should be easy and effortless. Remember to use the weight of the carcass to move the joints, creating clean lines for cutting.

DUCK COOKING BASICS

SCORE THE SKIN. For ease of cutting, always score the skin on duck breasts while the breasts are still cold from the refrigerator. Using a sharp knife, score the skin on the diagonal, spacing the cuts about ½ inch apart (or as directed in individual recipes) and being careful not to cut through to the meat. Rotate the breast 90 degrees and score the same way in the opposite direction to make a crosshatch pattern. Scoring the skin will help the fat render more quickly and the skin to brown and crisp.

DON'T OVERCOOK IT. Think of duck as more like steak than chicken. You want to cook breasts to rare, medium-rare, or, at most, medium.

WATCH THE TEMPERATURE. When cooking duck—whole duck or parts—keep an eye on its internal temperature by using an instant-read thermometer. This will help you know when it's cooked exactly how you like it.

Here are some temperatures to keep in mind:

DUCK BREASTS
Rare: 125°–130°F
Medium-rare: 130°–135°F
Medium: 135°–140°F

WHOLE DUCK OR DUCK LEGS
145°–165°F

KNOW YOUR OVEN. I always set my timer for the halfway point of the suggested cooking time. At that point, you should have a good idea if you will need to leave the duck to cook the full time or if you should pull it out earlier so it doesn't overcook.

SAVE YOUR RENDERED FAT. Whenever you sear duck breasts or legs, save any rendered fat not called for in the recipe for another use. Just pour it through a fine-mesh sieve set over a heatproof container, let cool, cap tightly, and refrigerate. It will keep for up to 6 months.

START WITH THE BASICS. In this chapter, you'll find all the basic recipes you will need to cook duck successfully, from pan-searing breasts and roasting duck legs to rendering fat and smoking a whole bird on the grill. These simple methods form the foundation of many of the recipes in this book. Once you have mastered these key techniques, moving on to the more complex recipes will be easier and more fun. Plus, knowing the basics will open up a whole new world of flavors through seasonings and other ingredients.

RENDERED DUCK FAT

It is easy to render a big batch of duck fat, and once you have the rendered fat on hand, it is a valuable kitchen staple. From cooking eggs and sautéing vegetables to frying potatoes and making frosting (yes!), a quart of rendered duck fat in the fridge will go a long way. It's also lower in saturated fat than butter, making it a healthier cooking fat. This recipe yields a quart of rendered fat, but you can render any amount you want by following these simple steps. The smaller you chop or process the pieces, the more efficient the rendering process will be.

3¼ lb duck skin and fat

Makes 1 quart rendered fat

Using a sharp cleaver or chef's knife, chop the skin and fat into small pieces. Alternatively, using kitchen shears, cut the skin and fat into 2- to 3-inch pieces, then, working in small batches, transfer the skin and fat to a food processor, add just enough water to keep things moving, and pulse until chopped into small pieces. (The water will evaporate while the fat is rendering.)

Transfer the skin and fat to a large stockpot and place over medium-low heat. Melt the skin and fat, stirring occasionally to prevent sticking. If the pieces begin to stick, add a little water and stir to dislodge them. If the pieces start burning, turn down the heat to low. It should take about 30 minutes to render all the fat.

When it seems like the bits of fat and skin are fully rendered, place a large fine-mesh sieve over a heatproof bowl and pour the contents of the pot into the sieve. Discard the solids. Transfer the fat to one or more heatproof containers, let cool, cap tightly, and refrigerate overnight.

The next day, when the fat has solidified and turned white, you will notice a clear, watery layer on the bottom of the container. This "water," which will be gelatinous, is a rich source of collagen and flavor. Scrape the fat into a clean airtight container and use the "water" in a stock. This step will keep the fat fresh and will provide a good way to flavor stock.

The fat will keep in the refrigerator for up to 6 months. When removing fat from the container, always use a clean utensil. Dipping an already-used utensil into the fat will lead to spoilage.

DUCK GIZZARD CONFIT

I was introduced to confit gizzards for the first time on a trip to France in 2010, and they flipped the script. A Périgord salad on nearly every menu in the Dordogne featured these tasty morsels. Made at home, they're a great addition to our duck gizzard salad (page 122) or make a delicious replacement for roasted duck meat on a pizza (page 165). You can even serve them as an appetizer, warmed and gently crisped in a frying pan, each one speared with a toothpick.

1½ lb duck gizzards
About 2 tablespoons kosher salt
1½ lb rendered duck fat (page 32)
3 garlic cloves
1 bay leaf

Makes 1½ lb gizzard confit

Put the gizzards into a large fine-mesh sieve, rinse them under cool running water, and drain well. Transfer the gizzards to a large bowl and toss with enough salt to coat them lightly and evenly. Cover and refrigerate for at least 12 hours or up to 24 hours (but no more).

Return the gizzards to the sieve and hold under cool running water to rinse off the salt. Drain and pat dry with paper towels.

In a large sauté pan over medium heat, melt the duck fat. Add the gizzards, garlic, and bay leaf and bring to a simmer, then turn down the heat to low. Cook the gizzards, stirring occasionally, until cooked through, about 1½ hours. You want them to retain their structure but be tender and easy to bite.

If using right away, set the large sieve over a heatproof bowl and pour the contents of the pan into it, reserving the fat for another use. If not using immediately, let sit in the pan until cool to the touch, then transfer the gizzards and the fat to an airtight container, making sure they are covered completely with the fat. Store in the refrigerator for up to 3 weeks.

DUCK LEG CONFIT

CHEF TRACEY SHEPOS CENAMI

Although the process is long, duck confit is one of the simpler—and one of the most famous—of all duck preparations. A centuries-old tradition, it was originally used as a way to preserve meat for eating during the long winter months. Nowadays, it's regularly sold in butcher shops and grocery stores. Homemade confit is wonderful, and this version from chef Tracey Shepos Cenami of Jackson Family Wines is foolproof. If stored correctly, the duck will last for months in the fridge. Some say it even gets better with age!

Duck Leg Confit
⅓ cup kosher salt
1 tablespoon sugar
5 fresh thyme sprigs
1 teaspoon fennel seeds
1 teaspoon black peppercorns
1 teaspoon juniper berries
1 bay leaf
6 duck legs
5 cups rendered duck fat (page 32), melted

To Crisp the Duck Confit
¼ cup neutral oil
Kosher salt and freshly ground black pepper

Makes 6 duck legs confit; about 6 servings

To confit the duck legs, first brine them. In a small bowl, stir together the salt, sugar, thyme, fennel seeds, peppercorns, juniper berries, and bay leaf. Place the duck legs in a single layer in a 9-by-13-inch baking dish. Evenly coat both sides of each leg with the salt mixture, then sprinkle any excess salt mixture evenly over the top. Cover with plastic wrap and place weights, such as bricks wrapped in aluminum foil, on top to weight down the legs. Refrigerate overnight.

To confit the duck, preheat the oven to 275°F. Rinse the duck legs under cool running water and pat dry with paper towels. Rinse and dry the baking dish and place it on a sheet pan. Return the duck legs to the dish and pour the duck fat over them, covering them completely. Cover the dish with aluminum foil.

Bake the legs until the meat is very tender and falling off the bone, 2½ to 3 hours. Remove from the oven and let sit until the duck is cool to the touch.

Transfer the duck legs and fat to an airtight container, making sure the legs are completely submerged in the fat. They will keep in the refrigerator for up to 6 months.

To crisp the duck, line a plate with paper towels. In a shallow frying pan over medium-low heat, warm the oil. (You will need a large frying pan to crisp 2 or 3 legs at a time.) Remove as many duck legs as needed from the fat, wiping off any excess fat. When the oil is hot, place the duck legs in the oil and cook, turning once, until crispy and golden brown all over, 2 to 3 minutes total. Transfer to the towel-lined plate to absorb any excess oil. Season lightly with salt and pepper and serve right away.

ROASTED DUCK LEGS

Cooking duck can be as complicated as you want to make it, but there is nothing simpler or more delicious than this recipe for roasted duck legs. Watch your oven the first time to make sure you don't overcook them, then you're ready to go from there. We sell our legs in bags of six or twelve pieces, so the recipe can be easily doubled, tripled, or more!

2 duck legs
Kosher salt and freshly ground black pepper

Makes 2 duck legs; 2 servings

Preheat the oven to 400°F. Season both sides of the legs liberally with salt and pepper. Place the legs, skin side up, on a small sheet pan.

Roast the legs, rotating the pan back to front halfway through roasting, until dark golden brown, about 1 hour. Let the legs rest on the pan on a wire rack for 5 minutes before serving. The legs sometimes stick a little to the bottom of the pan, so you may need to loosen them with a spatula.

Be sure to save the rendered fat from the sheet pan. Place a fine-mesh sieve over a heatproof container and pour the fat into the sieve. Let cool, then cap tightly and store in the refrigerator for up to 6 months.

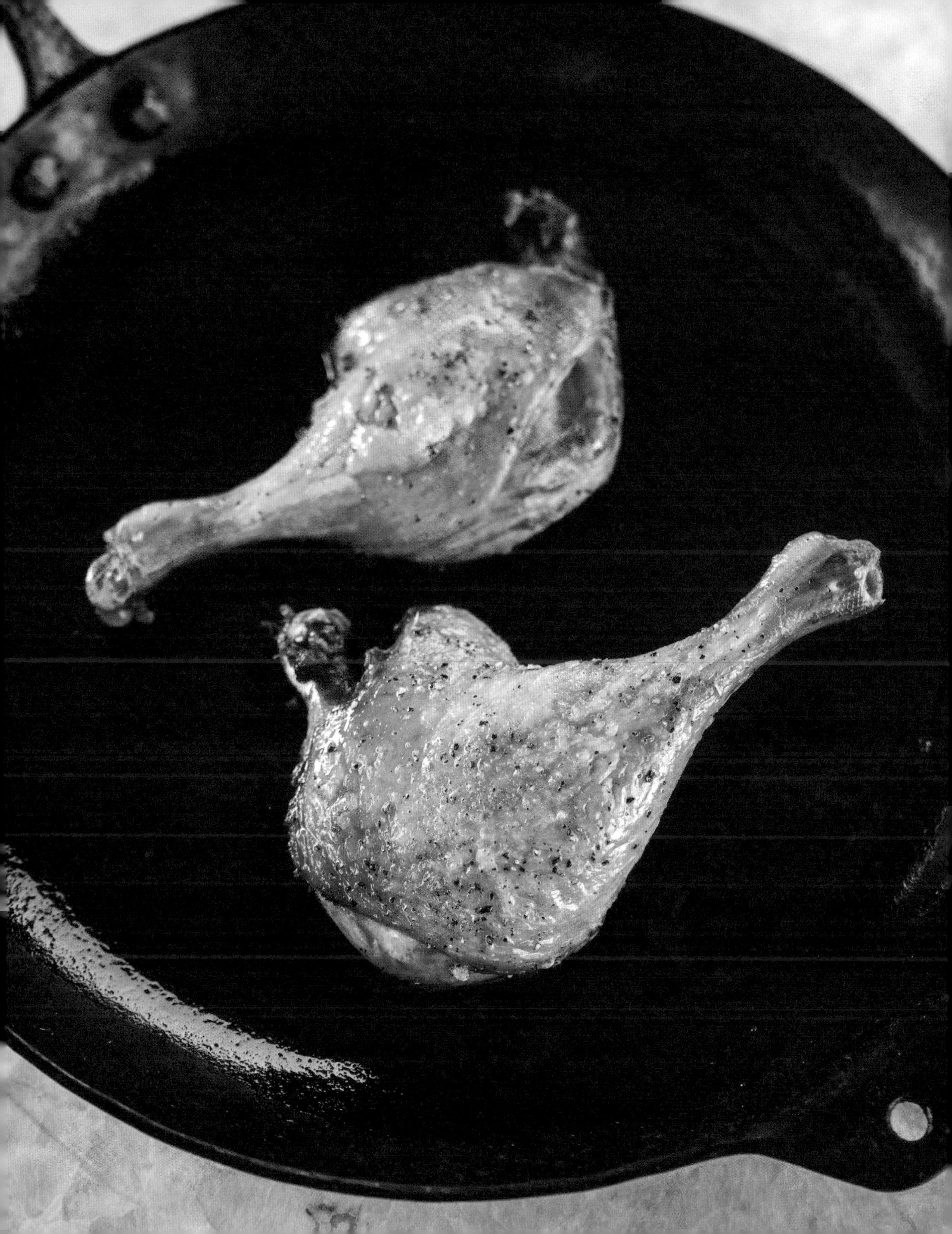

PAN-SEARED DUCK BREASTS

The rules of the game for duck breast are low and slow on the skin side and hot and fast on the meat side. The perfect result is golden brown and crisp skin, and meat cooked until still pink in the center. For the crosshatch step, be sure your knife is razor-sharp to ensure a clean cut through the skin without piercing the meat. Bring the breasts to room temperature before you cook them.

2 duck breasts
Kosher salt and freshly ground black pepper

Makes 2 duck breasts; 2 to 4 servings

Preheat the oven to 500°F.

While the duck breasts are still cold from the refrigerator, using a sharp knife and working with one duck breast at a time, score the skin on each breast on the diagonal, spacing the cuts about ½ inch apart and being careful not to cut through to the meat. Rotate the duck breast 90 degrees and score the same way in the opposite direction to make a crosshatch pattern. This will help the fat to render more quickly and the skin to brown. Season the duck breasts on both sides with salt and pepper and set aside for 20 minutes to come to room temperature.

Place the duck breasts, skin side down, in a cold cast-iron or other heavy frying pan. Turn on the heat to medium and let the breasts cook undisturbed until they have rendered their fat, about 10 minutes. Every so often, lift each breast with tongs to make sure the skin is not burning. If it is getting too dark, lower the heat.

Once the fat is rendered and is deep golden brown, transfer the breasts, skin side up, to a sheet pan, place in the oven, and roast until browned and medium-rare, 3 to 5 minutes longer. An instant-read thermometer inserted into the thickest part of a breast should register 130°F. Transfer to a cutting board and let rest for 5 to 10 minutes before serving.

Alternative Stove Top Method

Score the skin on the duck breasts as directed, then place the breasts, skin side down, in a cold cast-iron or other heavy frying pan. Turn on the heat to low and let the breasts cook undisturbed until they have rendered their fat, 10 to 15 minutes. Every so often, lift each breast with tongs to make sure the skin is not burning. If it is getting too dark, remove from the heat.

Once the fat is rendered and is deep golden brown, raise the heat to medium-high, turn the breasts over, and continue to cook until the meat is browned and the breasts are medium-rare, 2 to 4 minutes longer. An instant-read thermometer inserted into the thickest part of a breast should register 130°F. Transfer to a cutting board and let rest for 5 to 10 minutes before serving.

SMOKED DUCK BREASTS

CHEF JUSTIN WANGLER

Justin Wangler, executive chef at Kendall-Jackson Wine Estate & Gardens, is no stranger to all things smoked and barbecued from his childhood in Asheville, North Carolina. If you aren't using a grill or smoker, Justin suggests a Camerons (or similar) stove-top smoker, or make a DIY one as instructed below. If using a stove-top smoker, it's always a good idea to open a window as well!

4 duck breasts
Kosher salt
2 cups fruitwood chips, such as apple or cherry, soaked for 30 minutes

Makes 4 duck breasts; 4 to 8 servings

While the duck breasts are still cold from the refrigerator, score the skin in a crosshatch pattern as directed on page 31. Season on both sides with salt and transfer, skin side up, to a plate. Refrigerate, uncovered, for at least 8 hours or up to 2 days. Remove the duck from the refrigerator and let come to room temperature before cooking, about 30 minutes.

Prepare a charcoal or gas grill for indirect cooking over low heat (around 250°F), placing a drip pan on the indirect side. Alternatively, prepare a smoker for cooking with low heat (250°F).

Place the duck breasts, skin side down, into a cold, large cast-iron or other heavy frying pan and place on the stove top. Turn on the heat to medium-low and let the breasts cook undisturbed until they have rendered their fat and the skin is golden brown, 6 to 8 minutes. Drain off the excess fat and save for another use. Transfer the breasts, skin side up, to a plate.

Drain the wood chips and wrap them in an aluminum foil packet. Prick holes in the top of the packet. Place the wood chip packet over the heat source and close the grill. (If you have a gas grill with a smoking box, put the drained chips directly into the box.) When smoke starts rising from the grill, place the duck breasts, skin side up, over the indirect side of the grill (not over the heat) and cover the grill.

Smoke the duck until nicely browned, cooked to medium-rare, and an instant-read thermometer inserted into the thickest part of a breast registers 130°F, about 10 minutes. Transfer to a cutting board and let rest for at least 5 minutes before serving.

Alternative Stove Top Method
Score, season, and sear the skin side of the duck breasts as directed. Place 2 tablespoons finely ground fruitwood chips in the center of the bottom of a stove-top smoker. Top with the drip pan, then the rack. Alternatively, to make a DIY stove-top smoker, line the bottom of a large, heavy pot with aluminum foil. Place finely ground wood chips on the foil and top with a second layer of foil. Set a flat steaming basket on the foil and then place your meat on the basket. Finally, put the lid on the pot and secure the seam with some foil so no smoke leaks out.

Place the smoker over medium heat on the stove top. (Make sure you do this in a well-ventilated kitchen.) Smoke will begin to rise. When it turns from greenish to white, place the duck breasts, skin side up, on the rack or basket and cover the smoker. Smoke the breasts until an instant-read thermometer inserted into the thickest part of a breast registers 130°F (medium-rare), 3 to 6 minutes. Transfer to a cutting board. Let rest for 5 minutes before serving.

WHOLE SMOKED DUCK

This whole duck can be used in so many dishes! On its own, it's a flavor-packed main course, great with roasted root vegetables and sautéed winter greens. It's the star ingredient of chef Gavin Schmidt's smoked duck soup (page 124), and the meat can be shredded and used in tacos, on a salad, or even tossed with pasta. You can smoke the duck on a gas or charcoal grill or in a smoker. Pricking the skin all over allows the fat to render while the duck is smoking. Before cooking, the duck is salted (known as "dry brining") and refrigerated for at least 8 hours, so you'll need to plan ahead. Salting the duck adds flavor and helps it retain moisture during cooking, while refrigerating it uncovered dries out the skin so it absorbs the smoke flavor better.

1 whole duck
Kosher salt and freshly ground black pepper
2 cups fruitwood chips, such as apple or cherry
¼ cup fresh orange juice
2 tablespoons honey or maple syrup

Makes 4 to 6 servings

Using a thin metal skewer or the tip of a sharp paring knife, prick the skin of the duck all over, being careful not to pierce the meat. Pat the duck dry with paper towels and season all over, including the cavity, with salt and pepper. Place on a rack on a sheet pan and refrigerate, uncovered, for at least 8 hours or up to overnight.

Soak the wood chips in water for 30 minutes. Prepare a charcoal or gas grill for indirect cooking over low heat (around 250°F), placing a drip pan on the indirect side. Alternatively, prepare a smoker for cooking with low heat (250°F).

Drain the wood chips and wrap them in an aluminum foil packet. Prick holes in the top of the packet. Place the wood chip packet over the heat source and close the grill. (If you have a gas grill with a smoking box, put the drained chips directly into the box.) When smoke starts rising from the grill, place the duck, breast side up, over the indirect side of the grill (not over the heat) and cover the grill.

In a small saucepan over medium heat, warm the orange juice and honey together until the honey melts and the mixture is well blended, then remove from the heat and set aside.

Smoke the duck for 1 hour, then baste with the orange juice mixture. Continue to smoke, rotating the duck breast side down after about 1½ hours, until nicely browned all over and an instant-read thermometer inserted into the thickest part of the thigh registers 165°F, 3 to 4 hours. Baste the duck with the orange juice–honey mixture once every hour while smoking.

Transfer the duck to a cutting board and let rest for at least 15 minutes before carving or chopping to serve or to use as directed in individual recipes.

WHOLE ROASTED DUCK

CHEF DUSTIN VALETTE

A whole roasted duck is a great way to impress dinner guests and to shake up what typically is served when roasted poultry is on the menu. If you are hosting a holiday meal for a small group, it's a nice treat to have the same presentation and festive effect without jamming up your fridge with more leftovers than you need. This easy recipe for roasting a whole duck comes from chef Dustin Valette, who then glazes it with maple syrup and pairs it with butternut squash hash (see recipe page 174).

1 whole duck
1 teaspoon extra-virgin olive oil
Kosher salt and freshly ground black pepper
1 bunch fresh thyme

Makes 4 to 6 servings

Preheat the oven to 425°F. Set a rack in a roasting pan.

Rub the outside of the duck all over with the oil. Season the outside and the cavity of the duck with salt and pepper. Place the thyme in the cavity. Place the duck, breast side up, on the rack in the roasting pan. Tie the legs together with kitchen twine (or truss the whole duck).

Roast the duck for 15 minutes to brown. Turn down the oven temperature to 325°F and continue roasting, rotating the duck breast side down halfway through roasting, until the skin is richly browned and crisp and an instant-read thermometer inserted into the thickest part of the thigh (not touching bone) registers 145°F, 45 minutes to 1 hour.

Transfer the duck to a cutting board and let rest for at least 15 minutes before carving or chopping to serve or to use as directed in individual recipes.

BASIC DUCK STOCK

Stock is one of the easiest things to make, and the flavor of homemade stock is in an entirely different league from its store-bought counterpart. When chilled in the refrigerator, duck stock can be semisolid. That's because it's full of collagen, which contributes to its silky texture. I like to start a pot early in the morning and let it simmer all day long. It's just enough time to get all the goodness out of the ingredients. This recipe yields a versatile stock that can be used in many dishes. Freeze it in a mix of quart and pint containers so you always have just the right amount on hand when making soups, sauces, or other dishes.

3 to 4 lb bones from 2 whole duck carcasses
2 carrots, roughly chopped
2 celery stalks, roughly chopped
2 garlic cloves
Kosher salt and freshly ground black pepper (optional)

Makes about 4 quarts

Trim off the skin and any excess fat from the duck carcasses, specifically around the back, neck, and inside the cavity. Save the skin and trimmed fat for rendering into duck fat (see page 32). I put them into a ziplock plastic bag in the freezer and just keep adding to it until I have enough to render. Put the carcasses into a large stockpot along with the carrots, celery, and garlic and add water to cover all the ingredients by 1 inch.

Bring to a boil over high heat, skimming off any foam that forms on the surface. Reduce the heat to low and simmer, covered and skimming as needed, for 4 to 12 hours. The longer you simmer the stock, the more flavorful it will be.

When done to your liking, remove from the heat and let cool in the pot to room temperature. Set a fine-mesh sieve over a large bowl and pour the contents of the pot into the sieve. Discard the solids. Taste and season with salt and pepper, if you like.

Cover the bowl and refrigerate until chilled and the fat has solidified on top. Lift off the fat cap; store the fat in an airtight container in the refrigerator to use in recipes calling for rendered duck fat. Divide the stock into airtight containers and refrigerate for up to 5 days or freeze for up to 6 months.

CHEF'S NOTE: *I keep a large ziplock plastic bag in the freezer for storing vegetable scraps—onion skins, carrot peels, celery tops, mushroom stems, and the like—all of which I add to the stockpot along with the carrots, celery, and garlic called for in the recipe. When the bag is full, I know it's time to make another pot of stock! Each combination of vegetables and trimmings alters the flavor of the stock a little, plus using the scraps makes for very little waste in the kitchen and a delicious and nutritious stock.*

RICH DUCK STOCK

Roasting bones will give your stock a deep, full-bodied flavor and a rich brown color. This stock will add a concentrated burst of flavor—almost like a bouillon cube—to your dishes. Use it to add rich, pronounced flavor to hearty stews, pasta dishes, robust sauces, and more, reserving the basic stock (page **44**) for clear broth soups or lighter dishes. I use fresh bones from whole carcasses for stock. You can also use necks, wings, or feet, which will yield a more gelatinous stock.

- 1½ to 2 lb bones from 1 whole duck carcass
- 1 large yellow or white onion, roughly chopped
- ½ cup roughly chopped carrot
- ½ cup roughly chopped celery
- 1 cup dry white or red wine or warm water
- 2 teaspoons kosher salt
- 1 teaspoon black peppercorns
- 1 bay leaf

Makes about 2 quarts

Preheat the oven to 450°F.

To make roasting more efficient, prep the carcass. Trim off the skin and any excess fat from the duck, specifically around the back, neck, and inside the cavity. Save the skin and fat for rendering into duck fat (see page 32). I put them into a ziplock plastic bag in the freezer and just keep adding to the bag until I have enough to render. Break down the carcass into thirds to fit into a roasting pan, then put the pieces into the pan along with the onion, carrot, and celery.

Roast for about 15 minutes, then flip the bones onto their opposite side and continue to roast until the bones are golden and roasted on all sides but not burned, 15 to 30 minutes longer.

Transfer all the roasted ingredients to a stockpot. Place the warm roasting pan on the stove top over medium heat, pour in the wine, bring to a simmer, and deglaze the pan, using a spatula to dislodge the crispy browned bits from the pan bottom. Transfer the contents of the roasting pan to the stockpot, then add water to cover all the ingredients by about 1 inch along with the salt, peppercorns, and bay leaf.

Bring the mixture to a boil over high heat, skimming off any foam that forms on the surface. Reduce the heat to low and simmer, covered and skimming as needed, for at least 2 hours or up to 8 hours, stirring occasionally. The longer you simmer, the more intense the final flavor will be. Add more water if needed to ensure the bones are always covered with liquid.

When done to your liking, remove from the heat and let cool in the pot to room temperature. Set a fine-mesh sieve over a large bowl and pour the contents of the pot into the sieve. Discard the solids. Cover the bowl and refrigerate until chilled and the fat has solidified on top. Lift off the fat cap and store in an airtight container in the refrigerator to use in recipes calling for duck fat (it's great for cooking vegetables). Divide the stock into airtight containers and refrigerate for up to 5 days or freeze for up to 6 months.

CHAPTER TWO

CHARCUTERIE

HATCHO MISO DUCK LIVER PÂTÉ

CHEF ASUKA UCHIDA

Chef Asuka Uchida's parents owned a high-end Japanese restaurant in Okayama, Japan. She grew up in the kitchen, watching and helping her parents, then went on to study French cuisine and work at many French and Japanese restaurants, some of them with Michelin stars. This duck liver pâté combines her years of cooking and training into one incredibly special dish.

The making of Hatcho miso, an eight-hundred-year-old tradition, originated in the small Japanese town of Okazaki. It is made from local soybeans, salt, water, and koji (edible mold) and is aged in sealed wooden barrels for two years. The result is a deep, dark reddish miso that is saltier than other types of miso, is full of depth and umami, and has an earthy finish. It's worth the effort to seek it out at a well-stocked Japanese market or online. If Hatcho miso is unavailable, substitute red miso, which is made with toasted barley.

1 cup whole milk
1 cup water
Kosher salt and freshly ground black pepper
½ lb duck livers, cleaned
3½ tablespoons rendered duck fat (page 32) or canola oil
3 shallots, thinly sliced
3 garlic cloves, thinly sliced
4 fresh thyme sprigs
3½ tablespoons brandy or Cognac
3 tablespoons Hatcho miso, red miso, or barley miso
½ cup unsalted butter, at room temperature, cut into cubes
Toasted baguette slices, crostini, or crackers for serving

Makes two 6-oz ramekins; 6 to 8 servings

In a bowl, stir together the milk, ½ cup of the water, and 1 tablespoon salt. Add the livers and stir to coat evenly. Cover and refrigerate for at least 12 hours or up to overnight.

Drain the livers into a fine-mesh sieve, discarding the liquid. Pat the livers dry with paper towels and set aside.

Preheat a large cast-iron or other heavy frying pan over medium heat, then add the fat. When the fat has melted and is hot, add the shallots, garlic, and thyme and cook, stirring, until fragrant but not browned, about 3 minutes.

Add the livers and cook, stirring, just until cooked through, about 5 minutes total, being careful not to overcook. About 30 seconds before the livers finish cooking, add the brandy and simmer just until the alcohol cooks off. Remove from the heat and season with salt and pepper. Remove and discard the thyme sprigs.

While the mixture is still warm, transfer it to a food processor and process until a smooth paste forms, stopping as needed to scrape down the sides of the bowl with a spatula to ensure all the mixture is pureed. Add the miso, then, with the processor running, add the butter in two or three additions, processing until smooth after each addition. Taste and adjust the seasoning with salt and pepper if needed.

Divide the finished pâté between two 6-oz (¾-cup) ramekins and smooth the surface. Alternatively, to ensure a silky-smooth texture, press the pâté through a fine-mesh sieve before packing it into the ramekins. Cover with plastic wrap and refrigerate until well chilled and the flavors have blended, at least 4 hours or up to 24 hours. Serve with toasted baguette slices.

WINE: What a great opportunity to try some sake! Look for a Jyunmai-shu, which has rich body and high acidity to balance the liver pâté.

CREAMY DUCK LIVER PÂTÉ

CHEF TU DAVID PHU

A silky duck pâté is a showstopper every time. Oakland-based chef Tu David Phu uses this recipe, which is as simple and delicious as it gets, for his Duck Bánh Mì (page 139). It's also great served with crostini and cornichons in its more traditional role as an appetizer. I've even been known to make it into a full meal!

½ lb duck livers, cleaned
½ cup milk (1 or 2 percent)
Kosher salt
2 tablespoons neutral oil
½ medium yellow onion, thinly sliced
2 garlic cloves, minced
1 tablespoon coconut sugar or light brown sugar
¼ teaspoon freshly ground black pepper
½ cup unsalted butter, at room temperature

Makes two 4-oz ramekins; 4 to 6 servings

WINE: A crisp rosé, like a vin gris of Pinot Noir, with bright acidity to balance the creaminess of the dish.

In a bowl, combine the duck livers, milk, and ¼ teaspoon salt. Set aside at room temperature for 1 hour. Using a fine-mesh sieve, drain the livers and discard the liquid. Pat the livers dry with paper towels and set aside.

In a small frying pan over medium heat, warm 1 tablespoon of the oil. Add the onion and garlic and cook, stirring occasionally, until the onion is golden brown and starts to caramelize, about 10 minutes. Remove from the heat and lightly season with salt and pepper. Transfer to a small bowl and set aside.

Return the frying pan to medium-high heat and warm the remaining 1 tablespoon oil. Add the reserved duck livers and sear, turning once after about 2½ minutes, until browned on both sides and medium-rare in the center, about 7 minutes. Remove from the heat and add 1 tablespoon salt, the sugar, and the pepper. Mix thoroughly with a spoon.

Transfer the liver mixture to a food processor. Add the butter, 2 tablespoons at a time, pulsing once after each addition.

Transfer the mixture to the fine-mesh sieve placed over a bowl. Using the back of a spoon, press the mixture through the sieve. Discard any chunks remaining in the sieve. Transfer the liver mixture to two 4-oz (½-cup) jars or ramekins, cover, and refrigerate for at least 3 hours before serving. The pâté will keep in the refrigerator for up to 5 days.

DUCK LIVER MOUSSE

with duck fat financiers

CHEF STUART BRIOZA

Duck liver mousse—a creamier, fluffier version of pâté—is nothing short of ethereal. Chef Stuart Brioza of State Bird Provisions in San Francisco takes this already special starter and shoots it to the moon. Kissed with Madeira and port, the mousse is accompanied by mini *financiers* (French almond cakes)—the perfect bite-size pillows to spread the mousse on. Truthfully, the *financiers*, enriched with duck fat, are delicious on their own.

Duck Liver Mousse
½ lb duck livers, cleaned
1 cup heavy cream
1 large egg
1 tablespoon dry Madeira, plus ½ teaspoon
1 tablespoon tawny port, plus ½ teaspoon
1 teaspoon kosher salt
⅛ teaspoon freshly ground black pepper
2 dashes Tabasco sauce
¼ teaspoon freshly grated nutmeg
¾ cup unsalted butter, cut into 1-inch cubes, at room temperature

Financiers
⅓ cup plus 1 tablespoon all-purpose flour
¼ cup confectioners' sugar
½ teaspoon kosher salt
⅔ cup almond meal
4 large egg whites, at room temperature
¼ cup heavy cream, at room temperature
2 tablespoons orange blossom or wildflower honey
¼ cup plus 2 teaspoons rendered duck fat (page 32), melted
Flaky sea salt and ground pepper

Makes about 30 bites

WINE: A rich, sweet wine, such as Sauternes, would complement this dish. If you prefer a dry wine, try a bottle of Graves AOC. Graves white wines are predominantly Sauvignon Blanc, often with Sémillion, and medium-bodied compared to some of the other Bordeaux whites.

To make the mousse, preheat the oven to 350°F. In a blender, combine the livers, cream, egg, 1 tablespoon Madeira, 1 tablespoon port, salt, pepper, Tabasco, and nutmeg and puree until very smooth. Pass the mixture through a fine-mesh sieve set over a small baking dish, pressing against and stirring the solids in the sieve to extract as much liquid as possible. Discard the solids. Smooth the mixture in the dish to an even layer.

Put the baking dish into a small roasting pan and pour hot water into the pan just up to the level of the liver mixture in the dish. Tightly cover the dish with aluminum foil. Bake until the liver is mostly set but the center still jiggles slightly when you shake the dish, 30 to 35 minutes. Some cracks may form on the surface. That's nothing to worry about.

Rinse the blender, then transfer the hot duck mixture to it, add the butter, and blend until smooth. Add the remaining ½ teaspoon each Madeira and port and blend briefly to mix well. Let the mixture cool to room temperature, then transfer to an airtight container and refrigerate until chilled and thickened, at least 4 hours or up to 3 days.

To make the financiers, sift together the flour, sugar, and salt into a bowl. Add the almond meal and stir well. In a medium bowl, whisk together the egg whites, cream, and honey until the honey dissolves. Add the flour mixture to the egg white mixture and whisk until smooth. Add the warm duck fat, about one-third at a time, whisking after each addition until incorporated. Cover and refrigerate for at least 30 minutes or up to 3 days.

Preheat the oven to 400°F. Coat two silicone molds (see Chef's Note) with cooking spray and place on a large sheet pan. Divide the batter evenly among the forms in each mold, filling each to just below the rim. Bake the financiers, rotating the sheet pan back to front halfway through baking, until they are golden brown and rise slightly above the rim of the forms, about 20 minutes. Let cool slightly on the sheet pan on a wire rack, then remove the financiers from the molds.

Arrange the warm financiers on a platter and top each one with a smear of mousse. Crumble a little flaky salt and sprinkle a little pepper on each mousse-topped financier. Serve right away.

CHEF'S NOTE: *The silicone molds for the financiers are available at restaurant supply stores and online. Look for 12-by-7-inch (quarter-sheet-pan size) molds labeled "15 half rounds" with each form measuring 1½ inches in diameter. Mini muffin pans will also work in a pinch.*

DUCK RILLETTES

CHEF JOHN ASH

Preparing rillettes, like making confit, was traditionally a way to preserve meat, primarily pork, in its own fat for long storage. Today, you can find rillettes made from shredded or chopped duck, goose, rabbit, pork, fish, and even mushrooms! This recipe, from Sonoma County chef John Ash, calls for a whole duck, but it can also be made with duck legs. I have many memories of Dad cooking duck rillettes in the kitchen to bring to food festivals and functions. It's super easy to make up a big batch for a crowd.

Roasted Duck

1 tablespoon fine sea salt
1 tablespoon finely chopped fresh thyme, or 2 teaspoons dried thyme
1 teaspoon freshly ground black pepper
½ teaspoon red pepper flakes
1 whole duck
1½ cups dry white wine

Rillettes

½ cup finely chopped shallots
1½ tablespoons minced garlic
½ tablespoon fine sea salt
½ teaspoon dried thyme
½ teaspoon dried oregano
½ teaspoon dried rubbed sage
½ teaspoon freshly ground black pepper
3 tablespoons brandy
1½ tablespoons finely chopped fresh flat-leaf parsley leaves

Crostini, whole-grain mustard, fruit chutney, and cornichons, for serving

Makes 8 servings

WINE: A fuller rosé with good acidity. Look for a Tempranillo rosé from the Rioja region.

To roast the duck, preheat the oven to 350°F. In a small bowl, stir together the salt, thyme, black pepper, and red pepper flakes. Sprinkle the spice mixture evenly all over the outside of the duck and in the cavity. Using a cooking fork or the tip of a sharp paring knife, prick the skin of the duck all over, being careful not to pierce the meat. Place the duck, breast side up, in a deep, heavy roasting pan. Pour the wine into the pan and then cover the pan with aluminum foil.

Roast until the meat is tender and easily falls off the bone, 2½ to 3 hours. Transfer the duck to a cutting board to cool slightly.

To make the rillettes, transfer ½ cup of the cooking juices and fat from the roasting pan, including any scraped up browned bits from the pan bottom, to a small saucepan and warm over medium heat. Add the shallots, garlic, salt, thyme, oregano, sage, and black pepper and cook, stirring, until the shallots are softened but not browned, about 10 minutes. Carefully add the brandy, then continue to cook for about 5 minutes longer. Remove the pan from the heat and stir in the parsley.

Pull the meat off the duck, discarding the skin, cartilage, and bones. Shred the meat into bite-size pieces and transfer to a large bowl. Stir in the shallot mixture. Taste and adjust the seasoning with salt and pepper if needed. Remember, cold foods need just a bit more salt.

Line a 6-cup pâté mold with parchment paper or plastic wrap. Spoon the duck mixture into the mold and, using a rubber spatula or the back of a spoon, firmly press down the mixture. Wrap the mold in plastic wrap and place the mold on a sheet pan. Top with a weight, such as a brick wrapped in foil, so any excess fat is forced out. Alternatively, press the duck mixture into eight 6-oz (¾-cup) ramekins or ceramic cups and cover tightly with plastic wrap. Refrigerate the rillettes overnight before serving. They will keep refrigerated for up to 2 weeks.

To serve, if using a pâté mold, run a knife around the edge to loosen the rillettes, then invert the mold onto a cutting board or serving plate. Lift off the mold, peel away the parchment or plastic wrap, wipe off any excess fat, and cut into slices. If you have packed the rillettes into ramekins, serve each guest a ramekin. Accompany with crostini, mustard, chutney, and cornichons.

DUCK CRÉPINETTES

with ras el hanout and preserved meyer lemon

BUTCHER TAYLOR BOETTICHER

A popular North African spice blend, *ras el hanout* typically brings together more than a dozen different spices to produce a spectacularly aromatic mixture that just happens to be perfect for seasoning duck. Meyer lemons, a staple of Northern California, have a hearty constitution that makes them ideal for preserving in salt. Here, butcher Taylor Boetticher of Fatted Calf pairs this heady spice blend with preserved Meyer lemons in duck *crépinettes*, scrumptious little French-style sausage patties wrapped in caul fat. Taylor recommends serving them with a farro, arugula, nectarine, and pistachio salad.

½ lb pork caul fat (see Chef's Note)
1 tablespoon black peppercorns
1 teaspoon coriander seeds
1 whole star anise
½ teaspoon yellow mustard seeds
1 bay leaf, broken into small pieces
1½ teaspoons Aleppo pepper flakes
2 lb ground duck meat
½ lb ground pork fatback
1 tablespoon fine sea salt
2 teaspoons ras el hanout (page 22)
1½ teaspoons minced garlic
¼ cup diced preserved lemon peel, preferably Meyer lemon, rinsed (see Chef's Note, page 93)
¼ cup finely chopped fresh flat-leaf parsley leaves

Makes 14 crépinettes; 6 to 8 servings

WINE: A lightly floral Viognier is perfect for this dish.

Rinse the caul fat under cool running water to rid it of any blood, then immerse in a large bowl of water and set aside until needed.

In a dry small frying pan over medium heat, toast the peppercorns, coriander, star anise, and mustard seeds, shaking the pan often, until fragrant, about 1½ minutes. Pour onto a plate and let cool. Transfer to a spice grinder or clean coffee grinder, add the bay leaf and Aleppo pepper flakes, and grind to a fine powder.

In a large bowl, combine the duck and fatback. Sprinkle the salt over the top, followed by the ras el hanout, the ground spices, and the garlic. Mix all the seasonings into the ground meat and fat until evenly distributed. Add the preserved lemon and parsley and mix until evenly incorporated.

Divide the mixture into 14 equal portions each weighing about 3 ounces. Shape each portion into a patty ¾ inch thick and smooth the edges.

Remove the caul fat from the water and squeeze dry. Spread the caul fat out on a clean work surface. Lay a patty near one edge on the caul fat. Using a sharp knife, cut around the patty, leaving a 2-inch border of the caul fat on all sides. The piece of caul fat will be about 6 inches square. Pull the edges of the fat over the patty, covering it completely and trimming away any overlapping caul fat. Pinch the edges of the caul fat together to secure the seam. Place the crépinette, seam side down, on a large sheet pan. Repeat to wrap the remaining patties in caul fat the same way, adding them to the sheet pan. Cover the sheet pan with plastic wrap and chill the crépinettes in the refrigerator for about 30 minutes.

The crépinettes can be cooked on the stove top or on a grill. To cook on the stove top, arrange the crépinettes in two cold, dry large nonstick or cast-iron frying pans and place over medium heat. Cook until the underside is deeply golden brown, 4 to 5 minutes. Turn and cook until the second side is browned, about 5 minutes longer. Alternatively, prepare a charcoal or gas grill for direct cooking over medium heat (350°F) and grill the crépinettes, turning once, until nicely browned and crisp on both sides, 4 to 6 minutes on each side. Serve at once.

CHEF'S NOTE: *Caul fat, the lacy yet sturdy fat membrane that sheathes some of the organs of pigs, sheep, and cows, can be purchased at well-stocked butcher shops and online.*

COUNTRY-STYLE PÂTÉ

CHEF TRAVIS DAY

The Parisian restaurant L'Ami Jean is known for its country pâté, and after just one visit, I can vouch for that fame. Served with a crock of cornichons and sliced crusty bread, it's all a girl could desire. Luckily, chef Travis Day, owner of Thistle Meats in Petaluma, California, does a bang-up job making a country-style pâté with our Liberty Ducks. If you can't get to Paris or Petaluma, this recipe will bring those flavors straight into your home. To ensure the perfect cook, you'll need a 12-by-4-by-3-inch lidded terrine mold, ideally enameled to ensure even heat distribution in the water bath. Slices of this pâté can also be served with a mixed green salad as a light main course.

¼ cup brandy
4 teaspoons fine sea salt
1½ teaspoons freshly ground black pepper
1 teaspoon light brown sugar
½ teaspoon pink curing salt #2
¼ teaspoon quatre épices, homemade (page 23) or purchased
¾ lb skinless duck breast (1 large breast)
⅔ lb pork fat
¾ lb duck livers, cleaned
½ cup rendered duck fat (page 32)
1 large yellow onion or 3 large shallots (½ lb total weight), thinly sliced
1 duck egg or extra-large chicken egg, lightly beaten
Whole-grain mustard, cornichons, pickled vegetables, and crostini or toasted baguette slices, for serving

Makes one 2¼-lb loaf pâté; 8 to 10 servings

WINE / BEER: A full-fruit Zinfandel with dark stone fruit notes would pair beautifully with the duck in this *pâté de campagne*. A Belgian dubbel with its malt-forward mouthfeel would also complement this dish.

In a large bowl, stir together the brandy, sea salt, pepper, brown sugar, curing salt, and quatre épices.

Cut the duck meat and pork fat into 1-inch cubes. Add them and the livers to the bowl with the brandy mixture and mix until the meat, fat, and livers are evenly coated with the seasonings. Cover and refrigerate for at least 12 hours or up to overnight.

In a sauté pan over medium heat, melt the duck fat. Add the onion and cook, stirring often, until it is is translucent and just starting to brown, about 10 minutes. Remove from the heat and let cool to room temperature, then transfer to a small bowl, cover, and chill in the refrigerator until ready to use.

Freeze all the grinding parts, including the coarse die, of your meat grinder for at least 1 hour before removing the marinated meat mixture from the refrigerator. This will ensure that the friction of the grinding process won't warm or melt the fat, which can cause the texture of the pâté to be of lesser quality.

Preheat the oven to 250°F. Fit your grinder with the coarse die and pass the marinated meats through the grinder once, capturing them in a bowl. Fold the egg and chilled onion into the ground meats, distributing them evenly.

Line a 12-by-4-by-3-inch terrine mold with a large piece of plastic wrap, centering the wrap so an equal amount (at least 4 inches) overhangs the mold on all four sides.

Scrape the pâté mixture into the prepared terrine, then press against it firmly with a rubber spatula to remove any air pockets and to spread it to all four corners. As you work, make sure the mixture is an even thickness throughout the mold. Fold the overhanging plastic wrap over the top of the mold to fully enclose the pâté. If the terrine mold comes with a weight, place it atop the covered pâté.

Cover the terrine mold with its lid and place it in a roasting pan just large enough to accommodate it. Add boiling water to the pan to come two-thirds of the way up the sides of the mold. Bake the pâté until an instant-read thermometer inserted into the center registers 145°F, about 1 hour and 50 minutes. Remove the terrine mold from the water bath and return the mold to the oven. Continue to bake until the thermometer inserted into center registers 155°F, about 25 minutes longer (the total cooking time will be about 2¼ hours). Remove the pâté from the oven and let cool, still covered, to room temperature. Transfer to the refrigerator and chill for at least 8 hours or preferably overnight.

When ready to serve, if the fat has congealed around the pâté, place the mold in a roasting pan, add hot water to the pan to reach two-thirds of the way up the sides of the mold, and let stand for 2 minutes to melt the fat slightly around the perimeter. Invert the mold onto a cutting board, lift off the mold, and remove the plastic wrap.

To serve, cut the pâté into uniform slices and arrange on a serving plate or add to a charcuterie platter. Accompany the slices with mustard, cornichons, pickled vegetables, and toasted baguette slices.

DUCK PROSCIUTTO

This is truly beginner meat curing at its finest—simple in preparation, simple in ingredients. All you need is some cheesecloth and some refrigerator space. The first time I saw duck prosciutto (that I recall) was in France in 2006 at a gas station food court. To my disbelief, it was vacuum sealed and shelf stable, much like you'd see beef jerky sold at a gas station in the United States. Serve the prosciutto in very thin slices as part of a charcuterie board, with Brie on a sandwich, draped over chunks of fresh melon, or cut into small pieces and mixed with peas and cream sauce on pasta.

4 duck breasts, tenders removed
2 cups kosher salt
2 tablespoons sugar

Makes 4 breasts of duck prosciutto; serves 6 to 8

WINE: A crisp, light red, like Beaujolais or Bardolino, would complement the salt and meatiness of the prosciutto.

Leave as much fat on each duck breast as you can. In a 9-by-13-inch baking dish, mix together the salt and the sugar. Arrange the breasts, skin side down, on the salt mixture, pressing them firmly into the mixture. Scoop up some of the salt mixture and rub it all over the meaty side of the breasts. Then turn the breasts skin side up, making sure the meaty side is still resting in the salt mixture. Transfer the dish to the refrigerator and let the breasts cure, uncovered, for at least 24 hours or up to 36 hours.

Remove the breasts from the baking dish and rinse them under cool running water to remove the salt mixture. Pat the breasts completely dry with paper towels, then wrap each breast individually in a double thickness of cheesecloth. You should barely be able to see the meat through the wrapping but it should still be porous enough to allow for some airflow.

Place the wrapped duck breasts on a wire rack set in a small sheet pan. Alternatively, line up chopsticks on the sheet pan and place the breasts on top. Set the sheet pan in a dry place in the refrigerator where the duck breasts can cure. A top shelf away from anything that may spill is good. The airflow is important to make sure no spoilage occurs. Once a day, turn the breasts to make sure air is reaching all the surfaces equally.

In about 2 weeks, the duck breasts will be fully cured. You're looking for firm meat with some give to it. When you slice into it, the middle should be a rich, dark red, while the outside of the meat, which is drier, will be a dark purple. The air temperature and humidity of every refrigerator are a little different, so the timing may vary.

To serve, cut the prosciutto into paper-thin slices. The prosciutto will keep refrigerated in an airtight container for up to 1 month.

DUCK SKIN CHICHARRONES

CHEF SEAN Z. PAXTON

Using all parts of the animal has multiple benefits. In this recipe from chef Sean Z. Paxton, a batch of duck skin yields both rendered duck fat to use in other dishes and a delicious crispy snack. While the *chicharrones* can be seasoned with just salt and pepper, here they are treated to a heady mix of spices, orange peel, and thyme. Or you can try tossing them with *ras el hanout*, Creole seasoning, Sichuan spice mix, or even the *speculoos* spice mix, adding 1 tablespoon sugar to the blend for an intriguing sweet-and-savory snack. (See spice mix recipes on pages 22–23.)

2 lb duck skin
1 tablespoon Belgian Witbier Spice Blend (page 22)

Makes 8 servings

BEER: A Belgian witbier would highlight the orange and coriander while also being light and refreshing. A Belgian lambic or an American sour would help cut the fat.

To prepare the duck skin, inspect it carefully, removing any quills, pinfeathers, or wax. Rinse the skin well under cool running water. Using a sharp knife or kitchen shears, cut the skin into strips or squares about 2 inches wide. The duck skin will shrink as the fat renders, creating bite-size pieces when finished.

Transfer the prepared duck skin to a heavy pot and add water to cover. Place the pot over medium heat and bring the water to a boil, stirring occasionally to prevent the skin from sticking to the bottom of the pot. The liquid will turn cloudy and opaque as the fat melts and the water slowly evaporates, leaving behind rendered duck fat. When the water has evaporated and the fat is clear, after 30 to 45 minutes, the duck skin will cook and turn golden brown and crisp. Using a slotted spoon or metal skimmer, transfer the crisped skin pieces to a wire rack. Place a fine-mesh sieve over a heatproof bowl and pour the contents of the pot into the sieve. Transfer the rendered fat to a heatproof container, let cool, cap tightly, and refrigerate for up to 6 months.

While the chicharrones are still warm, transfer them to a large bowl, sprinkle with the spice blend, and toss to coat evenly. Serve right away.

GARLIC CONFIT IN DUCK FAT

CHEF JOSHUA TANGO

Garlic. Duck fat. What more do you need? This confit is a versatile ingredient to have in your kitchen, and the recipe is easily multiplied to stockpile. Napa Valley chef Joshua Tango loves it on garlic toast, smeared onto a duck taco, or, his personal favorite, tossed with fresh pasta mixed with plenty of Parmesan and butter.

1 cup rendered duck fat (page 32)
½ lb peeled garlic cloves (see Chef's Note)
4 fresh rosemary sprigs

Makes two ½-pint (8-oz) jars

WINE: Garlic is tough to pair on its own. You need to seek out something with acidity to cut through the spice and the fat. Look for a citrusy Sauvignon Blanc or a Chardonnay and Sauvignon Blanc blend.

Preheat the oven to 220°F. In a enameled cast-iron Dutch oven or other heavy pot over low heat, warm the duck fat until it liquefies. Carefully add the garlic cloves, submerging them completely in the fat. Top with the rosemary sprigs and transfer the pot, uncovered, to the oven. Cook gently until the garlic is soft and spreadable, at least 2 hours or up to 3 hours.

Remove and discard the rosemary sprigs. Using a slotted spoon, transfer the garlic cloves to two ½-pint jars, dividing them equally between the jars. Cover the cloves with just enough of the fat to submerge them. (Store the remaining garlic-infused fat in an airtight container in the refrigerator for cooking vegetables or other uses.) Let cool, then cover and store in the refrigerator for up to 1 month. Use on everything!

CHEF'S NOTE: *One head of garlic yields about 2 oz peeled cloves. It takes a lot of work to peel as much garlic as you need for this recipe, so no judgment if you buy already peeled cloves.*

DUCK HAM

CHEFS JEREMY FOX AND MATTHEW SCHALER

You'll need to prep the duck breasts five days in advance, but the effort is worth it. At his Santa Monica restaurant Birdie G's, chef and owner Jeremy Fox and chef de cuisine Matthew Schaler take classics and turn them into fun and exciting new dishes. For example, Jeremy pairs the duck ham with shredded Emmental or gruyère cheese in stuffed potato latkes he calls "goldbars." For a different take, make ham and cheese turnovers using the empanada dough recipe on page 98. Pressed for time? Simply make a duck ham and cheese sandwich on sliced sourdough.

Brine
2 quarts water
½ cup kosher salt
1 tablespoon pink curing salt #2
2 teaspoons brown mustard seeds
2 teaspoons black peppercorns
8 whole cloves
3 allspice berries
1 cinnamon stick
2 bay leaves

4 duck breasts (2½ to 3 lb)
1 tablespoon freshly ground black pepper
1 tablespoon ground coriander
1 teaspoon kosher salt

Makes 4 breasts of duck ham; serves 6 to 8

WINE: You want something with a little sweetness but still with some acidity. A nice Chenin Blanc, like one from Vouvray, would be good for balancing the saltiness of the meat.

To make the brine, in a large saucepan over high heat, combine the water, kosher salt, curing salt, mustard seeds, peppercorns, cloves, allspice, cinnamon, and bay leaves. Bring to a boil, stirring until the salt dissolves. Remove from the heat and let cool to room temperature. Transfer the brine to a nonreactive container, cover, and refrigerate until well chilled, at least 4 hours or up to overnight.

Trim the duck breasts of any excess fat or any errant bone fragments. Submerge the duck breasts in the cold brine, cover, and refrigerate for 4 days.

After 4 days, remove the duck breasts from the brine and pat dry with paper towels. Discard the brine.

Preheat the oven to 275°F. Place a rack in a roasting pan. In a small bowl, stir together the pepper, coriander, and kosher salt. Lightly but evenly coat each duck breast all over with the spice rub (you may not need all of it).

Place the seasoned duck breasts, skin side up, on the rack and bake until golden brown and an instant-read thermometer inserted into the thickest part of a breast registers 135°F, about 30 minutes.

Transfer the breasts to a plate and let cool to room temperature, then cover tightly and refrigerate until cold (the internal temperature should be below 40°F) before serving.

To serve, cut the ham into thin slices or as desired. The ham will keep refrigerated for up to 2 weeks.

DUCK CHARCUTERIE BOARD

Although charcuterie boards have been around since the fifteenth century, there's been an explosion in their popularity over the last decade. What started as a selection of cured meats has evolved to become beautiful boards heavily laden with meats, cheeses, dried fruits, nuts, condiments, and more. I love making a charcuterie board for appetizers for a crowd or for a simple yet delicious dinner for two (it's like grown-up snacks!).

The trick to a successful board is providing your guests (or yourself) with a variety of textures and flavors that complement one another. It's a great opportunity to source small-batch cheeses from a good cheesemonger, and it's best to have the meats freshly cut rather than buy them prepackaged. There's been a boon of artisanal butcher shops around the country making incredible cured meats, so seek one out if possible. Here are my suggestions for making a charcuterie board at home with all the fixings. Regard it as a good starting point for putting together what is available to you.

Cured meats
Duck prosciutto (page 58)
Smoked duck breast (page 40)
Spanish duck chorizo (page 66)
Salami and/or soppressata

Spreadable meats
Duck liver mousse (page 51)
Country-style duck pâté (page 56)
Duck rillettes (page 52)
Garlic confit in duck fat (page 62)

Cheeses
Aged hard, such as pecorino, Gouda, or Manchego
Fresh, such as mozzarella or feta
Semisoft, such as Camembert, Brie, or chèvre

Accompaniments
Pickled vegetables
Olives
Cornichons
Grainy mustards
Ripe, seasonal fruit, such as sliced apples, pears, or melon
Dried fruits, such as apricots, figs, or apples
Fruit chutney, such as plum or apricot
Nuts, such as toasted walnuts, pecans, almonds, and/or cashews
Crackers, sliced baguette, or crostini

WINE: Look for a wine with some acidity and structure that won't overpower the flavors on the board. I like an aged white from the southern Rhône, like Marsanne or Roussanne (or a blend), or a Beaujolais Villages.

Start by selecting two to four different thinly sliced cured meats; the amount depends on the number of people you are serving. Then, add one or two spreadable meats for a variety of texture. A good rule of thumb is to serve about 2 ounces of meats per person.

Offer a mix of both aged and fresh cheeses on the board, especially when serving a lot of guests.

Add flavors and textures to balance and complement the meats and cheeses. Something tangy, something sweet, as well as crunchy crackers or crostini and toasted nuts will bring the board to life.

For tangy accompaniments, I love pickled vegetables, olives, and cornichons. A grainy mustard is a savory, vinegary accompaniment that goes well with pâté.

For sweet accompaniments, fruits—both fresh and dried—or a dollop of sweet-tangy chutney is always nice.

And don't forget crackers or a sliced baguette for serving. Sometimes it's nice to have both, but toasted baguette slices can substitute for crackers. A little pile of nuts, such as walnuts, pecans, or almonds, is also a nice addition.

For assembling all the elements, select a large cutting board (or a few smaller ones) or a large platter. If you're going to have guests slicing cheeses or meats, set out proper knives and a good surface for cutting.

Make sure to provide napkins or small plates for guests for putting together their perfect bites. There's not a lot better in this world than a baguette slice, some country pâté with a smidgen of grainy mustard, and a cornichon, but you need to have a space to create it!

SPANISH DUCK CHORIZO

CHEF ANDY DOUBRAVA

Chef Andy Doubrava, who oversees the kitchen at Rustic Canyon in Santa Monica, is a wizard with ingredients. I'm forever inspired by his combinations, so it's a real treat to include here his rendition of a cured Spanish-style chorizo made with duck instead of the traditional pork. Just as in Spain, this chorizo is aged and dried like a salami, so you'll need a cool, dark place with stable temperature and humidity levels. To be instantly transported to a Madrid tapas bar, serve slices of the duck chorizo alongside some duck ham (page 63), a wedge of Manchego cheese, and a bowl of Manzanilla olives.

3 tablespoons kosher salt
½ teaspoon pink curing salt #2
1½ teaspoons dextrose (superfine corn sugar) or sugar
1 tablespoon spicy smoked paprika, preferably pimentón agridulce (medium) or pimentón picante (hot)
1 tablespoon ground guajillo chile
½ teaspoon cayenne pepper
1 garlic clove, minced, or ½ teaspoon garlic powder
2¼ lb duck breasts, skinned
1 large natural pork casing, about 3 feet long

Makes 1 large duck chorizo

WINE: A light, crisp red wine, such as a Spanish Mencía. If interested in some bubbles, pair with a Cava Rosado.

In a small bowl, stir together the kosher salt, curing salt, dextrose, paprika, ground chile, cayenne, and garlic. Be sure to mix well to remove any lumps or the seasonings will be unevenly distributed and will affect the color of the chorizo.

Cut the duck breasts into pieces the size of the opening of your meat grinder. In a bowl, toss together the duck meat and seasoning mixture, coating the duck evenly on all sides. Cover and place in the freezer for at least 4 hours or up to overnight. Placing the duck in the freezer will ensure a better texture once it is ground.

Rinse the casing well under cool running water, then immerse the casing in a large bowl of warm water for about 1 hour to make it soft and pliable. Freeze all the grinding parts, including the smallest die, of your meat grinder for at least 1 hour before removing the meat mixture from the freezer. If you have a sausage stuffer (or if you will be using a funnel), refrigerate it at the same time.

Remove the seasoned meat from the freezer. Fit your grinder with the smallest die and pass the meat through the grinder, capturing it in a bowl. Then pass the meat through the grinder a second time. (If you don't have a grinder, you can grind the meat in a food processor, pulsing it to a fine texture. Be careful not to overprocess until reduced to a puree or paste.)

Set up your sausage stuffer (or ready your funnel). Drain the casing and run cool water through it. Tie off one end of the casing with a knot and attach the other end to the nozzle of the sausage stuffer. Add the meat mixture to the stuffer and push it into the casing, squeezing and packing it into the casing as fully and as tightly as possible without tearing the casing. As you work, be sure to force out any air bubbles you see forming. When all of the sausage mixture is in the casing, tie off the other end, then cut off and discard any extra casing. Attach a 6-inch length of kitchen twine to the knot at the end of the casing, making a loop that can be used to hang the sausage from a hook, nail, or bar.

Weigh the chorizo, noting the weight. As some of the mixture will be lost in the grinding and stuffing process, this weight will have changed from the weight of the original ingredients. Hang the chorizo in a cool, dark place that will stay at a semi-stable temperature of 70° to 75°F and humidity level of 60 to 70 percent. Possible spots to hang the sausage include a clean refrigerator outfitted with a temperature probe or temperature controller, a wine cooler, a garage, or a dark cupboard.

Check the weight of the chorizo every 2 days; you are looking for a 35 percent loss in weight. For example, a 37-oz sausage is ready to use when the goal weight of 24 oz is reached. Plan on 6 to 8 days, though the timing will depend on how well the temperature and humidity levels are maintained. Once the sausage is at the desired weight, place it in the refrigerator until ready to use and/or serve. It will keep for up to 1 month in an airtight container.

CHEF'S NOTE: *A sausage stuffer is a game changer, as it simplifies packing the meat mixture into a casing so it is free of air pockets. Many meat grinders come with a sausage stuffer attachment or offer one for purchase. Curing salt, which is available at some butcher shops and online, is critical to helping prevent any unwanted bacteria, yeasts, or molds.*

CHAPTER THREE

STARTERS & SMALL PLATES

DUCK FAT FRIES

There is hardly a better combination than duck fat and potatoes. You can peel the potatoes for these fries if you like, but I prefer them with the peel on. J. Kenji López-Alt, a food columnist turned scientist, helped me learn about the mechanics of a fry. The first dip in the oil fries the water on the surface of the potato—that initial sizzle you hear and see. The second fry is when the real crispiness occurs. That's because the water in the potato now has a better pathway to release, resulting in a crispier, crunchier French fry. The yield on this recipe can easily be adjusted up; you just need more potatoes and more fat. Serve these with the Roasted Garlic Ranch (page 96) and/or the Smoky Tomato Sauce (page 77). Or go wild and make these "animal style," topping them with melted Cheddar and caramelized onions.

2 lb russet potatoes, unpeeled
Rendered duck fat (page 32), for frying (about 8 cups)
Kosher salt

Makes 4 to 6 servings

WINE: Fries and Champagne are a perfect pairing. In fact, if you ask me, they are a complete meal.

Fill a large pot two-thirds full with water and bring to a boil over high heat (you need enough water to cover the potatoes by 1 inch).

To cut the potatoes into fries, place a potato on its side on a cutting board. With a large chef's knife, cut a thin slice off one edge. Turn the potato cut side down and cut lengthwise into slabs about ¼ inch thick or the width you'd like your fries. Stack two or three of the slabs, then cut the stack lengthwise into pieces the same width as the slabs (about ¼ inch). The most important thing is to make sure all the fries are uniform in size.

When the water is boiling, add the potatoes and boil for 5 minutes. Drain well, then gently blot dry with paper towels.

Line a sheet pan with paper towels and place it next to the stove top. In a large, deep sauté pan, warm enough duck fat to yield a depth of 1 to 2 inches once it has melted and heat over medium-high heat to 325°F on a deep-frying thermometer. Make sure the pan is no more than half full of fat. Working in batches, add the potatoes, being careful not to crowd the pan or lower the heat of the fat too much. Fry the potatoes, turning them occasionally with tongs, until lightly browned on all sides, about 5 minutes. Using the tongs, transfer the fries to the prepared sheet pan. Repeat with the remaining potatoes.

Preheat the oven to 200°F. Line a second sheet pan with paper towels. Add more duck fat to the sauté pan if the level has dropped below 1 to 2 inches and reheat over medium-high heat to 375°F. Again working in batches, add the fries and fry, turning occasionally with the tongs, until golden brown on all sides, 3 to 4 minutes. You can add more fries per batch during this round, but be careful not to crowd the pan. Using the tongs, transfer the fries to the second prepared sheet pan and place in the oven to keep warm. Repeat with the remaining fries.

When all the fries are ready, sprinkle them with salt and toss to mix. Serve right away.

DUCK SLIDERS

with secret XO sauce

My dad would probably argue with me on this one, but the first duck burger I ever had was one made of duck tenders (*aiguillettes*) and beef in France. It was at least the one that stuck with me! We've upped our game and have a 70/30 blend of ground duck meat and fat to make the perfect burgers. Serving the sliders as a whole loaf of buns is a fun way to present them to diners. I mean, who doesn't love a good pull-apart, gooey, cheesy moment? I've mixed a little five-spice powder into the slider mixture for an unexpected flavor punch and paired the sliders with my XO sauce to make them the ultimate umami bite.

Secret XO Sauce
1 tablespoon XO sauce
1 tablespoon ketchup
1 tablespoon mayonnaise

Sliders
1 tablespoon rendered duck fat (page 32), plus more for the pan
1 lb ground duck meat
1½ teaspoons kosher salt
1 teaspoon five-spice powder
1 yellow onion, finely chopped
12 dinner-size rolls, such as King's Hawaiian Sweet Rolls
12 small slices white Cheddar cheese, plus ⅓ cup shredded

Makes 12 sliders; 4 to 6 servings

WINE: A friend suggested chilling Syrah to pair with burgers, and I've never looked back. Look for a Crozes-Hermitage or other northern Rhône wine and chill to nearly white wine temperature to serve.

To make the sauce, in a small bowl, combine all the ingredients and mix well. Set aside.

To make the sliders, preheat the oven to 350°F. Grease a sheet pan lightly with duck fat.

In a bowl, mix together the ground duck, salt, and five-spice powder. In a large frying pan over medium heat, melt the duck fat. Add the onion and cook, stirring occasionally, until caramelized, about 10 minutes. Transfer the onion to a small bowl and set aside. Return the pan to medium heat, add the duck mixture, and cook, stirring occasionally and breaking it up with a wooden spoon, until just cooked through, 5 to 7 minutes. Remove from the heat and discard any excess liquid or fat. Stir the reserved sauce into the duck mixture.

Remove the rolls from the packaging in one piece and slice them horizontally, keeping the sides of the rolls intact. Place the roll bottom halves, cut side up, on the prepared sheet pan. Top the roll bottoms evenly with the cheese slices, then spread the duck mixture on top of the cheese. Arrange the onion on top of the duck mixture in an even layer, then finish with the shredded cheese in an even layer. Close the sliders with the roll tops, cut side down.

Bake the sliders until the cheese is melted and the tops of the rolls are toasted, about 15 minutes. Serve right away.

FRIED DUCK NUGGETS

with dipping sauce

This recipe is the ultimate redo of a children's classic enjoyed by both kids and adults. It's inspired by popular YouTuber Nick DiGiovanni's chicken nuggets, which easily translate to duck. Serve these crisp bites with one or two of the dipping sauces suggested here or with your own favorite dipping sauce.

1 lb ground duck meat
4 large eggs
1⅓ cups panko (Japanese bread crumbs)
2 dashes hot-pepper sauce, such as Tapatío brand, or more if you like your food spicy
1 teaspoon kosher salt
1 teaspoon freshly ground black pepper
1 cup cornstarch
Canola oil, for frying
Roasted Garlic Ranch (page 96), Bachan's Japanese Barbecue Sauce, Kewpie mayonnaise, and/or your favorite dipping sauce, for serving

Makes 4 to 6 servings

BEER: These are simple, fun, and oh so delicious. Crack open a light beer of your choice to make this an easy meal.

Line a 9-by-13-inch baking dish with parchment paper. In a large bowl, combine the ground duck, 2 of the eggs, ⅓ cup of the panko, the hot sauce, salt, and pepper and mix together with your hands until all of the ingredients are evenly distributed. Spread the mixture evenly over the bottom of the prepared baking dish. The mixture will be about ¼ inch thick. Place the dish in the freezer until the meat mixture is solid, at least 2 hours or up to overnight.

When ready to cook, remove the baking dish from the freezer and let stand at room temperature for about 10 minutes. The meat mixture should be thawed just enough to cut with a cookie cutter. Using a 2-inch round cutter (or any shape you like!), cut out as many rounds as possible. Press together the scraps and cut out more rounds.

Preheat the oven to 200°F. Put the cornstarch, the remaining 1 cup panko, and the remaining 2 eggs in separate shallow bowls. Whisk the eggs until blended. Line a sheet pan with paper towels.

Pour the oil to a depth of ½ inch into a deep sauté pan and heat over medium-high heat to 350°F on a deep-frying thermometer. (Alternatively, if you have a countertop deep fryer, pour in the oil and set the temperature to 350°F.)

Working in batches to avoid crowding the pan, coat each round with the cornstarch, tapping off the excess, then dip it into the egg, allowing the excess to drip off, and finally coat with the panko. Carefully add the rounds to the hot oil and cook until golden brown on the bottom, about 2 minutes, then turn and cook until golden brown all over and cooked through, about 2 minutes longer. Using a slotted spatula, transfer the nuggets to the towel-lined sheet pan and place in the oven to keep warm. Repeat until all the rounds are fried.

Serve the nuggets hot with the sauce(s) of your choice alongside.

DUCK CHORIZO MINI TOSTADAS

Our Mexican-style duck chorizo has quickly become a favorite product of mine. Made with Boonville Farm's Spicy Piment d'Ville, it's a fun take on the Mexican staple. Piment d'Ville is a Californian-grown Espelette pepper, and the spicy version is picked young to make it almost cayenne-like, giving these tostadas a nice pop of spice! Boonville Farm is a small, women-owned operation in Mendocino, California, and the spices it produces are truly delicious. I sprinkle the Piment d'Ville on everything from eggs to lightly salted buttered toast.

Pickled Onion
1 small red onion, thinly sliced
2 cups boiling water
½ cup rice vinegar
1½ teaspoons sugar
½ teaspoon dried oregano, preferably Mexican
¼ teaspoon ground cumin
⅛ teaspoon fine sea salt

Slaw
3 cups finely shredded red or green cabbage, or a mixture
1 medium carrot, peeled and finely shredded
½ to 1 jalapeño chile, very thinly sliced
¼ cup chopped fresh cilantro
2 tablespoons avocado or canola oil
Juice of ½ lime
Fine sea salt and freshly ground black pepper

Avocado or canola oil, for frying
8 to 10 small (4-inch) corn tortillas
1 lb duck chorizo
Mexican crema, for serving
1 avocado, halved, pitted, peeled, and thinly sliced
8 to 10 fresh cilantro sprigs
1 lime, cut into 6 wedges

Makes 8 to 10 tostadas; 4 to 6 servings

WINE: A strong Sauvignon Blanc is ideal for these full-flavored mini bites. Look for one from New Zealand.

To make the pickled onion, put the onion into a small saucepan, pour in the boiling water, and set aside for 5 minutes. Drain the onions in a fine-mesh sieve, then rinse. Set aside.

In the same saucepan, combine the vinegar, sugar, oregano, cumin, and salt and bring to a boil over medium-high heat. Add the onion, stir to combine, and remove from the heat. Let cool to room temperature, then transfer to an airtight container and refrigerate for at least 30 minutes or up to 1 week before using.

To make the slaw, in a bowl, toss together the cabbage, carrot, jalapeño (adjusting amount to desired spiciness), and cilantro. Drizzle with the oil and lime juice, season with salt and pepper, and toss again. The slaw can be made up to 2 hours in advance, covered, and refrigerated.

To fry the tortillas, line a sheet pan with paper towels. Pour the oil to a depth of ½ inch into a large frying pan and heat over medium-high heat. Working in batches to avoid crowding the pan, fry the tortillas, turning once with tongs, until crisp and golden on both sides, about 1 minute total. Using the tongs, transfer to the prepared sheet pan. Repeat until all the tortillas are fried and then set aside. Discard the oil in the pan and wipe out the pan.

Return the frying pan to medium-high heat. Crumble the chorizo into the pan and cook, stirring occasionally and breaking up the meat with a wooden spoon, until browned and cooked through, 5 to 6 minutes. Drain off most of the excess fat (leave a little to keep the chorizo moist).

To assemble the tostadas, arrange the fried tortillas on a large platter and top with the chorizo, dividing it evenly. Top each tostada with a drizzle of crema and with some slaw, avocado, and pickled onion. Garnish with cilantro sprigs and serve with the lime wedges alongside.

DUCK FAT–CRISPED WHITE BEANS

with smoky tomato sauce and aioli

CHEF SARAH SCOTT

Although this recipe could be made with nearly any type of white bean, it is worth seeking out Royal Corona beans from Napa Valley–based Rancho Gordo. These plump beans give this dish the perfect ratio of crispy skin to creamy interior—they're unlike any other! If you can't find them, white gigante beans would work well. Chef Sarah Scott's two extraordinary sauces round out this seemingly simple, infectiously delicious dish.

Smoky Tomato Sauce

1 tablespoon extra-virgin olive oil
2 teaspoons minced garlic
1 tablespoon tomato paste
1½ tablespoons sherry vinegar
¾ cup canned crushed San Marzano tomatoes with juices
1½ teaspoons sugar
1½ teaspoons smoked paprika
½ teaspoon kosher salt

Aioli

1 large egg
2 garlic cloves, smashed
2 teaspoons fresh lemon juice
½ teaspoon kosher salt
1 cup extra-virgin olive oil, or ½ cup each neutral oil and extra-virgin olive oil

1 lb dried corona beans (large, meaty white beans), preferably Rancho Gordo brand Royal Corona (about 2 cups)
Kosher salt and freshly ground black pepper
¼ to ½ cup rendered duck fat (page 32)
Chopped fresh flat-leaf parsley leaves, for garnish
Fleur de sel, for garnish

Makes 6 to 8 servings

WINE: A rustic Italian red will complement the smoky tomato sauce and balance the richness of the beans. Seek out a Valpolicella blend.

To make the tomato sauce, in a small saucepan over medium heat, warm the oil with the garlic and cook, stirring, until fragrant, about 15 seconds. Add the tomato paste and vinegar and cook, stirring frequently, until the vinegar evaporates, about 1 minute. Add the tomatoes and sugar, stir well, turn down the heat to low, and cook, stirring occasionally, until the sauce has thickened and the flavors have melded, about 30 minutes.

Remove from the heat, stir in the paprika and salt, and let cool for a few minutes. Then transfer to a blender or food processor and puree until very smooth. Add water, 1 teaspoon at a time, until the mixture achieves a ketchup-like consistency. Transfer the sauce to a bowl and keep at room temperature if serving within a few hours. If not, transfer to an airtight container and refrigerate for up to 2 weeks.

To make the aioli, in a food processor, combine the egg, garlic, lemon juice, and salt and process for 30 seconds. Then, with the processor running, slowly add the oil in a fine, steady drizzle. Once the mixture emulsifies and thickens, you can add the oil a little faster. The moment all the oil has been incorporated, stop the processor, transfer the aioli to an airtight container, and refrigerate until ready to use or for up to 1 week.

To cook the beans, first pick over and rinse them, then transfer them to a large saucepan and add water to cover by 2 inches. Bring to a boil over high heat, then turn down the heat to low and simmer uncovered, stirring every so often, until tender, 1 to 3 hours; the timing depends on the age of the beans. Add water as needed to keep the beans covered during the cooking. Remove from the heat and season with salt and pepper, then drain well.

Preheat the oven to 200°F. Have a baking dish ready for the beans. In a large, heavy frying pan over medium-high heat, warm ¼ cup of the duck fat. When the fat has melted, add just enough of the beans to the pan to form a single layer and cook, stirring occasionally to make sure they color evenly on all sides, until crisped and golden, 8 to 10 minutes. Transfer the beans to the baking dish and place in the oven to keep warm. Repeat with the remaining beans, adding more fat to the pan between batches if needed. Keep the beans warm in the oven until ready to serve.

To serve, divide the beans among individual shallow bowls or spoon them into a large shallow serving bowl. Garnish with the parsley and fleur de sel. Serve right away with the sauces alongside for dipping.

BRITISH-STYLE ROASTIES

KIM LAIDLAW

These big, chunky potatoes are creamy on the inside, like mashed potatoes, and extra crispy on the outside. They get their texture from a quick precook on the stove top, then a long oven bath in plenty of duck fat, which adds flavor and deep crunch to the outside. Be sure to use a starchy potato like a russet to achieve the proper texture. Cookbook author and recipe developer Kim Laidlaw makes these every Christmas with her British husband and they are always a huge hit, but they would also be right at home alongside a whole roast duck and gravy for Sunday supper.

4 lb russet potatoes
Kosher salt
1 cup rendered duck fat (page 32)

Makes 6 servings

WINE / BEER: To keep with the theme, a British brown ale would give body and a touch of sweetness to balance the salty potatoes. For wine, a full-bodied red, like a good Zinfandel, would be nice.

Preheat the oven to 400°F. Have ready a large, heavy roasting pan that will hold the cut potatoes in a single layer with just a little space between the pieces. Line a large plate with paper towels.

Peel the potatoes and cut them into roughly 2- to 3-inch chunks; they should all be about the same size. Put the potatoes into a large saucepan, add just enough water to cover them, and season with plenty of salt. Bring to a boil over high heat, then lower the heat to medium and simmer uncovered, stirring once or twice, for 5 minutes.

While the potatoes simmer, add the duck fat to the roasting pan and place the pan in the oven to heat.

Using the lid of the saucepan slightly ajar to hold the potatoes in the pan, carefully drain off the water from the pan. Then cover the pan and give it a good shake to bash up the potatoes a bit (don't shake too hard, as you don't want to completely smash them). This creates a rough surface all over the potatoes, which helps them crisp in the hot fat. Uncover the pan and let the potatoes dry out in the pan for about 5 minutes.

Remove the hot roasting pan from the oven and carefully add the potatoes to the hot fat, arranging them, not touching, in a single layer. Return the pan to the oven and roast the potatoes, turning them about every 15 minutes or so, until they are deeply golden brown, very crispy on the outside, and meltingly tender inside, 1 to 1¼ hours.

Using tongs, transfer the potatoes to the towel-lined plate to drain. Sprinkle with salt and serve right away.

DUCK CONFIT ONION PANCAKES

with quince puree

CHEF DAVID BARZELAY

These perfectly portioned bite-size starters marry light, crisp pancakes—similar to Chinese scallion pancakes—with duck confit and a tart-sweet-savory quince puree. Chef David Barzelay of Lazy Bear in San Francisco tops these tasty bites with pickled quince as well. The recipe yields enough for a crowd, but the quince puree and the pancakes can be made in advance and refrigerated or frozen, so you can assemble only as many as you want. Lazy Bear makes a whole kit of other duck goodies at the restaurant, all of them with an inventive delivery.

Quince Puree
3 cups water
Juice of ½ lemon
1 quince, about ½ lb
1 tablespoon sugar
¼ teaspoon fine sea salt
1½ tablespoons extra-virgin olive oil
¾ cup fresh apple cider

Onion Pancakes
½ cup unsalted butter, melted and cooled slightly
½ cup finely chopped Walla Walla or other sweet yellow onion (about ½ small onion)
¼ cup finely chopped red or white spring onion, white or red and pale green parts (about 1 medium onion)
2 tablespoons chopped fresh chives
1 garlic clove, chopped
1¼ lb (about 4 cups) all-purpose flour
1½ teaspoons fine sea salt
1⅓ cups lukewarm water (105° to 110°F)
1 tablespoon sugar
½ teaspoon active dry yeast

To make the quince puree, in a bowl, combine the water and lemon juice. Peel and core the quince, then cut it into ¼-inch-thick wedges, adding them to the lemon water as they are cut. Turn to coat evenly, then drain and return the quince to the bowl. Sprinkle with the sugar and salt and toss to coat evenly. Set aside to cure for 15 minutes.

In a large frying pan over medium-high heat, warm 1 tablespoon of the oil. Add half of the quince wedges in a single layer and sear without turning until nicely browned and caramelized on the underside, 2 to 3 minutes. Transfer the wedges to a small saucepan. Rewarm the oil in the pan, add the remaining quince wedges, sear them the same way, and add them to the saucepan.

Add the apple cider to the quince, place the saucepan over medium-high heat, and bring to a boil. Turn down the heat to low, cover, and simmer, stirring occasionally, until the quince is very tender, 15 to 20 minutes.

Drain the quince into a fine-mesh sieve set over a bowl, reserving the cooking liquid. Transfer the quince to a blender and blend until very smooth, streaming in the remaining ½ tablespoon olive oil to give the puree a glossy finish. If the puree is very thick, add some of the cooking liquid, 1 teaspoon at a time, to achieve a spreadable consistency. Transfer the puree to a bowl or jar, taste, and season with more sugar and salt if needed. You should have about 2 cups. Set aside until needed. (The quince puree can be stored in an airtight container in the refrigerator for up to 1 week.)

To make the pancakes, first make the allium butter. In the blender, combine the butter, Walla Walla and spring onions, chives, and garlic and blend until smooth. You should have about 1 cup. Set aside at room temperature.

In the bowl of a stand mixer, stir together the flour and salt. In a small bowl, whisk together the water, sugar, and yeast, then let sit for 15 minutes to bloom the yeast. Fit the stand mixer with the paddle attachment, add the yeast mixture to the flour mixture, and mix on low speed until the mixture comes together in a rough mass. Add ½ cup of the reserved allium butter and beat on medium speed until a soft, slightly sticky dough forms. If the dough is very sticky, beat in a little more flour. Reserve the remaining

½ cup allium butter for lamination. Cover the bowl with a damp kitchen towel and let the dough rest for 30 minutes.

Divide the dough into thirds and shape each portion into a ball. (Each ball will weigh about ¾ lb.) On a well-floured work surface, roll out a ball into a round about 11 inches in diameter and ¼ inch thick. Gently spread one-third of the remaining allium butter (about 2½ tablespoons) evenly over the surface of the dough. Starting at one edge, roll the dough up tightly into a long rope, gradually stretching it as you roll so the finished rope is about 22 inches long. Starting with one end of the rope, coil the dough around itself into a tight spiral. Press the coils together, tuck the end underneath, and set aside on a floured surface. Repeat with the remaining dough portions. Cover the dough spirals with the damp towel and let rest for 30 minutes.

Line a large sheet pan with parchment paper and dust the parchment with flour. On a lightly floured work surface, roll out one dough spiral into a round about ¼ inch thick. Using a 2¾-inch round cutter, punch out as many rounds as possible. Transfer the rounds to the prepared sheet pan, making sure they are not touching. Repeat with the remaining dough spirals, adding the rounds to the sheet pan. If necessary, you can layer the rounds on the pan, separating the layers with sheets of floured parchment. Cover with plastic wrap and refrigerate for at least 1 hour or up to overnight, or freeze for up to 2 months.

Preheat the oven to 200°F. Line a second sheet pan with paper towels and place it in the oven. In a large frying pan over medium heat, warm 2 tablespoons duck fat until hot. Working in batches to avoid crowding, add the pancakes and fry, turning once or twice, until golden brown and crispy on both sides but still pliable, 2 to 3 minutes. Transfer to the towel-lined sheet pan and return the pan to the oven to keep the pancakes warm.

While you are cooking the pancakes, rewarm the quince puree in a small saucepan over low heat. Remove from the heat, cover to keep warm, and set aside. In a large cast-iron or other heavy frying pan over medium-high heat, warm 2 tablespoons duck fat. Add the shredded duck meat in an even layer and cook, without stirring, until the bottom is nicely crisped, about 3 minutes. Stir and continue to warm the duck, about 1 minute longer.

To assemble, arrange the warm pancakes on a platter. Spread 1 teaspoon quince puree onto each pancake, then top each pancake with a mound (about 1 tablespoon) of the warm duck confit. Garnish with a sprinkle of chives and serve right away.

Rendered duck fat (page 32), for frying
2½ cups shredded or chopped meat from duck leg confit (page 35) or roasted duck legs (page 36), including crispy skin (about 5 legs)
Chopped fresh chives, for garnish

Makes about 40 confit-topped pancakes; about 10 servings

WINE: A Loire Chenin Blanc, like the wines from Saumur.

DUCK FAT–FRIED EVERYTHING LATKES

CHEF CRAIG STOLL

Delfina is known for its extraordinary pastas and pizzas, but here we have a once-a-year treat that can be found on the menu at Hanukkah. Chef Craig Stoll serves these everything-spiced, shredded potato cakes crisped in duck fat with dollops of pear-quince butter and crème fraîche. Here, apple butter stands in for the pear-quince butter. Select medium-sized potatoes that are all about the same size so they cook evenly in the boiling water.

Seedy Mix
⅓ cup sesame seeds
1 tablespoon poppy seeds
1 tablespoon dehydrated chopped garlic
1 tablespoon dehydrated flaked onion
1 tablespoon caraway seeds
1½ teaspoons fennel seeds
¾ teaspoon flaky sea salt, preferably Maldon

About 3 lb (about 6) russet potatoes
1 large yellow onion
Kosher salt
1 large egg, beaten
¼ cup Wondra flour, potato starch, or all-purpose flour
2 to 3 cups rendered duck fat (page 32)
Chopped green onions, white and green parts, for garnish (optional)
Apple butter and crème fraîche, for serving

Makes about 16 latkes; 6 to 8 servings

WINE: Something with bubbles makes these latkes pop!

To make the seedy mix, in a small bowl, combine all the ingredients and mix well. Set aside.

Put the potatoes into a large pot and add water to cover by a few inches. Bring to a boil over high heat, then immediately remove from the heat and drain the potatoes into a colander. Transfer to a plate and refrigerate, uncovered, overnight.

Grate the onion on the fine holes of a box grater-shredder. Transfer to a fine-mesh sieve and set over a bowl. Using a rubber spatula, press as much moisture as possible out of the onion. Transfer the onion to a double layer of paper towels and top with a single paper towel. Press the onion to extract as much moisture as possible. Set aside.

Scrape the skin off the potatoes with a paring knife. Shred the potatoes on the coarse holes of a box grater-shredder or using the coarse shredding attachment on a food processor. Put the shredded potatoes into a large bowl and season with a little salt. Add the grated onion and all but 2 tablespoons of the seedy mix and gently toss together by hand. Add the egg and mix well to incorporate. Add the flour and mix gently so as not to break up the shredded potatoes.

Divide the potato mixture into 16 equal piles; each will weigh about 2½ oz. Shape each pile into a round about 4 inches in diameter.

Preheat the oven to 300°F. Place a wire rack over a large sheet pan and set the pan next to the stove top.

In a large, heavy frying pan (preferably cast iron) over medium-high heat, warm enough duck fat to yield a depth of ½ inch. Heat until the surface shimmers. The fat is ready if a bit of potato mix browns nicely within a minute or so. Add as many latkes to the pan as will fit without crowding, leaving enough space between them to maneuver a spatula. Once the fat regains its temperature, you might need to lower the heat a bit. Fry until the bottom is crisp and light golden brown, about 5 minutes. Turn and fry the second side until crisp and light golden brown, about 5 minutes longer. Transfer the latkes to the rack on the sheet pan and sprinkle with salt. Transfer the pan to the oven to keep warm. Fry the remaining latkes the same way, adding fat as needed to keep the original level.

Arrange the latkes on a platter and sprinkle the reserved seedy mix over the top. Garnish with the green onions, if desired. Serve right away with apple butter and crème fraîche.

SMOKEY BLACK CARDAMOM DUCK MOMOS

with roasted tomato–curry leaf dipping sauce

CHEF PREETI MISTRY

Smokey Black Cardamom masala, a spice blend made with black cardamom, fennel seeds, cumin, and cloves, was developed by chef Preeti Mistry with Spicewalla, a spice company founded by chef Meherwan Irani. Irani has collaborated with Preeti to put together spice mixes to go along with their *Juhu Beach Club Cookbook*, a vibrant take on Indian and San Francisco Bay Area cuisine. In this dish, the black cardamom masala dances with duck in plump dumplings that deliver an explosion of flavor. The recipe makes a lot of *momos* (dumplings popular in Nepal, India, and beyond), but they are terrific for a party, or you can freeze whatever you are not serving for another meal. It also offers a great opportunity to put your dinner guests—adults and kids alike—to work sealing the *momos*.

Dipping Sauce

1 medium-small tomato
1½ teaspoons neutral oil, such as rice bran or sunflower oil
⅓ cup reduced-sodium soy sauce or tamari
1 garlic clove, thinly sliced
½ jalapeño chile, finely diced
½ teaspoon toasted sesame oil
4 fresh curry leaves
½ tsp nigella seeds or black sesame seeds

Momos

4 tablespoons neutral oil, such as rice bran or sunflower oil, or as needed
¼ large yellow onion, finely chopped
1½ tablespoons peeled and minced fresh ginger
1 scant tablespoon Smokey Black Cardamom masala or homemade spice blend (see Chef's Note, page 88)
4 tablespoons water
1 lb ground duck meat
¼ cup finely chopped fresh cilantro, plus more for garnish
1 teaspoon fine sea salt
1 package (12 oz) round pot sticker wrappers

Makes about 46 dumplings; about 8 servings

To make the dipping sauce, preheat the oven to 350°F. Drizzle the tomato with ½ teaspoon of the neutral oil. Wrap the tomato in aluminum foil and place on a small sheet pan or pie pan. Bake until the tomato is totally soft, about 20 minutes. Let cool until it can be handled, then unwrap the tomato and, using the back of a spoon, push it through a fine-mesh sieve set over a small serving bowl. Discard the seeds and skin. Add the soy sauce, garlic, jalapeño, and sesame oil to the tomato pulp and stir to combine.

In a small nonstick frying pan over medium heat, warm the remaining 1 teaspoon neutral oil. When the oil is hot, add the curry leaves and nigella seeds, working carefully as they will pop. As soon as the leaves start to crisp, after 10 to 30 seconds, add the leaves and nigella seeds to the tomato mixture and stir briefly to mix. Set aside at room temperature for at least 2 hours before serving. (The sauce can be stored in an airtight container in the refrigerator for up to 3 days.)

To make the momos, first make the filling. In a frying pan over medium-low heat, warm 1 tablespoon of the neutral oil. Add the onion and cook, stirring, until slightly softened, about 5 minutes. Add the ginger and black cardamom masala and cook, stirring, until the spices and ginger start to brown and stick to the bottom of the pan, about 1 minute. Add 1 tablespoon of the water and scrape up any browned bits from the pan bottom. Remove from the heat and let cool.

In a bowl, combine the duck, ¼ cup cilantro, and salt and mix well with your hands. Add the cooled onion mixture to the duck mixture and mix with your hands until evenly distributed. If you like, cook a small nugget of the mixture in the frying pan, then taste for seasoning and add more salt if needed.

To fill and fold the momos, place the stack of pot sticker wrappers on a work surface, keeping them covered with a kitchen towel to prevent them from drying out. Set a small bowl of cold water alongside the wrappers.

continued . . .

WINE: A light, fruity red wine with great acidity. Try Blaufränkisch from Austria, which also has some nice tannin to match the full flavor of these dumplings.

To shape a momo, lay a wrapper on your nondominant hand. Spoon a scant tablespoon of the duck filling onto the center of the wrapper. Dip the index finger of your dominant hand into the water and run your finger across half of the wrapper to dampen lightly. Fold the other half of the wrapper over the filling, forming a half-moon, then, pushing out any air as you work, press the edges together to seal securely. Place the momo on a large sheet pan. Repeat until all the filling is used, adding the momos to the sheet pan as they are shaped.

To cook the momos, line a large plate with paper towels and set it near the stove top. In a large frying pan over medium-high heat, warm 2 tablespoons of the neutral oil. Working in batches, add as many momos to the pan as will fit without crowding. Cook, rotating the pan occasionally for even cooking, until the bottoms of the momos are nicely browned, 2 to 3 minutes. Using tongs, turn the momos and cook until the second side is browned, about 2 minutes. Lower the heat to medium, turn the momos over again, and add the remaining 3 tablespoons water to the pan. Immediately cover the pan with a lid (the addition of the water will make the oil pop and spit!) and let steam until cooked through and firm to the touch, 3 to 5 minutes. (To check for doneness, cut a momo in half.) Transfer the momos to the towel-lined plate to drain, then transfer to a serving platter. Cook the remaining momos in the same way, adding more neutral oil to the pan as needed. (If you like, keep the cooked momos warm on a sheet pan in a 200°F oven while you finish cooking the remaining momos.)

Garnish the momos with cilantro and accompany with the dipping sauce. Serve right away.

CHEF'S NOTE: *If you don't have the spice blend, you can make a similar version. Crack open 2 large black cardamom pods and remove the seeds. Grind the seeds to a fine powder with a mortar and pestle. Add ½ teaspoon ground cumin, ½ teaspoon ground fennel, and a pinch of ground cloves to the cardamom and stir to combine. You should have 1 scant tablespoon.*

To freeze the dumplings, arrange them (not touching) on a sheet pan, place in the freezer until frozen, and then transfer them to a ziplock plastic freezer bag and return to the freezer for up to 1 month. Then cook the dumplings straight from the freezer as directed, adding 1 to 2 minutes to each step.

ITALIAN DUCK MEATBALLS

with homemade marinara sauce

Plump, meaty duck meatballs are on regular rotation in my house. Once cooked, they are endlessly versatile (and can be easily frozen for quick weeknight meals too). Add them to a bowl of spaghetti and marinara, or arrange them on thick slabs of focaccia, top them with tomato sauce and cheese, and then brown under the broiler. They make a great addition to casseroles and are the primary ingredient in Italian wedding soup. Effortlessly comforting, these meatballs are like a big grandma hug.

Marinara

2 tablespoons rendered duck fat (page 32) or olive oil
1 yellow onion finely chopped
3 garlic cloves, minced
1 can (28 oz) crushed tomatoes with juices
1 teaspoon kosher salt
1 teaspoon dried oregano

Meatballs

Rendered duck fat (page 32) or olive oil, for greasing
2 lb ground duck meat
1 cup panko (Japanese bread crumbs)
1 tablespoon kosher salt
2 teaspoons dried oregano
2 teaspoons dried thyme
1 teaspoon ground piment d'Espelette or paprika
1 teaspoon freshly ground black pepper
2 large eggs
⅓ cup whole milk

Freshly grated Parmesan cheese, for serving

Makes 4 to 6 servings

WINE: These meatballs need a rich red Italian wine with bright tannins to balance the meat. Look for a Nero d'Avola from Sicily or California.

To make the marinara, in a large saucepan over medium heat, warm the duck fat. Add the onion and cook, stirring often, until translucent, about 5 minutes. Add the garlic and heat until it sizzles, then add the tomatoes, salt, and oregano and stir well. Turn down the heat to low and simmer, stirring occasionally, until the sauce thickens, about 15 minutes. Remove from the heat and cover to keep warm.

To make the meatballs, preheat the oven to 400°F. Grease a sheet pan with duck fat.

In a large bowl, combine the ground duck, panko, salt, oregano, thyme, piment d'Espelette, and black pepper and mix by hand just until all the ingredients are evenly distributed. In a small bowl, whisk together the eggs and milk until blended. Add the egg mixture to the duck mixture and again mix by hand until evenly incorporated.

Scoop up some of the duck mixture (about 2 oz), shape gently between your palms into a 1½-inch ball, and place on the prepared sheet pan. Repeat until all the duck mixture is used, arranging the meatballs, not touching, in a single layer on the pan. You should have about 20 meatballs.

Roast the meatballs, rotating the pan back to front halfway through roasting, until browned and cooked through, about 25 minutes.

Just before the meatballs are ready, reheat the marinara over medium-low heat. Then, when the meatballs are cooked, using a slotted spoon, transfer them to the sauce and stir gently to coat evenly.

Transfer the meatballs and sauce to a shallow serving bowl, top with plenty of Parmesan, and serve.

SPICY BARBECUE DUCK WINGS

CHEF TONY NAJIOLA

Ducks use their wings more often than chickens, which makes their wing meat a little tougher. But have no fear! Chef Tony Najiola of Petaluma's Central Market hit on sous vide cooking as the perfect way to turn out fall-off-the-bone-tender duck wings. Central Market is our local spot for celebrating birthdays and other milestones. This dish from Tony is a great tribute to all of life's celebrations. Just make sure you serve these wings with plenty of napkins!

Duck Wings
5 lb duck wings
2 teaspoons fine sea salt
1½ teaspoons smoked paprika
1½ teaspoons freshly ground black pepper
3 fresh rosemary sprigs, bruised

Spicy Barbecue Sauce
1 pasilla chile, seeded and roughly chopped
1 guajillo chile, seeded and roughly chopped
¾ cup ketchup
¼ cup honey
¼ cup red wine vinegar
3 tablespoons soy sauce
3 tablespoons dry red wine
2 tablespoons dark molasses (not blackstrap)
2 tablespoons light brown sugar
1½ tablespoons Dijon mustard
2 teaspoons freshly ground black pepper
2 teaspoons sweet or hot paprika
1 teaspoon cayenne pepper, or to taste
1 teaspoon mustard powder
1 teaspoon fine sea salt

Makes 6 to 8 servings

WINE / BEER: A crisp pale ale would make this a perfect tailgate party. For wine, an off-dry white will help balance the spicy sauce.

To prepare the wings, cut off the wing tips and reserve them for stock. Then cut each wing into the drumette and flat. You should have about 4 lb of wing pieces.

Fill a large bowl with water. In a small bowl, stir together the salt, smoked paprika, and black pepper. Add the wing pieces to a large, double-zippered plastic freezer bag. Add the spice mixture and rosemary and shake until the wings are evenly coated with the mixture. Arrange the wings in an even layer in the bag, then partially seal the bag closed. Gradually submerge the bag in the bowl of water, forcing out any air pockets around the wings as you do. When the zippered closing is just above the water level, force out the last bit of air and finish sealing the bag closed. (The pressure created by gradually submerging the bag in water forces out the air.) Alternatively, use a vacuum sealer to seal the wings inside a food-grade vacuum sealer bag.

Preheat a sous vide bath to 155°F. Add the bagged wings to the water bath, making sure the bag is completely submerged, and cook for 14 hours.

Remove the bag from the water bath. Let cool to room temperature, then drain off any liquid from the bag and transfer the wings to a large sheet pan, spreading them, not touching, in a single layer. Transfer to the refrigerator to chill for at least 2 hours or up to overnight.

Meanwhile, make the sauce. Put the pasilla and guajillo chiles in a heatproof bowl and add boiling water to cover. Set aside for 5 minutes to soften, then drain and transfer the softened chiles to a saucepan. Add the remaining sauce ingredients and place over medium-high heat. Bring to a boil, stirring constantly, then turn down the heat to low and simmer gently, stirring, until the chiles are softened and the sauce is slightly thickened, about 5 minutes. Remove from the heat and let cool slightly. Transfer to a blender and blend until smooth, or blend directly in the pan with an immersion blender. Taste and adjust the seasoning with salt, black pepper, honey, and cayenne if needed. (The sauce can be made up to 1 week in advance and stored in an airtight container in the refrigerator.)

Preheat the oven to 475°F. Pat the wings dry with paper towels. Bake the wings until they are crisp and golden brown, about 10 minutes.

While the wings are baking, rewarm the sauce. When the wings are ready, pour the warm sauce over them and toss to coat evenly. Transfer to a platter and serve.

SALT-AND-PEPPER FRIED DUCK TONGUES

CHEF BRANDON JEW

Mister Jiu's, chef Brandon Jew's modern Chinese restaurant, has quickly become a San Francisco classic. I celebrated my thirtieth birthday in the beautifully designed space because it has one of those menus that begs to be shared with the entire table. Brandon may be known for his whole duck dish, but here he is using one of the lesser cooked bits: the duck tongue! The spice mix has just enough zip to give your taste buds that quintessential numbing sensation from the Sichuan pepper. These small, delectable morsels are so beyond good that I may have eaten a half pound of them myself when testing the recipe. Trust me, try one and you'll want to come back for more.

½ lb duck tongues (about 35 tongues)
Kosher salt
1 cup rendered duck fat (page 32)

Spice Mix
¼ teaspoon Sichuan peppercorns
¼ teaspoon fennel seeds
¼ teaspoon coriander seeds
2 star anise points
½ teaspoon kosher salt
½ teaspoon ground white pepper

Neutral oil, for frying
½ cup cornstarch
2 tablespoons rice flour
Soy sauce or hoisin sauce, for serving

Makes 4 to 6 servings

WINE: A fruit-forward Gamay would be great. Red fruits will complement the Sichuan peppercorns, and the acidity is a nice balance to the richness of the tongues.

In a bowl, gently toss the duck tongues with enough salt to coat lightly, then cover and refrigerate for at least 12 hours or up to 24 hours.

Preheat the oven to 225°F. Transfer the tongues to a fine-mesh sieve and rinse off the salt under cool running water. Pat the tongues dry with paper towels. Put the duck fat into a small baking dish and place in the oven just until melted. Add the tongues to the fat, then return the baking dish to the oven. Bake the tongues until tender, about 1½ hours.

While the tongues are baking, make the spice mix. With a mortar and pestle (or using a spice grinder or clean coffee grinder), grind together the Sichuan peppercorns, fennel seeds, coriander seeds, and star anise until finely ground. Stir in the salt and white pepper.

Remove the tongues from the fat and let them cool until they can be handled. Reserve the duck fat for another use. Then, working with 1 tongue at a time, feel for the bone at the root end with your dominant hand and, while holding the tongue firmly with your other hand, pull out and discard the bone.

When all of the tongues have been boned, line a large plate with paper towels and place it near the stove top. Pour the oil to a depth of about 1 inch into a small, deep saucepan and heat over medium-high heat to 350°F on a deep-frying thermometer. In a bowl, stir together the cornstarch and rice flour.

Working in batches to avoid crowding the pan, lightly and evenly coat the tongues with the cornstarch mixture, tapping off the excess, and add to the hot oil. Fry until warm and crispy, about 1 minute. Using a slotted utensil, transfer the tongues to the towel-lined plate to drain. Repeat until all the tongues are fried.

Transfer the warm tongues to a serving plate. Using a fine-mesh sieve, dust the tongues with the spice mix. Serve right away with soy sauce for dipping.

DUCK FAT BAGNA CÀUDA

CHEF PILAR VALDES

A modern-day social media story is behind this recipe. Chef Pilar Valdes was in the middle of her own cookbook release when I noticed her wondering on Instagram if duck fat *bagna càuda* was a thing. A few quick back-and-forth messages and voilà, she made it a thing—specifically for us! *Bagna càuda* is a centuries-old dipping sauce of olive oil flavored with garlic and anchovy from the Piedmont, in northwest Italy. Here, Pilar makes a dish that is "part ode to *bagna càuda*, part Chinese-style sizzling oil technique, and 100 percent delicious." Because it is quite rich, she serves it with lots of crunchy vegetables—cucumber, carrot, fennel, green beans—and with some good crusty bread for sopping up the duck juices.

1 duck breast
Kosher salt

Bagna Càuda
¼ cup olive oil
1½ teaspoons grated garlic
6 olive oil–packed anchovy fillets, chopped
2 green onions, white and green parts, chopped
1 tablespoon finely chopped vinegar-packed guindilla chile or your favorite briny or pickled ingredient, such as capers, olives, or other pickled peppers
1½ teaspoons finely chopped preserved lemon peel (see Chef's Note)
½ teaspoon kosher salt
2 tablespoons rendered duck fat

Assorted raw vegetables, such as cabbage wedges, endive or other chicory wedges, cucumber spears, carrot sticks, and/or fennel slices
Crusty sourdough bread slices, toasted

Makes 4 servings

WINE: As this is a dish for sharing, a bottle—or two—of your favorite rosé will complete the meal.

While the duck breast is still cold from the refrigerator, using a sharp knife, score the skin on the diagonal, spacing the cuts about ¼ inch apart and being careful not to cut through to the meat. Rotate the duck breast and score the same way in the opposite direction to make a crosshatch pattern. Season the duck breast liberally on both sides with salt and set aside for 20 minutes to come to room temperature.

Place the duck breast, skin side down, in a cold cast-iron or other heavy frying pan. Turn on the heat to medium-low and let the breast cook undisturbed until it has rendered its fat and the skin is golden brown, about 15 minutes. As the fat renders, pour it off into a small heatproof bowl for the bagna càuda. Every so often, lift the breast with tongs to make sure the skin is not burning. If it is getting too dark, lower the heat.

When the skin is the desired color, raise the heat to medium and flip the breast. Continue to cook, flesh side down, until the flesh side is browned and the breast is done to medium, about 2 minutes more. An instant-read thermometer inserted into the thickest part of the breast should register 135° to 140°F. Transfer the duck to a cutting board and let rest for 15 minutes before slicing. Keep warm.

While the duck breast is cooking, make the bagna càuda. In a small saucepan over low heat, combine the oil, garlic, and anchovies and allow to warm, stirring occasionally. In a small, heatproof serving bowl, combine the green onions, guindilla chile, preserved lemon, and salt.

Add 2 tablespoons of the rendered fat from the frying pan to the pan holding the oil mixture and raise the heat to high. (Save the remaining rendered fat for another use.) As soon as the garlic and anchovies begin to sizzle, remove the pan from the heat and immediately (and carefully) pour the hot oil over the green onion mixture. Stir to mix well.

Assemble the vegetables around the rim of a platter and place the bowl of warm bagna càuda in the center. Add the bread to the platter and arrange the duck slices on top of the bread for maximum sopping up. Serve right away.

CHEF'S NOTE: *Preserved lemons, popular in Middle Eastern and North African dishes, are lemons cured in salt. They can be found at most well-stocked markets. To use, rinse the salt from the lemons, remove any pulp, and chop the peel as directed.*

DUCK HEART SKEWERS

CHEF CHRIS COSENTINO

Some of my most memorable culinary experiences have been at chef Chris Cosentino's head-to-tail dinners, where the food was always thoughtful, creative, and, most importantly, left no waste. I will never forget one night hearing a booming familiar voice. It was none other than Anthony Bourdain eating all the tasty morsels. On that occasion, Chris's most adventurous dish was an espresso made with pig's blood that was served at the end of the evening. Or perhaps it was the tender pasta noodles that turned out to be goose intestines. Either way, over the years, Chris has exposed me to dozens of dishes that I would never in my wildest dreams have imagined eating. In this recipe, he keeps it simple, preparing duck hearts in a style popular in Japanese *izakaya* (casual bars with snacks). The dish is traditionally made with chicken hearts and comes with a little bowl of toasted sesame oil. You dip the warm, tender hearts into the nutty oil and then dab them into another bowl of spicy black pepper. Chris riffs on that classic with meaty duck hearts and sweet hazelnut oil. *Kanpai!*

Soak 15 bamboo skewers in water for at least 30 minutes. Trim the hearts, making sure to remove any hard bits and squeezing to remove any excess clotted blood from the chambers. Rinse under running cool water and pat dry.

Divide the hearts evenly among the skewers, making sure there is a little space between the hearts. Season the hearts with salt.

Prepare a charcoal or gas grill for direct cooking over medium heat (350°F). Brush the grill rack clean, then oil the rack with olive oil.

Place the skewers directly over the fire and grill the hearts, rotating the skewers occasionally to brown the hearts evenly, until cooked to medium-rare, about 4 minutes total. They should be just golden and not at all burned.

Transfer the skewers to a serving plate and season with salt and pepper. Pour the hazelnut oil into a small bowl. Accompany the skewers with the lemon wedges and with the oil for dipping.

1 lb duck hearts
Fine sea salt and freshly coarse-ground black pepper
Olive oil, for oiling the grill rack
¼ cup hazelnut oil
4 to 6 lemon wedges

Makes 4 to 6 servings

BEER: A crisp beer, preferably Japanese.

DUCK, CHEDDAR, AND SHISHITO HUSH PUPPIES

with roasted garlic ranch

CHEF ANTHONY SECVIAR

These hush puppies are a delicious take on a Southern favorite. Chef Anthony Secviar makes them with roasted duck necks—four would give you plenty of meat to pick. Here, to simplify a bit, the recipe calls for a roasted duck leg. The excellent roasted garlic and herb ranch dressing makes way more than what you'll need to serve with this dish. But it is so good you'll want to use what's left over however you use ranch—on a salad, for dipping wings, and more.

Roasted Garlic Ranch
1 head garlic
2 teaspoons rendered duck fat (page 32), melted, or olive oil
1 cup fresh dill fronds
½ cup fresh flat-leaf parsley leaves
¼ cup chopped fresh chives
¾ cup sour cream
¾ cup buttermilk
¼ cup mayonnaise
Juice of 1 large lemon
1 tablespoon Worcestershire sauce
1 teaspoon kosher salt
1 teaspoon ground coriander
1 teaspoon ground cumin

Hush Puppies
1 roasted duck leg (page 36)
1 cup all-purpose flour
1 cup self-rising cornmeal (see Chef's Note)
1½ teaspoons baking powder
Kosher salt
1¼ cups buttermilk
1 large egg
½ cup seeded and thinly sliced shishito peppers
¼ cup shredded white Cheddar cheese
Canola oil, for frying

Makes about 15 hush puppies

DRINK: To compete with the fry and the strong garlic sauce, a dry cider or pale ale may be your best bet. In the wine arena, look for a pét-nat (sparkling wine) made from Chardonnay.

To make the ranch, preheat the oven to 400°F. Cut a ¼-inch-thick slice off the top of the garlic head to expose the cloves, then drizzle cloves with the duck fat. Wrap in aluminum foil and place on a small sheet pan. Bake until the cloves are soft, about 30 minutes. Unwrap the head, let cool slightly, and then squeeze the cloves out of their papery sheaths.

Transfer the garlic cloves to a blender and add the dill, parsley, chives, sour cream, buttermilk, mayonnaise, lemon juice, Worcestershire sauce, salt, coriander, and cumin. Blend until smooth, stopping to scrape down the sides of the jar once or twice. Taste and adjust the seasoning with salt if needed, then transfer to an airtight container and refrigerate until ready to use. The dressing can be made up to 3 days in advance.

To make the hush puppies, pull the meat and skin from the duck leg and discard the bones. Shred, then finely chop the meat and skin. You should have about ¾ cup. In a large bowl, mix together the flour, cornmeal, baking powder, and ¾ teaspoon salt. In a small bowl, whisk together the buttermilk and egg. Add the duck, shishitos, and cheese to the dry ingredients and stir to mix. Add the buttermilk mixture to the flour mixture and stir just until combined. The dough should be thick and sticky.

Preheat the oven to 200°F. Line a sheet pan with paper towels and set it near the stove top. Pour the oil to a depth of 2 inches into a wide saucepan and heat over medium-high heat to 350°F on a deep-frying thermometer. Working in batches to avoid crowding the pan, and using a ¾-oz ice cream scoop or a tablespoon, carefully drop the dough by rounded scoopfuls into the hot oil. The hush puppies will float to the surface. After about 30 seconds, using tongs, rotate the hush puppies and continue to cook. Rotate them again and continue to cook until golden brown and cooked through, 2 to 3 minutes longer. Using the tongs or a slotted utensil, transfer the hush puppies to the towel-lined sheet pan and immediately season with salt. Transfer the hush puppies to the oven to keep warm and then repeat until all the dough is cooked.

Serve the hush puppies hot with the roasted garlic ranch for dipping.

CHEF'S NOTE: *If you can't find self-rising cornmeal, you can make it yourself: mix together 1 cup fine-grind cornmeal, 1½ teaspoons baking powder, and ½ teaspoon kosher salt.*

DUCK EMPANADAS

with green olives and golden raisins

CHEF BRIAN STREETER

I made my first homemade empanada at a hostel in Mendoza, Argentina. At check-in, you could sign up for a cooking class, and I was quick to hit the list. A woman named Maria taught a group of us from all over the world the history of empanadas and how to make, fold, and bake them. At the time, I never thought about putting duck in one. Brian Streeter, the executive chef of Cakebread Cellars in Napa Valley, has adapted the traditional empanada flavors of green olives and raisins to our duck, and it's a match made in heaven. Some of my first culinary memories are from the American Harvest Workshop held annually at Cakebread. While my mom and dad cooked, my brother and I would visit the other food vendors and bring snacks back to them. Empanadas are the ultimate snack, and in the wildest of ways, this dish feels both wholesome and familiar to me.

Filling

3 tablespoons extra-virgin olive oil
1 medium yellow onion, minced
2 large carrots, peeled and finely chopped
¾ lb ground duck meat
¼ lb pork fatback, diced
3 garlic cloves, minced
2 canned plum tomatoes, seeded and finely chopped
1 chipotle chile in adobo sauce, finely chopped
1 cup golden raisins
½ cup pitted green olives, finely chopped
1 teaspoon smoked paprika
Pinch of ground cinnamon
Pinch of ground cloves
1 bay leaf
Kosher salt and freshly ground black pepper

Dough

3 cups all-purpose flour
1 tablespoon kosher salt
6 tablespoons cold unsalted butter, diced
6 tablespoons cold pork lard, diced
2 large eggs
½ cup ice-cold water
1 teaspoon cold water

Makes about 24 empanadas

To make the filling, place a large frying pan over high heat. When the pan is hot, add the oil and then add the onion and carrots and cook, stirring, until softened, about 10 minutes. Add the ground duck and pork fatback and continue cooking, stirring occasionally and breaking up the meat with a wooden spoon, until the duck is cooked through, about 5 minutes. Add the garlic and cook until softened, about 1 minute. Stir in the tomatoes, chipotle chile, raisins, olives, paprika, cinnamon, cloves, and bay leaf and season with salt and pepper. Turn down the heat to low, cover partially, and cook, stirring every so often, until the duck is tender and the mixture begins to thicken, about 25 minutes. Remove from the heat, uncover, and taste and adjust the seasoning with salt and pepper if needed. Remove and discard the bay leaf. Let cool to room temperature, then transfer to a bowl or other container, cover, and refrigerate until cold.

To make the dough, in the bowl of a stand mixer fitted with the paddle attachment, stir together the flour and salt. Add the butter and lard and mix on medium speed until the mixture is crumbly, about 3 minutes. Add 1 egg and the water and mix on low speed just until the dough starts to come together, about 2 minutes. Transfer the dough to a lightly floured work surface and knead just until smooth. Pat the dough into a thick disk, wrap in plastic wrap, and refrigerate until cold, at least 1 hour or up to overnight.

To make the empanadas, have ready a large sheet pan. On a lightly floured work surface, roll out the dough into a round about ⅛ inch thick. Using a 4½-inch round cutter, cut out as many rounds as possible and transfer them to the sheet pan. Gather up the dough scraps, press them together, and then roll out the dough ⅛ inch thick. (If the dough becomes too soft to roll easily, wrap it in plastic wrap and refrigerate it until slightly chilled, then try again.) Cut out more rounds and add them to the sheet pan. You should have about 24 rounds. Place the sheet pan in the refrigerator until the dough is chilled, about 30 minutes.

Meanwhile, preheat the oven to 400°F. Line a large sheet pan with parchment paper. In a small bowl, whisk the remaining egg with the cold water to make an egg wash.

Lay about one-third of the dough rounds on a floured work surface. Brush each round lightly with the egg wash. For each empanada, place a heaping tablespoon of the filling in the center of a round. Bring the two edges of the round together over the filling, then, starting from the middle and working toward the ends, press the edges together with your fingers to seal. Once sealed, crimp the seal to form a wavy pattern. Transfer the empanada to the prepared sheet pan. Repeat to use all of the dough rounds and filling, adding the empanadas to the sheet pan. Brush the empanadas lightly with the remaining egg wash.

Bake the empanadas until golden brown, about 15 minutes. Serve warm.

WINE: A Chardonnay with a hint of oak would be a great balance for the green olive–raisin filling of these empanadas. A pairing a little off the beaten path would be a dry sherry. Ask your bottle shop for a good fino sherry. It's light and delicate, with notes of almonds and dough.

DUCK CARNITAS TACOS

CHEF VALENTÍN ATAYDE

Chef Valentín Atayde of the Mercadito Food Truck knocks it out of the park with these tacos. He takes a pork classic, replaces it with duck cooked in its own fat, and then puts a Napa Valley spin on it. Valentín notes that after the duck fat cools off a bit, scoop it off the cooking liquid and save it for your next batch of carnitas or to fry other foods, such as *sopes*, refried beans, or tamales. Don't forget that the fat is already seasoned, so hold back when adding salt to the dishes you cook with it. The carnitas can also be presented as a main dish by serving the duck breasts and legs whole over Spanish-style rice.

Carnitas
3 cups water
5 guajillo chiles, seeded and deveined
Freshly squeezed juice of 2 oranges, peels reserved
Freshly squeezed juice of 2 limes, peels reserved
½ white onion, quartered
3 garlic cloves
3 tablespoons kosher salt
1 tablespoon cumin seeds
5 bay leaves
8 allspice berries
1 teaspoon dried Mexican oregano
6 duck breasts
4 duck legs
½ cup neutral oil
2 cups rendered duck fat (page 32), warmed

Pico de Gallo
2 large, ripe tomatoes, finely diced
¼ cup finely diced white onion
¼ cup finely chopped fresh cilantro, plus more for garnish
½ jalapeño chile, minced (optional)
Juice of 1 lime
Kosher salt

12 small (6-inch) corn tortillas, warmed
Purchased avocado-tomatillo salsa, for serving
Lime wedges, for serving

Makes 6 to 8 servings

BEER: It's hard not to pair a cold Mexican lager with these tacos—the perfect accompaniment to the bright, bold flavors.

To make the carnitas, in a blender, combine the water, chiles, orange and lime juices, onion, garlic, salt, cumin, bay leaves, allspice, and oregano. Blend until the chiles are fully incorporated and a smooth puree forms, about 3 minutes. Set aside.

Pat the duck breasts and legs dry with paper towels. In a large stockpot over medium-high heat, warm the oil until hot. Working in batches if needed to avoid crowding, add the duck breasts, skin side down, and sear until lightly golden brown on the underside, about 3 minutes. Turn and sear on the meat side for about 1 minute. Transfer the breasts to a plate and repeat with any remaining duck breasts. When all the breasts are seared, return them to the pot. Add the duck legs and the chile mixture, increase the heat to high, and bring to a simmer, stirring occasionally. This will take about 10 minutes.

Turn down the heat to medium-low and add the warm duck fat. Continue to cook, uncovered and stirring occasionally, for 30 minutes. Add the reserved citrus peels and simmer until the duck is tender when pierced with a paring knife, about 10 minutes longer. Remove from the heat and remove and discard the citrus peels. Let the duck rest for about 5 minutes.

Meanwhile, make the pico de gallo. In a small bowl, stir together the tomatoes, onion, cilantro, jalapeño (if using), and lime juice and season with salt. Taste and adjust with more salt and lime juice if needed.

Using tongs, transfer the duck breasts and legs to a cutting board. When cool enough to handle, pull the meat from the bones and shred it into bite-size pieces, discarding the skin and bones.

Strain the cooking liquid through a fine-mesh sieve set over a bowl and discard the solids. Using a large metal spoon, skim off the fat from the surface of the cooking liquid. (Alternatively, use a gravy separator.)

To serve, in a frying pan over medium heat, rewarm the meat gently with some of the cooking liquid. Pile the meat onto the warm tortillas and top with the pico de gallo and avocado-tomatillo salsa. Garnish with cilantro and lime wedges and serve right away.

TEA-SMOKED DUCK BREAST

with steamed buns

CHEF ZONGYI LIU

This recipe by chef Zongyi Liu was adapted by food writer Melanie Wong. At the Royal Feast Restaurant in Millbrae, California, chef Liu uses a whole duck. It's worth the trip to eat it there with all his other incredible dishes. Through an interview and tasting, Melanie adapted the recipe to use duck breast, a little more friendly for the home kitchen. The recipe takes planning and time, but the technique isn't difficult, and the result is almost as good as sitting at chef Liu's table. The smoker setup requires only everyday kitchen equipment. The *tian mian jiang* in the sauce and the lotus buns are available frozen at Asian markets. If you like, you can use jarred Sichuan or Peking duck sauce or Chinese plum sauce.

Brine
1-inch knob fresh ginger
6 tablespoons kosher salt
1 tablespoon Sichuan peppercorns
1 cinnamon stick
4 cups water
½ cup Shaoxing rice wine
2 green onions, white and green parts, cut into 1-inch lengths

Tea Smoked Duck
4 duck breasts
1¼ cups jasmine rice
⅓ cup sugar
½ cup fruitwood chips, such as cherry or apple
½ cup jasmine oolong tea leaves
¼ cup water

Sichuan Duck Sauce
½ cup tian mian jiang (sweet flour sauce)
1 tablespoon sugar
1 tablespoon toasted sesame oil
2 tablespoons water

Peanut oil or other neutral oil, for frying
12 frozen lotus buns, steamed and kept warm
4 green onions, white part only, julienned

Makes 6 to 8 servings

WINE: Look for an off-dry Riesling from Germany. A Spätlese would be perfect. If you prefer a dry wine, a Spätlese Trocken would still deliver a rich pairing minus the sweetness.

To make the brine, peel the ginger, smash it with a heavy knife, and then coarsely chop it. Set aside. In a dry frying pan over low heat, toast the salt, Sichuan peppercorns, and cinnamon, stirring often, until the salt darkens and turns yellowish, about 2 minutes. Transfer the salt mixture to a baking dish or other container just large enough to hold the duck breasts and brine. Add the water and stir until the salt dissolves. Add the wine, green onions, and ginger and stir to mix well.

Add the duck breasts, skin side up, to the brine. Cover and refrigerate for 12 hours, turning the duck breasts halfway through.

To set up the smoker, line the inside of a large, deep frying pan with a domed lid (or a wok or Dutch oven with a lid) with aluminum foil to make cleanup easier. Spread the rice in an even layer in the bottom of the pan. Sprinkle the rice evenly with the sugar, the wood chips, and then the tea leaves. Sprinkle the water evenly on top.

Position a small round rack in the center of the pan (or use a coil made out of aluminum foil). Place a shallow, heatproof bowl on the rack (good for catching the duck juices and shielding the duck from the direct heat source). Place a second round rack large enough to hold all the breasts in a single layer over the bowl.

Place the smoker setup on the stove top over medium-low heat and cover with the lid ajar until the steam dissipates. Listen for the sizzling of the water to stop. At that point, the fuel will reach combustion temperature, start to smolder, and create a head of smoke. Position the duck breasts on the top rack and then cover the pan with the lid. After 30 seconds, turn off the heat and allow the duck to smoke, covered, for 10 minutes. Leaving the cover on, turn on the heat to low for 3 minutes to refresh the smoke, then turn off the heat and continue to smoke for 15 minutes longer. At this point, the skin will be light to medium brown and an instant-read thermometer inserted into the thickest part of a duck breast will register 125° to 130°F. (For a heavier smoke flavor and a more traditional taste, repeat the cycle of refreshing the smoke over low heat for 3 minutes, then turning off the heat and letting the breasts sit for another 10 to 15 minutes.)

Remove the rack with the duck breasts from the smoker and set aside. Remove the bowl and second rack from the pan, then discard all the smoking materials and wipe out the pan. Place the smoked duck breasts on the rack in the pan and return the pan to the stove top. Pour just enough boiling water into the pan to come up to but not touch the rack or duck. Bring the water just to a simmer over medium heat, then turn down the heat to low, cover, and steam the duck until its fat is rendered and an instant-read thermometer inserted into the thickest part of a breast registers 165° to 175°F, 10 to 20 minutes.

While the duck is steaming, make the sauce. In a small saucepan over medium-low heat, stir together the tian mian jiang, sugar, sesame oil, and 2 tablespoons water. Bring to a simmer, stirring to combine. Cover and set aside off the heat until ready to use.

Remove the rack with the duck breasts from the pan and set aside. Discard the water in the pan and wipe the pan clean. Add peanut oil to a depth of ½ inch to the pan and heat over high heat to 375°F on a deep-frying thermometer. Adjust the heat as needed to maintain the temperature.

Pat the duck breasts dry with paper towels. Add the breasts, skin side down, and cook, ladling the hot oil over the duck meat, until the skin is dark mahogany brown, 2 to 3 minutes.

To serve, transfer the duck to a cutting board and let rest for 5 minutes. Cut the duck crosswise into ¼-inch-thick slices. Arrange the warm lotus buns on a large platter and spread some of the duck sauce on them. Fill each bun with 3 or 4 pieces of duck, drizzle with more sauce, and top with the green onions. Serve right away.

ROASTED DUCK LETTUCE CUPS

with sesame shiitake mushrooms

CHEFS DUSKIE ESTES AND JOHN STEWART

Chefs John Stewart and Duskie Estes are Sonoma County favorites. They cook with big hearts and are always at the center of community outreach. In that spirit, these lettuce cups are great for a party or other crowd. The pickled shiitake mushrooms and spice-roasted duck are an effortless pairing and will keep your guests coming back for more. Serve them with a bowl of rice and you've got yourself a whole meal.

Spiced Roasted Duck
1 teaspoon kosher salt
1 teaspoon ground Sichuan pepper
½ teaspoon ground cinnamon
¼ teaspoon ground star anise
¼ teaspoon ground fennel
Pinch of ground cloves
3 duck legs

Sesame Shiitake Mushrooms
1 cup stemmed and thinly sliced shiitake mushrooms
½ cup water
2 tablespoons sugar
¼ cup reduced-sodium tamari or soy sauce
¼ cup rice vinegar
1 slice fresh ginger
Pinch of Sichuan peppercorns
1 teaspoon sesame seeds, toasted

Sauce
½ cup hoisin sauce
1 tablespoon grated orange zest
1 teaspoon grated fresh ginger
½ teaspoon ground Sichuan pepper
¼ teaspoon ground cinnamon
Pinch of ground star anise
Pinch of ground fennel

1 head butter lettuce
Chopped fresh cilantro and mint
Sliced green onions, white and green parts, for garnish

Makes 6 servings

WINE / BEER: A German- or Czech-style pilsner with delicate hop bitterness would be a great accompaniment. For wine, look for a bright Pinot Noir. One from Austria, Germany, or Oregon would be great.

To roast the duck, preheat the oven to 400°F. In a small bowl, stir together the salt, Sichuan pepper, cinnamon, star anise, fennel, and cloves. Liberally season both sides of the duck legs with the spice mixture. Place the legs, skin side up, on a sheet pan.

Roast the legs, rotating the pan back to front halfway through roasting, until dark golden brown, about 1 hour. Let the legs rest on the pan on a wire rack for 5 minutes. The legs may stick a little to the bottom of the pan; use a spatula to loosen them. Pull the meat and crisp skin from the bones and discard the bones. Chop into bite-size pieces and transfer to a small serving bowl.

While the duck is roasting, make the mushrooms and the sauce. To make the mushrooms, put the mushrooms into a small heatproof bowl. In a medium saucepan, combine the water, sugar, tamari, vinegar, ginger, and Sichuan peppercorns and bring to a boil over medium-high heat, stirring until the sugar dissolves, about 1 minute. Pour the hot mixture over the mushrooms, then stir in the sesame seeds. Let sit for at least 10 minutes before using. The mushrooms will keep in an airtight container in the refrigerator for up to 1 week.

To make the sauce, in a small saucepan, combine all the sauce ingredients and bring to a simmer over medium heat, stirring constantly, for about 1 minute to blend the flavors. Thin the sauce with some of the mushroom marinade. Add half of the sauce to the warm duck and toss to combine. Transfer the remaining sauce to a small bowl.

To serve, separate the lettuce into individual leaves. Pile the lettuce leaves on a platter. Arrange the cilantro, mint, and green onions in separate mounds on a plate. Transfer the mushrooms to a small bowl. Set out the bowls of duck and sauce. To assemble the cups, spoon some duck meat onto a lettuce leaf and top with some of the mushrooms. Drizzle with extra sauce, if desired, and garnish with the cilantro, mint, and green onions. Enjoy at once.

CHAPTER FOUR

SOUPS & SALADS

ROASTED DUCK AND KURI SQUASH SALAD

with grapefruit, watercress, and toasted seeds

CHEF MELISSA PERELLO

Winter or summer, we love squashes! I am thrilled to finally see a bigger assortment of winter squashes—something other than just butternut—gracing store shelves. Kuri squash has dense orange flesh and dark orange skin, with a nutty, almost chestnut-like taste. While it can be used in both sweet and savory dishes, chef Melissa Perello of Frances in San Francisco finds the perfect home for it alongside duck legs. I've long been a big Melissa fan—not only of the way she presents her food in her kitchens, but also how she carries herself in the industry. She's been a rising force in the San Francisco Bay Area restaurant world for nearly two decades, and I'm happy to see it.

4 roasted duck legs (page 36)
1 small red kuri squash (about 1½ lb)
Olive oil, for drizzling and cooking
Kosher salt and freshly ground black pepper
¼ cup salted roasted pepitas
1 tablespoon coriander seeds, coarsely ground
1 tablespoon golden sesame seeds
1 Oro Blanco or ruby red grapefruit
Juice of 1 lemon
1 red Fresno or serrano chile, seeded and very thinly sliced
1 bunch purslane or watercress, tough stems discarded, and torn into bite-sized pieces
2 cups baby kale or chopped frisée
1 bunch fresh cilantro leaves, chopped
¼ cup sherry vinegar

Makes 4 servings

WINE: Rhône white wines are incredible for pairing with food. The fruit and nut notes of a Roussanne-Marsanne blend complement this salad.

Preheat the oven to 400°F and roast the duck legs as directed in the recipe, then set them aside. Leave the oven on. Line a sheet pan with parchment paper.

Cut the squash in half through the stem end and scoop out and discard the seeds and fibers. Cut each half lengthwise into 2-inch-wide wedges. Pile the squash onto the prepared sheet pan, drizzle with oil, sprinkle with salt, and toss to coat evenly. Spread the wedges in a single layer and roast, turning them about every 8 minutes, until fork-tender, 16 to 20 minutes. Let the wedges cool on the pan on a wire rack, then cut into smaller wedges. Leave the oven on.

While the squash roasts, in a large ovenproof frying pan over low heat, warm 1 tablespoon oil along with the pepitas. Slowly raise the heat to gently warm the pepitas, stirring occasionally, until golden, about 1 minute. Using a slotted spoon, transfer the pepitas to paper towels to drain, then roughly chop the pepitas. Transfer to a bowl, add the coriander and sesame seeds, and toss to mix. Set aside. Wipe out the pan and reserve.

Cut a thin slice off the top and the bottom of the grapefruit. Stand the fruit on a flat end on a cutting board and, using a sharp knife, cut downward in wide strips to remove the peel and white pith, following the contour of the fruit. Working over a bowl, cut along each side of the membrane between the segments, dropping the segments in the bowl.

Return the frying pan to medium-high heat and warm 2 tablespoons oil. Add the roasted duck legs, skin side down, and sear to recrisp the skin, then transfer the pan to the oven to rewarm the duck, about 7 minutes. Remove the duck from the pan and set aside. Add the squash to the hot pan, place over medium-high heat, and sear until hot and caramelized, with nice golden brown edges. Transfer the squash to a plate and drizzle with about half of the lemon juice. Taste and season with salt if needed.

In a bowl, toss together the chile, purslane, kale, and half the cilantro. Dress lightly with the remaining lemon juice, the vinegar, a few tablespoons oil, and salt. Divide the mixture evenly among 4 plates. Arrange a duck leg and an equal amount of the squash and grapefruit on top of each mound of greens and then garnish with the remaining cilantro. Sprinkle with the pepita mixture, dividing it evenly, and serve.

SEED-CRUSTED DUCK BREAST

with couscous-fig salad and beet-honey vinaigrette

CHEFS JOSIAH CITRIN AND KEN TAKAYAMA

Couscous is a fun ingredient to play with—it can be added to so many dishes—and is one of my favorite sides. Here, Southern California–based chefs Josiah Citrin and Ken Takayama combine roasted beets, dried figs, and plenty of chives with couscous to create a colorful salad that serves as the base of the dish. The seed-crusted, honey-glazed duck breasts and sweet-tangy vinaigrette round out the incredible flavor and varied texture of this memorable meal.

Beets

9 small (not baby) red beets (about 1 lb total), trimmed
3 tablespoons extra-virgin olive oil
Fine sea salt and freshly ground black pepper

Beet-Honey Vinaigrette

¼ cup Banyuls vinegar or sherry vinegar
1 tablespoon red wine vinegar
1½ tablespoons honey, preferably orange blossom
1 tablespoon finely chopped shallot
1 small garlic clove, minced
1 tablespoon finely chopped fresh herbs, such as basil, flat-leaf parsley, thyme, and/or rosemary
½ tablespoon Dijon mustard
½ teaspoon fine sea salt
¾ cup grapeseed oil
½ cup extra-virgin olive oil
2 tablespoons fresh lemon juice

Seed Crust

1 teaspoon fennel seeds
1 teaspoon coriander seeds
1 teaspoon sunflower seeds
1 teaspoon sesame seeds
1 teaspoon raw pepitas
¼ teaspoon freshly coarse-ground black pepper

Couscous

1⅓ cups water
1 teaspoon fine sea salt
2 teaspoons extra-virgin olive oil
1 tablespoon unsalted butter
1 cup instant couscous
¾ cup rich duck stock (page 45) or chicken bone broth, warm

To roast the beets, preheat the oven to 375°F. In a medium bowl, toss the beets with the oil and season with salt and pepper. Wrap the beets in aluminum foil, place in a baking dish, and add a little water to the dish. Roast the beets until they are knife-tender, about 1½ hours, adding water to the dish as needed to prevent the beets from burning. Unwrap the beets, let them cool until they can be handled, and then gently rub off the skins with a paper towel. Dice the beets. Reserve ¼ cup of the diced beets for the vinaigrette and set aside the remaining beets for the couscous. The beets can be roasted and diced up to 1 day in advance and refrigerated in an airtight container.

To make the vinaigrette, in a jar with a tight-fitting kid, combine the Banyuls and red wine vinegars, the honey, shallot, garlic, herbs, mustard, and salt. Cover and shake well. Add the grapeseed and olive oils and shake well again. Add the lemon juice and the reserved ¼ cup diced beets and shake one more time. Set aside.

To make the seed crust, heat a large cast-iron or other heavy frying pan over medium-high heat. Add the fennel, coriander, sunflower, and sesame seeds and the pepitas and heat, stirring often, until fragrant and toasted, 2 to 3 minutes. Pour onto a cutting board and let cool to room temperature, then coarsely chop. Transfer to a small bowl, add the pepper, and mix well. Set aside. Set the pan aside.

To make the couscous, in a small saucepan, combine the water, salt, olive oil, and ½ tablespoon of the butter and bring to a boil over high heat. Remove from the heat, add the couscous, and stir to combine. Cover and let steam for 10 minutes. Fluff the couscous with a fork. Add the duck stock, figs, and the remaining ½ tablespoon butter and toss and fluff to mix evenly. Season with fine sea salt and white pepper. Re-cover to keep warm.

While the couscous steams, prepare the duck breasts. While the duck breasts are still cold from the refrigerator, using a sharp knife and working with one duck breast at a time, score the skin on each breast on the diagonal, spacing the cuts about ½ inch apart and being careful not to cut through to the meat. Rotate the duck breast 90 degrees and score the same way in the opposite direction to make a crosshatch pattern. Season the duck breasts on both sides with fine sea salt.

continued . . .

⅔ cup finely diced dried figs
Fine sea salt and ground white pepper

Duck Breasts

3 duck breasts
Fine sea salt
1 tablespoon grapeseed or other neutral oil
½ cup honey, preferably orange blossom

2 tablespoons chopped fresh chives
Fleur de sel and freshly cracked black pepper
½ lb wild or baby arugula

Makes 6 servings

WINE: A Pinot Gris from Alsace has notes of cinnamon and clove that pair well with the seeded crust of the duck breasts.

Preheat the broiler. Set a wire rack on a sheet pan and place the pan near the stove top. Return the reserved frying pan to high heat and add the neutral oil. When the oil is hot, add the duck breasts, skin side down, and cook for 2 minutes. Lower the heat to medium and let the breasts cook until they have rendered their fat, about 7 minutes longer. Then baste the breasts with the rendered fat for 2 more minutes. Transfer the breasts, skin side up, to the wire rack and brush the skin with the honey. Sprinkle the reserved toasted seed mixture evenly over the skin on each breast. Transfer the duck breasts, skin side up, to a sheet pan and broil until the honey and seeds form a crust on the skin, 30 to 45 seconds. Transfer to a cutting board and let rest for 5 minutes.

Stir the reserved beets and the chives into the warm couscous, mixing well. Divide the couscous among 6 plates or shallow bowls. Thinly slice the duck breasts crosswise and arrange on top of the couscous, dividing the slices evenly. Shake the vinaigrette well, spoon a little of the vinaigrette over the duck, and then sprinkle the duck with fleur de sel and pepper. In a bowl, toss the arugula with a little of the vinaigrette to coat lightly, then divide the arugula among the plates or bowls, placing it on top of the duck. Spoon more vinaigrette over the arugula and around the dish and serve.

SEARED DUCK AND ORANGE SALAD

with roasted peanuts and pickled onion

This bright, filling, healthy salad was the result of one of those nights when I looked in the fridge and said to myself, "Hmmm, what can I make with what I've got?" In my senior year of college, I lived with *nine* other girls, and we all shared one standard-size refrigerator. It was almost a Division I sport to try and eat the food creatively before it got lost in the back of the fridge, where it invariably spoiled. There were a few casualties, but I tried my hardest to perfect the art of making wilted lettuce taste delicious. Luckily, you don't need to be that adventurous to make this delightful, clean-out-the-fridge salad.

In a jar with a tight-fitting lid, combine the onion, vinegar, salt, and sugar. Cover and shake well. Set aside at room temperature to "pickle" the onion for at least 1 hour or up to 3 hours before serving.

About 30 minutes before serving, pan-sear the duck breasts as directed and let rest before slicing.

While the duck breasts are cooking, add the lettuce to a large, wide salad bowl. Cut a thin slice off the top and the bottom of 1 of the oranges. Stand the orange on a flat end on a cutting board and, using a sharp knife, cut downward in wide strips to remove all the peel and white pith, following the contour of the fruit. Working over a bowl, cut along each side of the membrane of the segments, capturing the freed segments in the bowl. Repeat with the second orange. Transfer the segments to a cutting board and cut each segment crosswise into thirds. Add the orange pieces, peanuts, cheese, and sesame seeds to the bowl with the lettuces.

Add the oil, vinegar, and herbes de Provence to the jar with the pickled onion and season with pepper. Cover and shake well. Pour half of the dressing over the salad and toss to coat evenly.

Slice the warm duck breasts crosswise into ¼-inch-thick slices.

Divide the salad among 4 to 6 bowls, then divide the duck breast slices evenly among the salads. Drizzle with more of the vinaigrette and serve.

½ red onion, minced
2 tablespoons white wine vinegar
½ teaspoon kosher salt
¼ teaspoon sugar
2 pan-seared duck breasts (page 39)
8 cups chopped mixed lettuces, such as red leaf, frisée, and butter
2 navel oranges
¾ cup dry-roasted peanuts, chopped
¼ cup freshly shredded Parmesan or pecorino romano cheese
2 tablespoons sesame seeds
3 tablespoons extra-virgin olive oil
1 tablespoon balsamic vinegar
¼ teaspoon herbes de Provence
¼ teaspoon freshly ground black pepper

Makes 4 to 6 servings

WINE: A New World Grenache, lighter in body and alcohol, to balance, not overpower, the salad.

TANGY DUCK NOODLE SALAD

with herbs and cucumber

If I had to quantify this salad with adjectives, they would be "fun," "fresh," and "oh so good!" You know those days when it's so hot that you can't think of what you want to eat? This salad is the solution to that problem. A tangy lime-based dressing with a hint of fish sauce and spice cloaks tender rice noodles tossed with plenty of garlicky, gingery ground duck, crunchy cucumbers and carrots, and fresh herbs.

Dressing

¼ cup fresh lime juice
¼ cup rice vinegar
2 tablespoons fish sauce
2 tablespoons avocado or canola oil
1 small garlic clove, minced
1 teaspoon agave nectar or sugar
½ teaspoon red pepper flakes

Duck Noodle Salad

½ lb pad thai rice noodles, or ¾ lb rice vermicelli
1 tablespoon avocado or canola oil
1 large shallot, halved lengthwise and thinly sliced
2 garlic cloves, minced
2 teaspoons peeled and finely grated fresh ginger
1 Thai or serrano chile, seeded and very thinly sliced (optional)
1 lb ground duck meat
Fine sea salt and freshly ground black pepper
1 cucumber, 5 to 6 inches long, peeled if desired, halved lengthwise, and very thinly sliced crosswise (about ⅓ cup)
1 medium carrot, shredded
3 green onions, white and green parts, thinly sliced on the diagonal
¼ cup shredded fresh basil leaves, preferably Thai, plus more for garnish
¼ cup chopped fresh cilantro, plus more for garnish
¼ cup chopped fresh mint leaves, plus more for garnish
⅓ cup chopped salted roasted peanuts or cashews

Makes 4 to 6 servings

WINE: An aromatic white wine with good acid; a Riesling or Gewürztraminer will lighten every bite.

To make the dressing, in a bowl, whisk together all the ingredients until well combined. Taste and adjust the seasoning with agave nectar and pepper flakes if needed. Set aside.

To make the salad, cook the noodles in salted water according to the package directions. Drain and rinse under cool running water to stop the cooking. Transfer to a large, shallow serving bowl.

In a large frying pan over medium heat, warm the oil. Add the shallot, garlic, ginger, and chile (if using) and cook, stirring often, until fragrant, about 1 minute. Crumble the ground duck into the pan, raise the heat to medium-high, and cook, stirring occasionally and breaking up the meat with a wooden spoon, until the duck is browned and the fat has rendered, 5 to 8 minutes. Pour off the excess fat if you like. Add 3 tablespoons of the dressing, turn down the heat to low, and simmer gently, stirring to coat the duck with the seasonings, until most of the liquid has evaporated, about 1 minute. Season with salt and pepper. Remove from the heat and let cool to room temperature.

Add the duck mixture to the noodles and toss to combine. Scatter the cucumber, carrot, green onions, and the ¼ cup each basil, cilantro, and mint over the noodle mixture. Drizzle enough of the dressing over the salad to coat lightly and toss to mix evenly. Taste and adjust the seasoning with salt and pepper and more dressing if needed.

Divide the salad evenly among 4 to 6 plates. Sprinkle with the peanuts, garnish with the basil, cilantro, and mint, and serve.

DUCK CONFIT AND STONE FRUIT SALAD

with shaved cheddar and mustard vinaigrette

CHEF DAISY RYAN

Located roughly halfway between San Francisco and Los Angeles is the unassuming little wine country town of Los Alamos. This community of about sixteen hundred is an incredible culinary mecca, at the heart of which is Bell's, led by chef Daisy Ryan. Daisy's culinary training took her to New York City, and she brought that East Coast style and pizzazz back to Bell's. A good-quality aged Cheddar combines beautifully with ripe stone fruits, such as plums, peaches, and apricots, in this simple yet inspired recipe. This is one salad you can serve all summer long—from May to October—as the different fruits ripen.

Vinaigrette

½ cup champagne vinegar
2 tablespoons whole-grain mustard
2 tablespoons finely chopped shallot
1½ teaspoons honey
1 teaspoon Dijon mustard
¾ cup extra-virgin olive oil
Kosher salt and freshly ground black pepper

2 duck legs confit (page 35)
6 ripe plums or pluots, 3 ripe peaches or nectarines, or a combination
1 large head green or red leaf lettuce, leaves separated and torn into bite-size pieces
¼ lb aged clothbound Cheddar cheese
¼ cup chopped fresh flat-leaf parsley leaves

Makes 4 servings

WINE: The peach blossom aromatics of a lighter version of Viognier will make the stone fruits sing.

To make the vinaigrette, in a bowl, whisk together the vinegar, whole-grain mustard, shallot, honey, and Dijon mustard. Slowly add the oil in a thin stream while whisking constantly until emulsified. Season with salt and pepper.

Pick and shred the meat from the confit duck legs, discarding the skin and bones. Halve and pit the stone fruits and cut lengthwise into ⅛-inch-thick wedges. In a large, shallow salad bowl, toss together the lettuce, stone fruits, and shredded duck. Drizzle with just enough of the vinaigrette to coat lightly and toss to coat evenly.

Divide the salad among 4 salad plates or shallow bowls. Using a vegetable peeler, shave an equal amount of the Cheddar over the top of each salad. Garnish with the parsley and serve, passing any remaining vinaigrette at the table.

DUCK LEG CONFIT AND BEET SALAD

with medjool date vinaigrette

CHEF TRACEY SHEPOS CENAMI

One of the things that I love most about eating at Kendall-Jackson is that the culinary team takes the basics and makes them even better. This is true of chef Tracey Shepos Cenami's duck confit, which stars in this perfect salad (and is so good it's become our go-to recipe for the book). Every summer, the Kendall-Jackson team hosts a farm-to-table dinner featuring the products of Liberty Ducks and of Dry Creek Peach, another Sonoma County favorite. Tucker Taylor, director of culinary gardens for Kendall-Jackson, picks produce at its peak from the on-site winery gardens for the dinner. That kind of care makes the flavors of even a simple salad like this one absolutely pop. We're lucky that in California beets are truly "in season" year-round. Both earthy and sweet, they are the perfect accompaniment to the salty confit legs.

Date Vinaigrette

6 oz pitted Medjool dates, chopped
¼ cup sherry vinegar
2 tablespoons pomegranate molasses
1½ tablespoons Dijon mustard
1 teaspoon ground cumin
1 teaspoon fennel seeds
Kosher salt and freshly ground black pepper
1 cup extra-virgin olive oil

1 lb mixed baby beets, such as red, golden, and Chioggia, trimmed
2 tablespoons kosher salt
3 tablespoons rice bran or other neutral oil
1 cup water
8 cups mixed baby salad greens
4 duck legs confit (page 35), crisped

Makes 4 servings

WINE: With the beets and confit legs, a red wine is a great choice for this salad. Look for a Pinot Noir from the Sonoma Coast.

To make the vinaigrette, in a blender, combine the dates, vinegar, molasses, mustard, cumin, and fennel seeds and season with salt and pepper. Blend to a smooth puree, adding a little water as needed to keep the blades spinning. With the blender running, slowly add the olive oil in a thin stream, blending until the mixture is emulsified and all the oil is incorporated. Transfer to a jar or other glass container. Taste and adjust the seasoning with vinegar and salt if needed. Set aside.

To roast the beets, preheat the oven to 350°F. Pile the beets in a roasting pan, sprinkle with the salt, drizzle with the neutral oil and water, and then turn the beets to coat evenly. Spread the beets in a single layer. (If the beets vary significantly in size, separate them by size and use 2 pans.) Cover the pan with aluminum foil, transfer to the oven, and cook until the beets are knife-tender, 30 to 40 minutes; the timing will depend on their size. Remove the beets from the pan and, while still warm, gently rub off the skins with a paper towel. Quarter the beets lengthwise and let cool completely.

To assemble the salad, in a bowl, toss the salad greens with a little of the vinaigrette, coating the leaves lightly, then divide the greens evenly among 4 salad plates. Add the beets to the bowl and toss with a little more of the vinaigrette, then place the beets atop the salad greens, dividing them evenly among the plates. Top each salad with a crispy duck leg and serve, passing any remaining vinaigrette at the table.

CRISPY DUCK, KUMQUAT, AND DATE SALAD

with pistachios and sherry vinaigrette

CHEF TRACI DES JARDINS

During my senior year of high school, Dad asked if I wanted to go to an *Iron Chef America* viewing party. "A what a what a what?" I asked. Although I had earlier met chef Traci Des Jardins at Jardinière, her San Francisco restaurant, I was just beginning to be interested in culinary endeavors, and I was not sure what an Iron Chef was. As we all watched her cooking on the big screen, I remember looking over at her in-person at the party, where she sat beaming with joy and pride. When she (spoiler alert!) won, the room erupted in celebration. That party remains one of my favorite culinary memories and is one of the reasons I am doing what I do now. After that evening, I dove headfirst into watching more *Iron Chef America* episodes and started flipping through cookbooks and food magazines. You don't know how important those moments are when you're in them, but it's wonderful to look back at them and think about how they shaped your future.

- 1½ cups sliced kumquats, in ⅛-inch crosswise slices, seeded
- ½ cup pitted and julienned Medjool dates
- 1 tablespoon minced shallot
- 3 tablespoons sherry vinegar
- ½ cup extra-virgin olive oil
- Kosher salt and freshly ground black pepper
- 1 tablespoon grapeseed or other neutral oil
- 6 duck legs confit (page 35)
- 1 head frisée, cored and roughly chopped
- 2 cups baby arugula
- 1 cup mizuna or other salad greens
- ½ cup fresh flat-leaf parsley leaves
- 1 tablespoon shredded fresh mint leaves
- ½ cup toasted salted pistachio nuts

To make the vinaigrette, finely chop ¼ cup of the kumquat slices and 1 tablespoon of the dates. Add to a small bowl with the shallot and vinegar and whisk to combine. Slowly add the olive oil in a thin stream while whisking constantly until emulsified. Season with salt and pepper. Set aside.

Preheat the oven to 425°F. In a large sauté pan over medium-high heat, warm the grapeseed oil. Carefully add the duck legs, skin side down, to the pan. Turn down the heat to medium and cook for 3 to 4 minutes, then transfer pan to the oven until the duck is hot, 7 to 10 minutes longer. Remove from the oven and make sure all of the skin is crisp and rendered. If there are pieces that need additional browning, return the pan to medium heat on the stove top until browned. Transfer the legs to a cutting board. Remove the bones, including the small pin bones, from each leg by carefully twisting and pulling them loose from the duck meat. The duck legs should remain whole, so that they can be served whole on top of the salad.

In a large, shallow bowl, combine the frisée, arugula, mizuna, parsley, mint, and the remaining kumquats and dates. Drizzle with enough of the vinaigrette to coat lightly, season with salt and pepper, and toss to coat evenly.

Divide the salad among 6 plates or arrange on a large platter. Top each with a whole crispy duck leg confit, drizzle with a little more vinaigrette, and garnish with the pistachios. Serve right away, passing the remaining vinaigrette at the table.

Makes 6 servings

WINE: The brightness of the kumquats calls for a bright Sauvignon Blanc.

SMOKED DUCK FRISÉE SALAD

with duck egg and herb vinaigrette

This is my riff on the famed *salade lyonnaise* of France. The best version in Paris, according to Julia Child, was the *salade frisée aux lardons* at Chez Georges, and it remains one the restaurant's signature dishes. Using David Tanis's recipe from the *New York Times* as both inspiration and a starting point, I swapped out the chicken egg for a duck egg and the bacon for smoked duck breast. The results are just as satisfying as the original—if not more so.

2 tablespoons champagne vinegar
2 teaspoons Dijon mustard
1 teaspoon minced fresh herbs, such as chives and thyme
½ teaspoon finely grated garlic
3 tablespoons extra-virgin olive oil
12 baguette slices, about ½ inch thick
About 2 tablespoons salted butter
1 tablespoon distilled white vinegar
4 duck eggs or large chicken eggs
1 smoked duck breast (page 40), with skin, cut into ⅛-inch cubes
1 head frisée, cored and roughly chopped
Freshly ground black pepper

Makes 4 servings

WINE: A full-bodied white wine, such as a Chardonnay or Grenache Blanc that has had a little time in neutral oak barrels.

To make the vinaigrette, in a small bowl, whisk together the champagne vinegar, mustard, herbs, and garlic. Slowly add the oil in a thin stream while whisking constantly until emulsified. Set aside.

Preheat the oven to 425°F. Arrange the baguette slices on a sheet pan and toast, turning once, until crisp and golden brown on both sides, about 5 minutes total. Remove from the oven and butter the slices.

Line a plate with paper towels. Fill a wide saucepan half full of salted water and add the white vinegar. Bring to a simmer over medium heat. Crack an egg into a cup, being careful not to break the yolk, then carefully slip the egg into the water; repeat to add a second egg. Cook until the whites have set but the yolks are still runny, about 3 minutes. Using a slotted spoon, transfer the eggs to the prepared plate. Repeat to cook the remaining 2 eggs the same way.

While the eggs are cooking, in a dry frying pan over low heat, warm the duck, stirring occasionally, until slightly crisped but still tender, about 10 minutes.

To assemble the salad, add the frisée to a bowl, drizzle with some of the vinaigrette, and toss to coat evenly. Divide the frisée among 4 shallow bowls. Top each salad with an egg and one-fourth of the warmed duck, then drizzle with more vinaigrette and grind on some pepper. Accompany each salad with 3 baguette slices.

DUCK GIZZARD CONFIT SALAD

with almonds and duck fat croutons

No single trip may have impacted my life more than the two months I spent in the Périgord region in Southwest France, where local cooks are known for using duck in the area's signature dishes. This recipe is a direct copy of the *salade périgourdine* I ate there time and again, with one glaring exception: in the decade-plus since I left, I developed an allergy to walnuts, another Périgord region specialty. Much like its famous AOC regions for wine, France has AOC qualifications for other products, and its Noix du Périgord AOC meant there was an exceptional product around that regularly turned up in this salad. Because of this, I reworked the recipe with chopped almonds and with almond oil in the dressing. Making croutons is my favorite way to use up a day-old baguette, and they are fresher and more flavorful than commercial ones. But if you don't time or want to make them, just use your favorite commercial brand.

Duck Fat Croutons

2 cups cubed day-old baguette, in ½-inch cubes
1 tablespoon rendered duck fat (page 32), melted
Kosher salt and freshly ground black pepper

2 tablespoons rendered duck fat (page 32)
1 shallot, finely chopped
12 duck gizzards confit (page 33), quartered
2 tablespoons red wine vinegar
1 head red leaf lettuce, leaves separated and cut into bite-size pieces
¼ cup chopped salted roasted almonds (skin on)
2 teaspoons almond oil
1 teaspoon Dijon mustard

Makes 4 servings

WINE: A full-bodied rosé, such as a rosé of Mondeuse or Syrah, will balance the acidity in the dressing and the richness of the gizzards confit.

To make the croutons, preheat the oven to 350°F. Put the bread cubes onto a sheet pan and drizzle with the duck fat. Toss to coat evenly, then season with salt and pepper and toss again. Spread the cubes in a single layer and bake, stirring once halfway through baking, until golden brown, about 20 minutes. Set aside.

In a frying pan over medium heat, melt the duck fat. Add the shallot and cook, stirring, until softened, about 5 minutes. Add the gizzards and cook, stirring, until the gizzards are heated through and starting to brown, about 10 minutes. Transfer the gizzards and shallot to a plate. Deglaze the pan with 1 tablespoon of the vinegar, stirring with a wooden spoon to get all the crispy browned bits from the pan bottom. Transfer the vinegar mixture to a small bowl.

In a salad bowl, toss together the lettuce, almonds, croutons, and gizzard-shallot mixture. Add the remaining 1 tablespoon vinegar, the oil, and the mustard to the vinegar mixture in the small bowl and whisk to emulsify. Drizzle the dressing over the salad and toss to coat evenly. Divide among 4 salad plates or shallow bowls and serve.

SMOKED DUCK NOODLE SOUP

with napa cabbage, broccoli rabe, and marinated eggs

CHEF GAVIN SCHMIDT

The Morris in San Francisco has crafted a signature smoked duck, and we're honored that it's a staple on their restaurant menu. Chef Gavin Schmidt uses the whole smoked duck to make this multidimensional soup for the staff meal. At every turn, it's another addition of umami and flavor. The habanero adds *just* enough warmth, and the browning of the onion and orange slices delivers a delicate sweetness. At the restaurant, the hard-boiled eggs are marinated for over 24 hours in *shiro-dashi* (soy-flavored soup base), which can be found at Japanese and other Asian grocery stores. You'll want to make more eggs than you need for the soup, as they are also a great snack on their own. Save your Parmesan rinds, as they add good flavor to soup broths. If you don't have any rind on hand, ask your cheesemonger to slice a piece off for you.

Marinated Eggs
1 tablespoon distilled white vinegar
6 large eggs
¾ cup low-sodium soy sauce
1 tablespoon sugar
1 tablespoon sherry vinegar

Smoked Duck Soup
1 large yellow onion, cut crosswise into ½-inch-thick rounds
1 orange, cut crosswise into ½-inch-thick rounds
1 whole smoked duck (page 41)
3 qt basic duck stock (page 44) or chicken stock
3 fresh basil sprigs, plus shredded leaves for garnish
2 Parmesan cheese rinds (3 to 4 oz)
1 habanero or jalapeño chile, halved and seeded (optional)
Fine sea salt
1 head Napa or Savoy cabbage, cored and leaves thinly sliced
4 stems broccoli rabe, trimmed and diced

Egg Noodles
9 oz (about 1¾ cups) all-purpose flour
2 large eggs
4 large egg yolks
½ teaspoon fine sea salt

Makes 6 servings

To make the marinated eggs, prepare an ice bath in a medium bowl and set aside. In a saucepan over high heat, bring 3 qt water to a boil. Add the white vinegar. Add the eggs and boil for 10 minutes. Using a slotted spoon, transfer the eggs to the ice bath. In a medium bowl, whisk together ¾ cup water, the soy sauce, sugar, and sherry vinegar. When the eggs are cool enough to handle, peel them and add them to the soy sauce mixture. Refrigerate for at least 6 hours or up to 24 hours.

To make the soup, heat a large cast-iron or other heavy frying pan over medium heat. Add the onion slices in a single layer and cook, turning a few times to make sure the slices color evenly, until browned, 15 to 20 minutes. Transfer to a large stockpot. Add the orange slices to the cast-iron pan and cook, turning, until browned, about 15 minutes. Transfer to the stockpot.

Cut the smoked duck into 4 to 6 pieces and add to the stockpot. Add the duck stock, basil sprigs, Parmesan rinds, and habanero (if using) and bring to a gentle boil over high heat. Reduce the heat to low, cover partially, and simmer gently until rich and fragrant, about 1½ hours.

Transfer the duck to a cutting board. Place a fine-mesh sieve over a large heatproof bowl and pour the contents of the pot into the sieve. Discard the solids. Return the strained soup to the stockpot and season with salt. Set aside off the heat.

While the soup is simmering, make the noodle dough. Put the flour into a large bowl and make a well in the center of the flour. Add the whole eggs, egg yolks, and salt to the well and whisk the eggs with a fork just until blended. Then, using the fork, start pulling the flour into the eggs from the inside walls of the well. When a lumpy, thick dough begins to form in the center, use your hands to draw the remaining flour into the well, then continue to mix with your hands until a smooth and springy dough forms, 10 to 15 minutes. Wrap the dough in plastic wrap and let rest at room temperature for at least 1 hour or refrigerate for up to 2 days.

When the duck is cool enough to handle, pick the meat into bite-size pieces, discarding the bones. Chop the skin into bite-sized pieces and place in a small bowl. Add the meat to the stockpot.

Once the dough has rested, set up a pasta machine and adjust the rollers to the widest setting (#1 on most pasta machines). Divide the dough into 4 equal pieces. Working with 1 piece at a time, and keeping the other pieces covered with plastic wrap, flatten the dough slightly into a rectangle and feed it through the rollers, lightly flouring the dough and rollers as needed to prevent sticking. Fold the dough in half and roll again through the same setting. Repeat the folding and rolling as needed through the widest setting until the dough is silky smooth. Adjust the rollers to the next narrower setting (#2), then feed the dough through the rollers twice. Adjust the rollers to the next narrower setting (#3) and feed the dough through twice. Continue sending the dough strip through the rollers, adjust the setting narrower each time, until the pasta is smooth and about 1⁄16 inch thick.

Lay the pasta sheet on a work surface and trim the edges so they are even. Cut the sheet in half lengthwise and stack the two halves. Cut the stacked sheets in half crosswise, then once again, stack the two halves. Cut the stack lengthwise into ½-inch-wide noodles. Dust a sheet pan with flour, transfer the noodles to the pan, and toss the noodles with the flour. Cover with a clean kitchen towel while you roll out and cut the remaining dough into noodles.

When ready to serve, reheat the soup and duck meat over medium heat. When hot, add the cabbage and broccoli rabe. Reduce the heat to low and simmer, stirring, until the vegetables are tender.

Meanwhile, warm the cast-iron pan over medium heat. Add the reserved duck skin and cook, stirring occasionally, until the skin is crisp. Bring a large saucepan two-thirds full of salted water to a boil over high heat. Add the noodles to the boiling water and cook, stirring occasionally, until al dente, about 2 minutes.

Drain the noodles and divide them among 6 bowls. Ladle the hot soup over the noodles. Halve the eggs lengthwise and add to the bowls. Garnish with the crisp duck skin and shredded basil and serve.

WINE: A citrusy or floral white like Albariño or Sémillon will give lift to the smoky character of the soup.

DUCK POZOLE

CHEF DOMINICA RICE-CISNEROS

Bombera, chef Dominica Rice-Cisneros's restaurant in Oakland, California, is an homage to ancestral cooking, combining Californian and Mexican ingredients in a warm and inviting community-driven space. When speaking to her about this pozole, she spoke of her aunties cooking it over the fire and of how it is a sacred family recipe that can never be quite duplicated outside of that space. This pozole is full of spice from a whole head of garlic, a dream for me! Thank you to Dominica's family for gifting everyone with this extraordinary dish.

4 duck legs
12 cups water
Kosher salt and freshly ground black pepper
1 lb dried prepared hominy, preferably Rancho Gordo brand, soaked in cold water overnight (see Chef's Note)
½ yellow onion
½ to 1 head garlic, cloves separated and peeled
1 bunch fresh cilantro, tough stems trimmed
1 bunch green onions, green parts only, coarsely chopped
1 to 2 jalapeño chiles
½ cup raw pepitas, lightly toasted in a dry pan
1½ teaspoons dried Mexican oregano

Toppings
1 tablespoon dried Mexican oregano
1 white onion, diced
1 cup sliced radishes
3 to 4 cups shredded green cabbage
2 to 3 avocados, halved, pitted, peeled, and sliced
1 cup Mexican crema or sour cream
12 to 16 purchased small tostada shells
4 limes, cut into wedges

Makes 6 to 8 servings

In a large stockpot over high heat, combine the duck legs, 8 cups of the water, 1 tablespoon salt, and 1 teaspoon pepper and bring to a boil over high heat, skimming off any impurities that rise to the surface. Drain the hominy and add it to the pot along with the onion, half of the garlic (amount depends on personal taste), and the remaining 4 cups water. Bring back to a simmer, skimming off any impurities that rise to the surface, then turn down the heat to low and simmer gently, uncovered, until the duck is very tender, about 1½ hours.

Transfer the duck legs to a cutting board, then continue simmering the soup until the hominy is tender (al dente), 1 to 1½ hours longer. Add more water if needed to make sure the pozole stays soupy.

Pull the duck meat from the bones and shred it into bite-size pieces; discard the skin and bones. Using a large metal spoon, skim off the fat from the surface of the soup. Return the shredded duck meat to the soup and keep warm over low heat. (Alternatively, leave the duck legs whole, then just before serving, cut each leg in half and divide evenly among the bowls of pozole.)

In a blender, combine the remaining garlic, the cilantro, green onions, jalapeño(s) (amount depends on personal taste), pepitas, oregano, and 1 cup of the pozole broth (avoiding the duck and hominy). Puree until the mixture is smooth, season with salt, and then add to the pot. Continue to simmer for 10 minutes to blend the flavors. Taste and adjust the seasoning with salt and pepper if needed.

To serve, put the oregano, onion, radishes, cabbage, avocados, crema, tostadas, and limes in separate small bowls and on small plates or a large platter and set on the table. Ladle the pozole into 6 to 8 bowls and invite diners to add the toppings to their bowls to taste.

CHEF'S NOTE: *It's worth sourcing dried hominy for this recipe, but if you cannot find it, you can substitute 1 large can (29 oz) hominy, drained. Canned hominy has a softer texture and will be ready when the duck is cooked, after 1½ hours. It's also worth visiting a Mexican market for the Mexican oregano and tostadas.*

BEER: There's a lot of garlic in this incredibly tasty pozole, which makes it a great pairing for a light lager, preferably one from Mexico.

DUCK GUMBO

CHEF ALON SHAYA

Chef Alon Shaya came to Liberty Ducks through chef Chris Cosentino. Chris was running a series of dinners with chefs from all over the country, and Chris and Alon had duck on their collaborative menu. A few months later, Alon called up looking for some duck to serve for a special menu he was preparing in New Orleans. Fast-forward to 2021 and Alon has a new restaurant called Miss River, which is a love letter from this Israeli-born chef to his adopted city of New Orleans. Using duck legs and our duck andouille, you can now re-create his gumbo at home. My husband's family has close ties to New Orleans, and when I cook this dish, all I hear are "mmmms" and "yumms," so you know it's good.

¼ cup canola oil
4 duck legs, thighs and drumsticks separated
¼ cup all-purpose flour, plus more if needed
1 large yellow onion, finely chopped
2 celery stalks, finely chopped
1 green bell pepper, seeded and finely chopped
1 small jalapeño chile, seeded and minced
2 garlic cloves, thinly sliced
3 fresh bay leaves, or 1 dried bay leaf
2 teaspoons chopped fresh thyme leaves
3 tablespoons Creole seasoning, homemade (page 23) or purchased
4 cups basic duck stock (page 44) or chicken stock
1 lb duck andouille sausage or other smoked pork sausage, casing removed, cut into large dice
2 teaspoons hot-pepper sauce, such as Tabasco brand
1 tablespoon Worcestershire sauce
2 teaspoons sherry vinegar or apple cider vinegar
2 teaspoons kosher salt
Warm steamed white rice, for serving
1 bunch green onions, white and green parts, sliced

Makes 4 to 6 servings

WINE: As there's a little spice, a wine lower in alcohol is best. A fruit-forward Gamay (look for a Beaujolais Villages) or Russian River Chardonnay would be great.

In a large Dutch oven or other large, heavy pot over medium heat, warm the oil. Add the duck legs, skin side down, and cook until the skin is golden brown and crispy and the fat renders out, about 12 minutes. (Do this in batches if the pot is too crowded.) Remove the pot from the heat and transfer the duck legs to a sheet pan.

Add the flour to the oil and fat in the pot and stir well with a wooden spoon. Return the pot to medium heat and cook, scraping the bottom of the pot constantly, until a very dark brown roux develops, about 15 minutes.

Add the onion to the roux and cook, stirring constantly, for another 15 minutes. The roux will seize up around the onion and the pot will look dry, but that is normal. If this doesn't happen, add up to 2 tablespoons more flour and stir until the pot is dry. Add the celery, bell pepper, jalapeño, garlic, bay leaves, and thyme to the onions and stir until well combined. Add the Creole seasoning and cook, stirring, until the spices are fragrant and lightly toasted, about 3 minutes. Slowly pour in the stock while stirring constantly, then add the reserved duck legs and the duck andouille and stir to combine.

Turn down the heat to low, cover, and continue to cook, stirring occasionally, until the duck meat has begun to fall off the bone, about 1½ hours.

Remove the gumbo from the heat and stir in the hot sauce, Worcestershire sauce, vinegar, and salt, mixing well. Taste and adjust the seasoning with salt if needed. Remove and discard the bay leaves.

Ladle the gumbo over rice in individual bowls, garnish with the green onions, and serve.

CONFIT DUCK, FRENCH LENTIL, AND PORCINI MUSHROOM SOUP

CHEFS JOSIAH CITRIN AND KEN TAKAYAMA

This flavorful soup is reminiscent of the duck-mushroom broth with lentil cream and truffle mousse served at Mélisse, developed by chef/owner Josiah Citrin and chef/partner Ken Takayama. Simplified for home cooks, the recipe retains the character and flavors of the original. For a meatier soup, add another duck leg. To take this up a level, stir in some heavy cream, then shave a fresh truffle over the top.

½ oz dried porcini mushrooms (about ⅔ cup)
1 cup boiling water
2 tablespoons unsalted butter
2 tablespoons extra-virgin olive oil
1 large shallot, finely chopped
1 medium leek, white and pale green parts, halved or quartered lengthwise and thinly sliced crosswise
1 large carrot, peeled and finely diced
1 large celery stalk, finely diced
1 garlic clove, minced
1 teaspoon finely chopped fresh thyme leaves
1 bay leaf
3 tablespoons sherry, Cognac, or Madeira wine
1 cup French (Puy) green lentils or black lentils, picked over and rinsed
6 cups rich duck stock (page 45) or basic duck stock (page 44), plus more if needed
2 duck legs confit (page 35)
1 tablespoon duck fat (from the confit) or unsalted butter
6 oz fresh porcini, trumpet, or cremini mushrooms, brushed clean and finely chopped
Fine sea salt and freshly ground black pepper
Chopped fresh chives, for garnish

Makes 6 servings

WINE: Pour an herbal Pinot Noir with red fruits. Look for one from Burgundy to lend an additional umami mushroom note to the soup.

In a heatproof bowl, combine the dried mushrooms and boiling water and let stand for 30 minutes. Line a fine-mesh sieve with cheesecloth or a coffee filter and set over a bowl. Drain the mushrooms into the prepared sieve. Set the liquid aside. Finely chop the rehydrated mushrooms and set aside separately.

In a large saucepan or stockpot over medium heat, melt the butter with the oil. Add the shallot, leek, carrot, and celery and cook, stirring often, until translucent, about 5 minutes. Add the garlic, thyme, and bay leaf and cook, stirring, until fragrant, about 1 minute. Stir in the rehydrated mushrooms and the lentils, then pour in the stock and reserved mushroom liquid. Raise the heat to high and bring to a boil. Turn down the heat to low, cover partially, and cook, stirring occasionally, until the lentils are tender but still hold their shape, 20 to 35 minutes; the timing will depend on the type and age of the lentils.

Meanwhile, in a frying pan over medium-low heat, rewarm the duck legs, turning them once, about 4 minutes total. Transfer to a cutting board, let cool just until they can be handled, and then pull the meat and skin from the legs and shred or chop it into bite-size pieces.

Pour off all but about 1 tablespoon fat from the frying pan and return the pan to medium heat. Alternatively, pour off all the fat and melt the butter over medium heat. Add the fresh porcini and cook, stirring occasionally, until tender, about 4 minutes.

When the lentils are tender, stir in the duck meat and the cooked fresh porcini and continue to simmer until the soup reaches serving temperature, about 5 minutes. Season with salt and pepper. Ladle into 6 bowls, garnish each bowl with a sprinkle of chives, and serve.

DUCK CHILI

CHEF KEN FRANK

Chef Ken Frank's celebrated Napa Valley restaurant, La Toque, serves gorgeous modern French cuisine with a California touch. What's not on his menu is this chili. But what I love about this dish is that it's what Ken cooks at home. See a winter storm in the forecast? Make this a day before it's slated to hit and serve it with homemade corn bread on that stormy night. I promise you it will warm you right up.

2 cups water
1 mulato chile
1 ancho chile
1 pasilla chile
6 tablespoons rendered duck fat (page 32)
3 lb ground duck meat
Kosher salt
1 large yellow onion, finely diced
4 garlic cloves, finely chopped
½ cup mild chili powder
2 tablespoons tomato paste
1 can (28 oz) crushed fire-roasted tomatoes with juices
1 bottle (12 oz) brown ale, stout, or porter-style beer
3 cups basic duck stock (page 44) or water
2 to 3 dashes hot-pepper sauce (optional)

For Serving (Optional)

Shredded Monterey Jack or Cheddar cheese
Mexican crema or sour cream
Sliced green onions, white and green parts
Chopped fresh cilantro leaves
Diced avocado
Lime wedges

Makes 8 servings

In a medium saucepan over high heat, bring the water to a boil. Turn down the heat to low, add the mulato, ancho, and pasilla chiles, cover, and simmer until the chiles are rehydrated and tender, about 5 minutes. Transfer the chiles to a cutting board, reserving the cooking liquid. When the chiles are cool enough to handle, remove and discard the seeds and roughly chop. In a blender, combine the chiles and ¼ cup of the cooking liquid and blend until a smooth puree forms, adding up to ¼ cup more liquid as needed to achieve a smooth consistency. Scrape the puree into a small bowl and set aside.

In a large Dutch oven or other large, heavy pot over medium-high heat, warm the duck fat until sizzling. Add the ground duck and 1 tablespoon salt and cook, stirring often and breaking up the meat with a wooden spoon, until all the moisture has evaporated and the meat begins to brown, 8 to 10 minutes. Using a slotted spoon, transfer the duck to a bowl and set aside.

Add the onion to the drippings in the pot and cook over medium-high heat, stirring often, until golden brown, about 10 minutes. Add the garlic and cook, stirring, until fragrant, about 30 seconds. Return the duck meat to the pot along with the chili powder and tomato paste and cook, stirring to coat the meat and toast the spices, for about 2 minutes. Stir in the tomatoes, reserved chile puree, beer, and 1 teaspoon salt. Pour in the stock, raise the heat to high, and bring to a boil. Turn down the heat to medium-low and simmer gently uncovered, stirring occasionally so the chili doesn't settle and stick, until the chili thickens, about 1½ hours. Taste and adjust the seasoning with salt if needed and with a few dashes of hot sauce if more spicy heat is desired.

As with most chilis, this one can be served when ready, or it can be cooled to room temperature and stored overnight in the refrigerator to allow the flavors to meld, then reheated just before serving. Ladle into 8 bowls and serve with any of the toppings that you like. Leftover chili will keep in an airtight container in the refrigerator for up to 5 days.

BEER / WINE: Best with a cold beer, like a red ale. If looking for wine, go for a Malbec or Syrah from California or Australia.

DUCK PHỞ

CHEF MARK MALICKI

Mark Malicki has been a Sonoma County chef for ages. My first trip to the Casino Bar & Grill, a dive bar in the middle of nowhere where he cooks Friday through Sunday nights, was on St. Patrick's Day in 2011. I was mesmerized not only by the fact that his incredible corned beef and cabbage dish had so much flavor and texture but also that his kitchen was just a tiny griddle and two burners. Time and time again, I go back to Mark to taste the menu of the day, which, because he purchases from local farmers and markets, is always changing and evolving. What's on offer starts the weekend as one thing and finishes as something entirely different. Mark says the best duck he ever had was in Laos, roasted over a live fire and tended to by a woman basting it with fish sauce: "How big of a duck? Don't know. The fire was hot, the wood was smoky. The fish sauce was fishy and salty. How much fish sauce? Enough to make it taste good!"

Duck Broth

- 1 yellow onion, halved
- 2-inch knob fresh ginger, unpeeled, halved lengthwise
- 6 green cardamom pods
- 6 whole cloves
- 1 tablespoon coriander seeds
- 1 tablespoon fennel seeds
- 2 whole star anise
- 3 lb mixed duck bones, necks, and feet
- 3 tablespoons sugar
- 2 tablespoons kosher salt
- 2 tablespoons fish sauce
- 1 bunch green onions, white and green parts, sliced

Garnishes

- ¼ lb mung bean sprouts
- ½ bunch fresh cilantro sprigs
- ½ bunch fresh Thai basil sprigs
- 1 jalapeño chile, thinly sliced
- 1 lime, cut into 8 wedges
- Hot-pepper sauce
- Hoisin sauce

- 1 lb rice vermicelli, such as Three Ladies brand
- 2 duck breasts, skinned and very thinly sliced
- 1 small yellow onion, thinly sliced

Makes 4 servings

WINE: A light-bodied red wine, such as Trousseau.

To make the broth, preheat the oven to 400°F. Put the onion and ginger on a small sheet pan and roast, turning occasionally, until caramel-like and soft, about 1 hour.

In a dry small frying pan over medium heat, toast the cardamom, cloves, coriander seeds, fennel seeds, and star anise, shaking the pan often, until fragrant, 1 to 2 minutes. Remove from the heat.

In a large stockpot, combine the duck bones, roasted onion and ginger, toasted spices, sugar, salt, and water to cover by at least 1 inch (about 4 quarts) and bring to a boil over high heat, skimming off any impurities that rise to the surface. Turn down the heat to low and simmer gently uncovered, continuing to skim as necessary and adding more water if needed to keep the bones covered, for 2 hours.

Place a fine-mesh sieve over a saucepan and pour the contents of the pot into the sieve. Discard the solids. Stir in the fish sauce and green onions, then taste and adjust the seasoning with more fish sauce to taste if needed. Place the pan over very low heat to keep the broth warm.

Arrange the garnishes—bean sprouts, cilantro, basil, jalapeño, and lime wedges—on a large plate. Put the hot sauce and hoisin sauce into separate small bowls. Then cook the noodles according to the package directions and drain well.

To serve, divide the noodles evenly among 4 bowls, then divide the duck and onion slices evenly among the bowls, arranging them on top of the noodles. Bring the broth just to a boil and immediately ladle it over the ingredients in each bowl. The hot broth will cook the duck breast slices.

Serve the soup with the plate of garnishes and the sauces for diners to add to their bowls to taste.

CHAPTER FIVE

MAINS

DUCK MOLE CHILAQUILES

with fried eggs and avocado

CHEF NEAL FRASER

Chilaquiles are, at their simplest, a Mexican dish of fried corn tortillas simmered in a flavorful sauce. Chef Neal Fraser has had duck mole chilaquiles on the brunch menu at Redbird, his Los Angeles restaurant, for quite some time, and I can see why. Redbird's dishes are often shared by the whole table, and these chilaquiles are no exception. Make them for a crowd, and no guest will be disappointed. The spicy mole sauce makes more than you need, but the extra freezes well for another round of chilaquiles, for slathering on roasted duck legs, or, if you're feeling adventurous, for making duck enchiladas. If you don't have duck confit on hand, roast a couple of duck legs and use the shredded meat.

Mole

2 guajillo chilies, seeded and chopped
2 ancho chilies, seeded and chopped
⅔ cup water
2 tablespoons canola or avocado oil
1 small yellow onion, halved and thinly sliced
2 garlic cloves, roughly chopped
2 teaspoons ground coriander
2 teaspoons ground cumin
1 can (14 oz) crushed tomatoes with juices or tomato puree
1 cup basic duck stock (page 44) or chicken stock
¼ cup chopped chipotles in adobo
2 tablespoons cocoa nibs (optional)
2 tablespoons sesame seeds
2 tablespoons toasted pepitas
Fine sea salt
½ Mexican hot chocolate tablet (about 1⅔ oz), preferably Ibarra brand, chopped

2 duck legs confit (page 35)
About 8 oz thick-cut tortilla chips
1 tablespoon canola or avocado oil
4 large eggs
1 avocado, halved, pitted, peeled, and thinly sliced
Pico de gallo, homemade (page 101) or purchased
About ½ cup crumbled Cotija cheese or queso fresco

Makes 4 servings

WINE: As chilaquiles are a traditional breakfast dish, a Prosecco or cava would bring a celebratory feel to any weekend brunch.

To make the mole, in a small saucepan over high heat, combine the guajillo and ancho chiles and the water and bring to a boil. Remove from the heat, cover, and set aside for 15 minutes to soften. Transfer the chiles and their liquid to a blender and puree until smooth, adding a little water if needed for a smooth puree. You should have ⅔ cup. Scrape into a bowl and set aside. (The chile puree can be stored in an airtight container in the refrigerator for up to 1 week or in the freezer for up to 3 months.)

In a large saucepan over medium-low heat, warm the oil. Add the onion and cook, stirring, until translucent, about 7 minutes. Add the garlic, coriander, and cumin and cook, stirring, until fragrant, about 3 minutes. Add the reserved chile puree, tomatoes, stock, chipotles, cocoa nibs (if using), sesame seeds, pepitas, and ½ teaspoon salt. Raise the heat to medium and bring to a simmer, then turn down the heat to low and simmer, stirring occasionally, until all the ingredients are very tender and the sauce is thickened, about 30 minutes. Add the chocolate, cover, and set aside off the heat for 10 minutes. Stir, making sure the chocolate is melted, then transfer to a blender and blend to a smooth puree. Taste and adjust the seasoning with salt if needed. You should have about 4 cups. You will need only 1½ cups mole for the chilaquiles; store the remainder in an airtight container in the refrigerator for up to 4 days or in the freezer for up to 2 months.

While the mole simmers, pick the meat from the duck legs, discarding the skin and bones. Chop or shred into bite-sized pieces.

To assemble, in a large frying pan over medium-low heat, warm 1½ cups of the mole with the duck, stirring constantly, for about 3 minutes. If the mole is too thick, add a little water. Add the tortilla chips and toss and stir until evenly coated with the sauce and meat, about 3 minutes.

In another large, nonstick or well-seasoned frying pan over medium heat, warm the oil. Crack the eggs into the pan and cook over easy or to your liking.

Divide the chilaquiles among 4 individual plates and top each serving with a fried egg. Add a quarter of the avocado slices to each plate, then garnish with the pico de gallo and cheese. Serve at once.

DUCK BÁNH MÌ

CHEF TU DAVID PHU

When we first announced this cookbook, I put out a call for recipe requests and ideas, and *bánh mì* came in at the top of the list! I quickly got in touch with Bay Area chef Tu David Phu to see if he was interested in creating this beloved sandwich for us, and the rest is history! Tu is a first-generation Vietnamese American and has worked with our duck in multiple stops along his culinary career. His newsletter is filled with the history and culture of Vietnamese cuisine, and I save every issue in my inbox for reference later. A *bánh mì* is not a *bánh mì* without the pâté, so don't skip that step! His recipe on page 50 is the perfect complement to the duck meat, pickled vegetables, and crunchy bread.

Pickled Carrots
1 cup water
½ cup rice vinegar
½ jalapeño chile, halved
2 garlic cloves, smashed
1 coin-size slice fresh ginger
½ teaspoon coconut sugar or granulated sugar
¼ teaspoon kosher salt
2 small carrots, peeled and cut into matchsticks

Duck Breast Char Siu
3 duck breasts
3 tablespoons hoisin sauce
1 tablespoon coconut aminos or fish sauce
1 tablespoon honey
1 tablespoon apple cider vinegar
½ teaspoon kosher salt
½ teaspoon garlic powder
½ teaspoon five-spice powder
½ teaspoon gochugaru (Korean red pepper flakes), optional
½ teaspoon sweet paprika
¼ teaspoon peeled and minced fresh ginger

1 small English cucumber
Four 6-inch pieces baguette, split horizontally
About ¼ cup mayonnaise
½ cup duck liver pâté, homemade (page 50) or purchased
1 or 2 jalapeño chiles, thinly sliced (optional)
12 fresh cilantro sprigs

Makes 4 sandwiches

To make the pickled carrots, in a small saucepan over medium heat, combine the water, vinegar, jalapeño, garlic, ginger, sugar, and salt. Bring to a simmer, then remove from the heat and add the carrots. Place a small plate on top of the mixture to submerge the carrots in the pickling liquid. Let steep at room temperature for at least 15 minutes. To store, transfer the carrots in their pickling liquid to an airtight container and refrigerate for up to 14 days.

Next, make the duck breast char siu. While the duck breasts are still cold from the refrigerator, using a sharp knife and working with one breast at a time, score the skin on each breast on the diagonal, spacing the cuts about ½ inch apart and being careful not to cut through to the meat. Rotate the duck breast 90 degrees and score the same way in the opposite direction to make a crosshatch pattern. Set the breasts aside for 20 minutes to come to room temperature.

Place the duck breasts, skin side down, in a cold large nonstick frying pan. Turn on the heat to medium-low and let the breasts cook undisturbed until they have rendered their fat and the skin is golden brown, about 8 minutes. Transfer to a plate, skin side up, and pat with paper towels to remove any excess fat.

In a small bowl, whisk together the hoisin sauce, coconut aminos, honey, vinegar, salt, garlic powder, five-spice powder, gochugaru (if using), paprika, and ginger. Spoon the marinade over the duck breasts, spreading it all over each one. Set aside at room temperature to marinate for 30 minutes.

While the duck marinates, preheat the oven to 350°F. Line a roasting pan with aluminum foil.

Transfer the duck breasts, skin side up, to the prepared roasting pan. Roast the duck until browned and cooked to your liking, about 3 minutes for medium-rare and about 5 minutes for medium. An instant-read thermometer inserted into the thickest part of a breast should register 130° to 135°F for medium-rare and 135° to 140°F for medium. Transfer the duck breasts to a cutting board and let rest for 5 minutes, then thinly slice on the diagonal. Leave the oven on.

continued . . .

BEER: Saison beer often has a lemon note, which balances well with the spices and pickled elements of this delicious sandwich.

To assemble the sandwiches, cut both ends off the cucumber and cut the cucumber crosswise into pieces about 6 inches long. Cut each piece lengthwise into ¼-inch-thick slices.

Put the baguette pieces into the oven to toast for 5 minutes. Arrange all the baguette halves cut side up on a work surface. Smear the cut side of each baguette bottom with about 1 tablespoon mayonnaise and smear the cut side of each baguette top with 2 tablespoons pâté.

Place one-fourth of the duck breast slices on each baguette bottom, then layer with one-fourth each of the pickled carrots, cucumber slices, and jalapeño slices (if using) and finish with 3 cilantro sprigs. Close with the baguette tops and serve at once.

COFFEE-CRUSTED DUCK BREASTS

with whipped polenta and pickled cherries

CHEF KEVIN MEEHAN

The night before my bachelorette party, my two best girlfriends and I went to eat at Kali in Los Angeles. I had been there a couple of times before and liked the warm, friendly feeling of the place. Perhaps that's because you walk in and see chef Kevin Meehan and the team in the kitchen straightaway, as if they've invited you into their world. Or maybe it's because Drew Langley is behind the counter, ready to serve you a glass of something special he's found. Whatever the reason, we had an amazing meal that night. Kevin dry ages whole ducks for this dish at the restaurant. But because home fridges have limited space, the recipe has been adapted for duck breasts. Black peppercorns are a main ingredient, so use the good stuff, such as Diaspora Company's Aranya peppercorns, a single-origin pepper from southwest India. Coffee is a natural meat tenderizer, so the resulting texture of these duck breasts is otherworldly.

Pickled Cherries
1 lb Bing cherries, pitted (about 2 cups)
½ cup black tea kombucha
⅓ cup port wine
⅓ cup sugar
1 tablespoon fine sea salt
1 whole star anise

Coffee-Rubbed Duck
⅓ cup ground coffee
2 teaspoons freshly ground black pepper
6 garlic cloves, minced
1 teaspoon fine sea salt
4 duck breasts

Whipped Polenta
2 cups whole milk
2 cups water
1 cup fine-grind polenta
2 tablespoons unsalted butter
Fine sea salt and freshly ground black pepper

Flaky sea salt, such as Maldon, for garnish

Makes 6 to 8 servings

WINE: Merlot often shows notes of coffee and dark chocolate with supple tannins and medium acidity, all of which pair exceptionally well with this dish.

To make the pickled cherries, put the cherries into a heatproof wide-mouthed glass jar with a tight-fitting lid. In a saucepan over high heat, combine the kombucha, port, sugar, salt, and star anise and bring to a boil, stirring until the sugar dissolves. Pour the kombucha mixture into the jar, covering the cherries, and tightly cap the jar. Set aside to cool to room temperature. Refrigerate for at least 6 hours before using. The cherries can be made up to 2 weeks in advance.

To make the duck, in a bowl, stir together the coffee, pepper, garlic, and salt. Rub the mixture all over the duck breasts. Place the breasts on a small sheet pan and refrigerate uncovered for 24 to 48 hours. Remove the duck breasts from the refrigerator 1 hour before cooking. Rinse the coffee mixture off the breasts and pat dry with paper towels. Score the skin as directed on page 31.

To make the whipped polenta, in a large saucepan over medium heat, combine the milk and water and bring to a boil. Turn down the heat to medium-low, then slowly add the polenta while stirring constantly with a whisk. Cook, stirring constantly with a whisk, until the polenta is thick and creamy, about 30 minutes. Remove from the heat, add the butter, and season with salt and pepper. Let cool for a few minutes, then transfer to a blender and blend until whipped.

While the polenta is cooking, place the duck breasts, skin side down, in a cold large cast-iron or heavy frying pan. Turn on the heat to low and let the breasts cook undisturbed until they have rendered their fat, 12 to 15 minutes. Every so often, lift each breast with tongs to make sure the skin is not burning. If it is getting too dark, remove from the heat. Once the fat has rendered out and is deep golden brown, raise the heat to medium-high, turn the breasts over, and continue to cook until browned and medium-rare (an instant-read thermometer inserted into the thickest part of a breast should register 130°F), 2 to 4 minutes longer. Transfer to a cutting board and let rest for 10 minutes before serving.

To serve, slice the duck breasts crosswise into thin slices. Divide the polenta evenly among 6 or 8 shallow bowls or plates and arrange the duck slices on the polenta, dividing them evenly. Top with the pickled cherries and some of their juices, finish with flaky salt, and serve.

JEN'S DUCK BREAST RICE BOWL

The recipe for this rice bowl is a template. Use this method as a starting point and pop in whatever you have on hand or love. Among the other things I like to add are kimchi, nori, sliced avocado, Kewpie mayonnaise, and crunchy fried onions. For a more intense flavor, use duck stock instead of water to cook the rice. This versatile bowl has quickly become one of my go-to weeknight meals.

2 pan-seared duck breasts (page 39)
4 cups steamed white rice, warm
3 tablespoons olive oil or rendered duck fat (page 32)
2 cups chopped braising greens, such as cabbage, kale, Swiss chard, and/or bok choy
1 tablespoon toasted sesame oil
1 teaspoon soy sauce
1 teaspoon rice vinegar
1 cup sliced cremini mushrooms (or your favorite mushrooms)
2 tablespoons rendered duck fat (page 32) or olive oil
4 duck eggs or large chicken eggs
2 green onions, white and green parts, thinly sliced
Sesame seeds, for sprinkling
XO sauce, chile crisp sauce, Sriracha sauce, or other hot-pepper sauce, for serving

Makes 4 servings

BEER / WINE: A Japanese rice-based beer is a nice break from my traditional pairing. Given the clean-out-the-fridge nature of this dish, the half bottle of wine left over from the night before is what's typical at our house.

Prepare the pan-seared duck breasts as directed and keep warm. Have ready the cooked rice, covered to keep warm.

In a large nonstick frying pan over medium heat, warm 1 tablespoon of the olive oil. Add the greens and cook, stirring, until the greens are wilted and tender, about 3 minutes. Remove from the heat and stir in the sesame oil, soy sauce, and vinegar. Transfer the greens to a bowl and cover to keep warm.

Return the pan to medium heat and warm the remaining 2 tablespoons olive oil. Add the mushrooms and cook, stirring, until tender, 5 to 7 minutes. Transfer the mushrooms to a second bowl and cover to keep warm.

With the pan still over medium heat, add the duck fat. When the fat has melted, crack the eggs into the pan. Cook, turning once if you like, until done to your liking (over easy or medium is my favorite!).

To assemble the bowls, divide the warm rice among 4 shallow bowls. Slice the duck breasts crosswise into ¼-inch-thick slices. Arrange one-fourth of the duck slices on one side of the rice in each bowl. Divide the cooked greens evenly among the bowls, piling them on top of the rice apart from the duck. Add the mushrooms to the bowls, dividing them evenly and keeping them separate from the greens and duck. Top each bowl with a fried egg. Finish the bowls with the sesame seeds, green onions, and XO sauce and serve.

DUCK CONFIT CASSOULET

with tarbais beans, leek, and bacon

CHEF RUPERT BLEASE

Cassoulet is a traditional dish of Southwest France that dates back to medieval times. Its makeup differs from town to town but always includes white beans and meat, though the types of both vary. For example, the Grande Confrérie du Cassoulet de Castelnaudary, a forty-year-old group dedicated to the history and historical preservation of its local cassoulet, uses Castelnaudry white beans in its recipe. Here, chef Rupert Blease, of San Francisco's Lord Stanley restaurant, calls for Tarbais beans, which are typically used in the Toulouse version of the dish. No matter which creamy white bean you find for this recipe (it is also okay to use flageolets or cannellini), you'll be happy with how this dish turns out.

Beans
1 lb dried Tarbais, flageolet, or cannellini beans, picked over, then soaked overnight in water
½ carrot, peeled
1 celery stalk
¼ white onion
2 tablespoons kosher salt

Cassoulet
1 tablespoon rice bran or other neutral oil
1 carrot, peeled and diced
½ white onion, diced
1 medium leek, white part only, diced
1 celery stalk, diced
2 garlic cloves, minced
3 slices bacon, diced
Kosher salt and freshly ground black pepper
⅓ cup dry white wine
2 tablespoons rendered duck fat (from confit legs)
1 cup fresh bread crumbs
½ cup chopped fresh flat-leaf parsley
4 duck legs confit (page 35)
½ lemon

Makes 4 servings

WINE: A Côte du Rhône or Minervois from Southern France nicely rounds out the warming sensation of this quintessential fall dish.

To cook the beans, drain the beans and add to a large saucepan or soup pot with a lid. Add the carrot, celery, onion, and water to cover by 1 inch. Do not add salt at this point, as it will make the skins of the beans wrinkle. Cover and bring to a boil over medium-high heat, then turn down the heat to medium-low, cover partially, and cook, stirring occasionally, until the beans are evenly cooked and soft all the way through and you can bite through the skin easily, about 1 hour. Season to taste with salt, then let cool to room temperature.

To make the cassoulet, preheat the oven to 350°F. In a large Dutch oven or other large, heavy pot over medium heat, warm the oil. Add the carrot, onion, leek, celery, garlic, and bacon and season generously with salt and pepper. Cook, stirring constantly so the ingredients don't caramelize, until the vegetables are soft, about 4 minutes.

Drain the beans into a fine-mesh sieve set over a bowl, reserving the cooking liquid. Remove and discard the carrot, onion, and celery pieces from the beans. Add the beans to the Dutch oven with the vegetable mixture and add the wine. Place over low heat and stir to combine. Slowly spoon the bean cooking liquid into the Dutch oven until the ingredients are just covered. Continue cooking at a low simmer for about 20 minutes until all the flavors mingle.

In a frying pan over medium heat, warm the duck fat. Add the bread crumbs and toast, stirring, until browned, about 3 minutes. Spread the bread crumbs in an even layer on top of the beans, then top the bread crumbs evenly with the parsley. Place the duck legs on top of the parsley layer and transfer the pot to the oven.

Bake uncovered until the duck skin is brown and crisp, about 25 minutes. Remove the finished cassoulet from the oven, season with a squeeze of lemon juice to cut through the fattiness, and serve.

DUCK JAMBALAYA

CHEF TANYA HOLLAND

Chef Tanya Holland and I were first introduced by mutual friend Stevie Stacionis of Bay Grape, who had graciously suggested my Raft Wines Viognier to Tanya. Tanya has a wonderful warmth to her, like you've known her for years, and you can feel that warmth through her cooking. Brown Sugar Kitchen takeout was a highlight for us during the pandemic. When I brought home her food, our then five-year-old neighbor (and his parents) would join us outside for dinner, and he would quickly exclaim how the fried chicken was "the best" and the biscuits were "so good I want to eat more." If that's not a five-star review, I don't know what is!

2 duck legs confit (page 35)
1 small yellow onion, diced
2 celery stalks, diced
1 green bell pepper, seeded and diced
2 teaspoons Creole seasoning, homemade (page 23) or purchased
1 cup chopped fresh tomatoes or canned diced tomatoes (optional)
2 garlic cloves, chopped
2 teaspoons Worcestershire sauce
1 teaspoon Louisiana hot sauce
2 cups long-grain white rice
4 cups basic duck stock (page 44) or chicken stock
2 duck breasts
Fine sea salt and freshly ground black pepper
2 green onions, white and green parts, thinly sliced

Makes 6 servings

WINE: An unoaked Chardonnay or Chenin Blanc would bring a light lift to the dish.

Pull the meat from the confit duck legs, discarding the skin and bones; reserve 2 tablespoons of the duck fat from the confit. Roughly chop the meat and reserve.

In a Dutch oven or other heavy pot over medium heat, warm the duck fat. Add the onion, celery, bell pepper, and Creole seasoning and cook, stirring occasionally, until tender but not browned, about 6 minutes. Add the tomatoes (if using), garlic, Worcestershire sauce, and hot sauce and cook, stirring, until fragrant, about 1 minute. Stir in the rice, stock, and reserved duck confit and bring to a simmer. Turn down the heat to low, cover, and cook until the rice is tender, about 20 minutes. Turn off the heat and let sit for 10 minutes.

While the rice mixture is cooking, sear the duck breasts. While the duck breasts are still cold from the refrigerator, using a sharp knife and working with one duck breast at a time, score the skin on each breast on the diagonal, spacing the cuts about ½ inch apart and being careful not to cut through to the meat. Rotate the duck breast 90 degrees and score the same way in the opposite direction to make a crosshatch pattern. Season the duck breasts on both sides with salt and pepper and set aside for 20 minutes to come to room temperature.

Place the duck breasts, skin side down, in a cold large cast-iron or other heavy frying pan. Turn on the heat to low and let the breasts cook undisturbed until they have rendered their fat, 12 to 15 minutes. Once the fat is rendered and is deep golden brown, raise the heat to medium-high, turn the breasts over, and continue to cook until the meat side is browned and the breasts are medium-rare, 2 to 4 minutes longer. An instant-read thermometer inserted into the thickest part of a breast should register 130°F. Transfer to a cutting board and let rest for 5 to 10 minutes before serving.

Uncover the jambalaya and stir in all but 2 tablespoons of the green onions. Slice the duck breasts crosswise into thin slices. Divide the jambalaya evenly among 6 bowls or spoon onto a warmed serving platter. Top the jambalaya with the duck breast slices, garnish with the remaining green onions, and serve at once.

DUCK RAGÙ PAPPARDELLE

with red wine and chestnuts

CHEF STAFFAN TERJE

Perbacco, the upscale Italian restaurant in San Francisco, is associated with a very specific holiday memory of mine. Every year my dad and I would go to an event that was notoriously lean on passed appetizers but delightfully close to the front door of Perbacco. So every year we'd sneak out a little early and grab a seat at the bar to chat with Umberto, or hope that chef Staffan Terje would come out of the kitchen to say hello. The Italian word *perbacco* is an interjection that emphasizes the positive as well as surprise and pleasure. It roughly translates as "wow" or more fully as "good times," and I can safely say the restaurant's name was well chosen. This dish is appropriate for the winter season, when chestnuts are on menus. You can try your hand at roasting them yourself, or you can purchase already roasted and peeled chestnuts vacuum packed, in jars, or frozen.

- 6 duck legs, skinned
- 2 cups dry red wine
- Fine sea salt and freshly ground black pepper
- 2 tablespoons rendered duck fat (page 32)
- ½ large yellow onion, finely chopped
- 1 medium carrot, peeled and finely chopped
- 1 celery stalk, finely chopped
- 6 fresh sage leaves, roughly chopped
- 2 cups rich duck stock (page 45) or chicken stock
- 1 cup roasted and peeled chestnuts
- 1½ lb fresh pappardelle
- Freshly grated Parmesan, for serving

Makes 6 servings

WINE: A beautiful Italian Nebbiolo from the Piedmont will be a nice balance to the chestnuts. I swoon over a wine with high acidity and tannin.

Place the duck legs, meatier side down, in a baking dish and pour the wine over the legs. Cover and refrigerate for at least 6 hours or up to 24 hours. Transfer the duck legs to a large plate or sheet pan and pat dry with paper towels. Season the legs on both sides with salt and pepper. Reserve the wine.

In a large Dutch oven or other heavy pot over medium heat, warm the duck fat. Working in batches to avoid crowding, add the duck legs and cook, turning once, until browned on both sides, about 5 minutes on each side. Return them to the plate or sheet pan and set aside.

Add the onion, carrot, and celery to the Dutch oven and cook over medium heat, stirring occasionally, until lightly browned, 12 to 15 minutes. Add the sage and stir to combine. Return the duck legs to the pot and add the reserved wine and the stock. Season with salt and pepper.

Bring to a simmer, then turn down the heat to low, cover partially, and cook gently until the duck legs are very tender and the meat comes off the bone easily, about 1 hour.

Transfer the legs to a plate or sheet pan and let cool slightly. Add the chestnuts to the Dutch oven and continue to simmer over low heat; the chestnuts will start to fall apart into small pieces after about 20 minutes.

When the duck legs are cool enough to handle, remove the meat from the bones, discarding the bones and any excess fat. Shred the meat into bite-size pieces and return it to the pot. Let the ragù simmer until the sauce is slightly thickened, about 10 minutes. Taste and adjust the seasoning with salt and pepper if needed.

Fill a large pot half full with salted water and bring to a boil over high heat. Add the pasta and cook, stirring occasionally, until al dente, 3 to 4 minutes. Drain the pasta and add to the duck ragù. Toss the pasta in the sauce until all the ribbons are evenly coated.

Divide the pasta and its clinging sauce among 6 plates or shallow bowls or transfer to a platter. Spoon more ragù from the pan over the top. Sprinkle with Parmesan and serve.

DUCK CONFIT BASTEEYA

CHEF MOURAD LAHLOU

Basteeya is one of the signature dishes at Aziza, chef Mourad Lahlou's San Francisco restaurant. In the restaurant, he uses chicken confit in the elaborate "pie," but he developed this duck version for us. Mourad believes that *basteeya* is the most representative dish of his native Morocco—sweet and savory and incredibly unique. In the past, he used Moroccan *warqa*, which is a thinner, more glutinous pastry sheet than filo. But he made the change to filo for a better bake in the oven (*basteeya* is traditionally baked over embers). As a child, Mourad says he "was obsessed with *basteeya*, and the way I liked it best was a little piece that I had discreetly carved off in secret early in the morning or late at night from the leftover pie that was draped in towels in the kitchen." This recipe makes a large pie, but it will keep for a while because of the sugar in it. Mourad suggests having any leftovers in slices for lunch or as snack with tea.

6 duck legs confit (page 35)
2 tablespoons unsalted butter
2 tablespoons extra-virgin olive oil
3 medium yellow onions, halved and thinly sliced
1½ tablespoons apple cider vinegar
1 tablespoon balsamic vinegar
1 teaspoon kosher salt
½ teaspoon freshly ground black pepper
1 teaspoon ground cinnamon
⅛ teaspoon freshly grated nutmeg
Pinch of ground cloves

Almonds
2½ cups whole natural (raw) almonds (about 13 oz)
⅓ cup granulated sugar
½ teaspoon ground cinnamon
⅛ teaspoon freshly grated nutmeg
Pinch of ground cloves
¼ cup clarified butter or ghee, melted and cooled (see Chef's Note)
1½ teaspoons orange blossom water

To Assemble
½ cup clarified butter or ghee, melted and cooled
½ lemon
9 large filo sheets, each about 13 by 18 inches
2 to 3 tablespoons confectioners' sugar

Makes 8 to 10 servings

Pull the meat from the duck legs, discarding the skin and bones. Shred the meat into bite-size pieces; you should have about 4 cups. Set aside.

In a Dutch oven or a large, deep sauté pan over medium heat, melt the butter with the oil. Add the onions and cook, stirring constantly, until nicely browned and caramelized, about 30 minutes. Lower the heat if the onions start browning too quickly; you want them to cook slowly so they caramelize. Add the cider and balsamic vinegars, salt, pepper, cinnamon, nutmeg, and cloves and stir to mix well. Remove from the heat and set aside to cool.

To prepare the almonds, preheat the oven to 325°F. Spread the almonds in a single layer on a small sheet pan and toast, stirring occasionally, until golden brown in the center when a nut is broken open, 20 to 25 minutes. Let the almonds cool to room temperature. Leave the oven on.

In a large bowl, whisk together the granulated sugar, cinnamon, nutmeg, and cloves. Process the almonds in a food processor until finely ground. Add to the sugar mixture and stir to combine. Add the clarified butter and then the orange blossom water. Stir to mix well. The mixture should be thoroughly moistened but not oily; if it seems too dry, add up to 2 tablespoons more clarified butter.

Add the cooled onion mixture and the reserved confit duck meat to the almond mixture and stir gently until well mixed.

To assemble the basteeya, raise the oven temperature to 400°F. Have ready a 9-inch springform pan with 3-inch sides. Add the clarified butter to a spray bottle. Put the cut lemon on the work surface. You will run your fingertip over the cut lemon just before you lift each filo sheet, which will help to separate them more easily. Lay a dry kitchen towel on the work surface, open up the filo sheets (if they are rolled), and lay the sheets flat on the towel. Cover the sheets with a slightly damp kitchen towel.

continued . . .

WINE: This dish is full of flavor and texture. I think a Barbera, a high-acid, high-toned red, stands up to the flavors and brings a nice pop to the beautiful plate.

Spray the inside of the springform pan with butter. Lift 1 filo sheet, fold it in half, and place the folded sheet in the pan so you have about 3 inches overhanging the rim. Spray the folded sheet with butter. Repeat with another piece of filo, first folding it, then overlapping the first sheet in the pan, and finally spraying it with butter. Continue to work around the bottom of the pan, folding, placing, and spraying each sheet. It should take 4 filo sheets to cover the pan. Spray the layer with butter. Repeat with the remaining 5 filo sheets, but this time, pull the folded sheets of filo out so you have 8 to 9 inches of overhang; this will allow the filo to reach to the center of the basteeya once the pan is filled and the filo is folded in over the top. As you add each filo layer, always remember to spray it with butter.

Spoon the duck mixture into the filo-lined pan, spreading it evenly; it should fill the pan. Starting with the sheet of phyllo that was placed last, fold the sheet over the filling toward the center, folding in the edge as needed for the sheet to lie evenly over the top. Spray with butter. Continue in the same manner with all of the sheets in the reverse order they were added until the basteeya is completely encased in filo, spraying each layer with butter. Finally, spray the top with butter.

Bake until all of the visible filo is golden brown and crisp and the center of the basteeya is very hot when probed with a cake tester, 1 to 1¼ hours. If the basteeya starts to get too brown, lay a piece of aluminum foil lightly over the top. Transfer to a wire rack and let cool for 10 minutes.

Unclasp and remove the pan sides and carefully slide the basteeya onto a serving platter. Dust the basteeya with an even layer of the confectioners' sugar. Cut into wedges and serve warm.

CHEF'S NOTE: *You can make clarified butter at home by gently simmering unsalted butter until the milk solids settle to the bottom of the pan, then pouring off the clear, golden liquid, leaving the milk solids behind. Or you can purchase it at specialty food shops. Ghee, which is used in Indian cooking, is more widely available and is made the same way, but it is simmered longer, which results in a nuttier flavor and darker color. It can also be used in a pinch.*

DUCK-FIG SAUSAGES

with sour cream and onion mash

CHEFS DUSKIE ESTES AND JOHN STEWART

I love a modern-day update to an old classic! Sausage and mash is traditionally British, but chefs John Stewart and Duskie Estes put a Sonoma County twist on the dish by mixing chopped dried figs, orange zest, and fresh thyme with our ground duck to create a flavorful sausage. Combined with rich sour cream and onion mash, this is a crave-worthy meal, especially on a chilly evening. To keep things easier for home cooks, the sausage mixture is shaped into patties, so anyone can get the hang of this dish. But if you have a sausage stuffer and casings, you can stuff these into sausage links like they do at their restaurant.

Duck-Fig Sausages

- 1 cup stemmed and finely chopped dried figs
- Juice of 1 orange
- 1 cup red wine
- 1½ teaspoons minced fresh thyme leaves
- ¾ teaspoon Dijon mustard
- 2 lb ground duck meat
- 2 teaspoons kosher salt
- 1½ teaspoons smoked paprika
- 1½ teaspoons onion powder
- ½ teaspoon ground fennel

Sour Cream and Onion Mash

- 1 lb Yukon Gold potatoes, peeled and cut into 1-inch chunks
- 1 lb russet potatoes, peeled and cut into 1-inch chunks
- 6 tablespoons unsalted butter, at room temperature
- ½ cup buttermilk, warmed
- ¼ cup sour cream
- Kosher salt and freshly ground black pepper
- 4 green onions, white and pale green parts, thinly sliced

Makes 4 servings

To make the sausages, in a saucepan over medium-high heat, combine the figs, orange juice, wine, thyme, and mustard and cook, stirring, until the figs are plumped and the liquid is slightly reduced, about 10 minutes. Transfer the fig mixture to a bowl and let cool completely. When cool, add the ground duck, salt, paprika, onion powder, and fennel and stir to combine. Form the mixture into 12 equal portions and shape each portion into a patty about ⅓ inch thick.

To make the mash, fill a large saucepan half full with water, add all the potatoes, and bring to a boil over high heat. Turn down the heat to low and simmer uncovered, stirring occasionally, until the potatoes are soft when pierced with a small knife, about 25 minutes. Drain the potatoes into a colander, then pass them through a ricer or food mill back into the saucepan. Add the butter, buttermilk, and sour cream and, using a fork, whip until fluffy. Season with salt and pepper and stir in the green onions. Keep warm.

While the potatoes are cooking, cook the sausages. Heat a large cast-iron or other large, heavy frying pan over medium heat. When the pan is hot, add the patties in a single layer (if they won't fit without crowding, cook them in two batches). Cook until browned on the bottom, 3 to 5 minutes, then turn and cook until browned on the second side and cooked through, 3 to 5 minutes longer.

To serve, divide the mash evenly among 4 bowls and top each bowl with 3 sausage patties. Serve at once.

BEER / WINE: A rich stout is a fun pairing for this take on bangers and mash. For wine, a rich Zinfandel would pair nicely with the fig and duck.

GRANNY'S DUCK MEAT LOAF

My husband's sweet parents reworked his grandmother's meat loaf recipe to use ground duck rather than her traditional beef. Granny and Mike's mother are from Virginia, and I think of this meat loaf as quintessential Americana. To adjust the seasoning to your taste, cook a nugget of the meat mixture in a small frying pan, taste, and season with more salt and pepper if needed. Granny served her meat loaf with mashed potatoes and sautéed green beans.

2 tablespoons extra-virgin olive oil, plus more for the loaf pan
1½ cups finely chopped Vidalia or other sweet yellow onion (about 1 large onion)
1 cup finely chopped celery (about 3 stalks)
1 cup seeded and finely chopped green or red bell pepper, or a mixture
1½ lb ground duck meat
1½ cups quick-cooking rolled oats
1 cup fresh flat-leaf parsley leaves, chopped
1 teaspoon finely chopped fresh thyme or marjoram leaves
1 teaspoon kosher salt
1 teaspoon freshly ground black pepper
2 large eggs, lightly beaten
¼ cup whole milk, plus more if needed
⅓ cup ketchup or tomato sauce (optional)

Makes 4 to 6 servings

WINE: Something simple, fruity, and delicious pairs well with this dish. I love a juicy Zinfandel from California's Dry Creek Valley or Alexander Valley.

In a large frying pan over medium-low heat, warm the 2 tablespoons oil. Add the onion, celery, and bell pepper and cook, stirring, until tender, about 5 minutes. Set aside to cool.

Preheat the oven to 350°F. Lightly grease a 9-by-5-inch loaf pan or a 1½- to 2-quart baking dish with oil.

In a large bowl, combine the cooled cooked vegetables, ground duck, oats, parsley, thyme, salt, and pepper. Mix with your hands just until the ingredients are fairly evenly incorporated, then add the eggs and milk and continue to mix with your hands just until well mixed. Do not overwork the mixture or your meat loaf will be dry and dense. If the mixture seems dry, add a little more milk.

Transfer the duck mixture to the prepared loaf pan. Bake the meat loaf until it pulls away from the sides of the pan, the top is nicely browned, and an instant-read thermometer inserted into the center registers 160°F, 1 to 1¼ hours. If you like, spread the ketchup over the top of the meat loaf after it has been baking for 45 minutes.

Let the meat loaf cool in the pan on a wire rack for 5 minutes, then cut into slices and serve.

SUMMER DUCK LEG AU VIN

with rosé and summer vegetables

CHEFS GILBERT PILGRAM AND NATHAN NORRIS

The corner seat at Zuni Café, right where Rose and Market Streets join, is a special spot. It's where you can simply sit and watch the world go by. It's also where my husband and I celebrated his thirtieth birthday and his first visit to the acclaimed restaurant. That night we ate many of the classic dishes that have kept customers returning again and again over the last forty years. We left feeling as though we had tasted a bite of San Francisco culinary history. At the restaurant's fortieth anniversary party in 2019, the space was packed with vendors, past and present employees, and loyal customers, many of whom had watched Zuni grow dramatically in size and evolve from the Southwest and Mexican cuisine of its early days to its Eurocentric table of today. This duck recipe, a relatively new addition to the menu, was created by chef and owner Gilbert Pilgram and chef de cuisine Nathan Norris for the summer vegetable season. The kitchen uses Ronde de Nice or Costata Romanesco summer squash in the mix.

- 4 duck legs
- 1½ teaspoons fine sea salt
- 4 tablespoons unsalted butter
- 2 tablespoons all-purpose flour
- 2 cups dry rosé
- 1 medium yellow onion, cut into 1-inch chunks
- 1 medium carrot, peeled and cut into 1-inch chunks
- 2 celery stalks, cut into 1-inch chunks
- ½ lb green beans, trimmed
- 4 tomatoes, such as Early Girl, cored and halved crosswise
- 2 zucchini, trimmed
- 1 tablespoon extra-virgin olive oil
- ⅓ cup aioli, homemade (page 77) or purchased, for serving (optional)

Makes 4 servings

WINE: A Provençal rosé with notes of crisp berry and citrus completes the picture-perfect moment of this summer supper dish.

The day before you plan on cooking the duck legs, season them on both sides with the salt, then refrigerate them uncovered on a plate or small sheet pan.

Preheat the oven to 550°F. To make a roux, in a small saucepan over medium-low heat, melt 2 tablespoons of the butter. Add the flour and whisk to combine, breaking up any lumps. Continue to cook the butter-flour mixture, whisking constantly, until it turns golden brown, about 6 minutes. Remove from the heat and set aside.

In another small saucepan, bring the wine just to a simmer over medium heat, then turn down the heat to keep the wine at a very gentle simmer.

In a frying pan over medium-high heat, melt the remaining 2 tablespoons butter. Add the onion, carrot, and celery, turn down the heat to medium, and cook the vegetables, stirring occasionally, until lightly caramelized, about 5 minutes. Stir in the roux. Slowly add the simmering wine in small amounts, stirring after each addition to ensure a smooth consistency before adding more. If you add the wine too quickly, the roux will develop lumps. When all the wine is incorporated, remove the pan from the heat.

Arrange the duck legs, skin side down, in a 9-inch square baking dish and pour the hot vegetable-wine mixture over the legs. Cover the dish tightly with aluminum foil and transfer to the oven. After about 10 minutes, check to make sure the liquid is simmering, then vent the foil covering and turn down the oven temperature to 350°F. Bake until the duck is cooked through and a thin-bladed knife can be inserted easily into the thickest part of a thigh, about 1 hour and 10 minutes.

While the duck is cooking, prepare the remaining vegetables. Fill a saucepan half full with salted water and bring to a boil over high heat. Add the green beans and boil until tender-crisp, 3 to 6 minutes; the timing depends on how firm you like them. Drain into a colander and

continued . . .

rinse under cold water to stop the cooking. Season the cut sides of the tomatoes with salt. Cut the zucchini in half lengthwise and then cut the halves crosswise on the diagonal into pieces about ½ inch thick.

Remove the dish from the oven and turn up the oven temperature to 450°F. Remove the foil and turn the legs skin side up. Drain off enough of the liquid from the dish so the skin on each leg is uncovered but the flesh remains submerged. Reserve the liquid. Tuck the tomato halves, cut side up, among the duck legs. Return the dish, uncovered, to the oven and bake until the duck skin is golden brown, about 10 minutes.

Transfer the duck legs and tomatoes to a warmed large plate and cover to keep warm. Set a fine-mesh sieve over a bowl and pour the contents of the baking dish and the reserved liquid into the sieve. Discard the solids. Using a large metal spoon, skim off the fat from the surface of the cooking liquid. Pour the liquid into a small saucepan and reheat over medium-low heat until hot just before serving.

In a frying pan over medium heat, warm the oil. Add the zucchini and green beans, season with salt, and cook, stirring occasionally, until tender, about 5 minutes.

To serve, arrange the duck, tomatoes, and zucchini and green beans on 4 plates, dividing them evenly. Top with the warm cooking liquid, dividing it evenly (about ¼ cup per serving). Finish each serving with a generous tablespoon of aioli, if desired, and serve.

PAN-SEARED DUCK BREASTS SALSA VERDE

CHEF SARAH SCOTT

Trust me when I say you'll find any excuse to make this *salsa verde* from chef Sarah Scott of Oakville's Opus One Winery. Here in California, we see a lot of *salsa verde* full of tomatillos and green chiles in Mexican fare. But it Italy, you'll see this green sauce loaded with fresh herbs, capers, and anchovies. Serve this dish with a loaf of ciabatta or *panzanella* (Tuscan bread salad).

4 duck breasts
Kosher salt and freshly ground black pepper

Salsa Verde
1 shallot, minced
1 tablespoon red wine vinegar
1 tablespoon fresh lemon juice
⅓ cup chopped fresh flat-leaf parsley
2 tablespoons minced fresh chives
2 tablespoons minced fresh tarragon leaves
2 tablespoons chopped fresh basil leaves
1 tablespoon finely chopped capers
1 olive oil–packed anchovy fillet, rinsed and finely chopped
Finely grated zest of 1 lemon
½ cup extra-virgin olive oil
1 teaspoon kosher salt
¼ teaspoon freshly ground black pepper

Fleur de sel, for garnishing

Makes 4 to 6 servings

WINE: A rich, full-bodied Chardonnay brings out the herbal zest of the *salsa verde* and stands up to the texture of the duck breast.

While the duck breasts are still cold from the refrigerator, using a sharp knife and working with one duck breast at a time, score the skin on each breast on the diagonal, spacing the cuts about ½ inch apart and being careful not to cut through to the meat. Rotate the duck breast 90 degrees and score the same way in the opposite direction to make a crosshatch pattern. Season the duck breasts on both sides with salt and pepper, transfer to a plate, and refrigerate uncovered for at least 6 hours or up to overnight. Let the duck breasts sit at room temperature for 1 hour before cooking.

To make the salsa verde, in a bowl, combine the shallot, vinegar, and lemon juice and let sit for 15 minutes. Stir in the parsley, chives, tarragon, basil, capers, anchovy, and lemon zest, mixing well. Slowly drizzle in the oil while whisking continuously, then add the salt and pepper and mix well. Taste and adjust with more salt and lemon juice if needed. Set aside at room temperature.

Place the duck breasts, skin side down, in a cold large cast-iron or other heavy frying pan. Turn on the heat to low and let the breasts cook undisturbed until they render their fat, 12 to 15 minutes. Every so often, lift each breast with tongs to make sure the skin is not burning. If it is getting too dark, remove from the heat.

Once the fat is rendered and is deep golden brown, raise the heat to medium-high, turn the breasts over, and continue to cook until the meat side is browned and the breasts are medium-rare, 2 to 4 minutes longer. An instant-read thermometer inserted into the thickest part of a breast should register 130°F. Transfer to a cutting board and let rest for 10 minutes before serving.

To serve, slice the duck breasts crosswise and arrange on a platter. Spoon the salsa verde over the duck. Sprinkle with fleur de sel and serve at once.

DUCK SUGO CAVATELLI

with herbs and orange zest

CHEF TONY FERRARI

Chef Tony Ferrari has long been like a brother to me. In 2009, while exploring food in the San Francisco Bay Area, he reached out to my dad, asking if he could shadow him at the farm to learn about Liberty Ducks. And because I was away working on a goat farm in Spain for the summer, Tony ended up taking my room for a month. When he and his brother, Austin, lived in San Francisco, they would come to our house for the holidays. They'd also bring friends up, all crashing at Dad's after hours and hours of eating and drinking and the occasional sing-along. When their family would come out to visit them, there was often a big meal at Dad's. The brothers have since moved back to Cincinnati, but they're still family to us. This dish is representative of family: it's a large portion of sugo—"sauce" in Italian—and is big enough for a crowd. It makes twice the amount of sugo that you'll need to serve four people, but the sauce freezes well. Or just double the amount of pasta to serve eight people. I am the first to say that there's nothing better than a bursting-at-the-seams table, as it's always full of love.

2 lb ground duck meat
1 large yellow onion, finely chopped
2 medium carrots, peeled and finely chopped
2 celery stalks, finely chopped
4 garlic cloves, minced
3 tablespoons red wine vinegar
1 can (28 oz) diced tomatoes with juices
1 can (28 oz) tomato sauce
1 to 2 tablespoons finely grated orange zest
2 bay leaves
1 teaspoon dried thyme
1 teaspoon dried oregano
1 teaspoon dried basil
Kosher salt and freshly ground black pepper
1 lb cavatelli, rigatoni, or other short ridged pasta
Freshly grated Parmesan cheese, for serving

Makes 4 servings

WINE: From Austin Ferrari: For a high-end bottle, look for Montevertine Le Pergole Torte—a true and pure wine that shows Sangiovese at its fullest extent. For a more modest price tag, pick out a Nebbiolo d'Alba, a wine with soft tannin and mouthwatering acidity.

To make the sugo, place a large cast-iron or other large, heavy frying pan over medium heat. Crumble the ground duck into the pan and cook, stirring occasionally and breaking up the meat with a wooden spoon, until the meat is browned, about 15 minutes. Using a slotted spoon, transfer the meat to a bowl.

In the same pan over medium heat, add the onion, carrots, and celery and cook, stirring, until the onion is translucent, 5 to 7 minutes. Add the garlic and cook, stirring occasionally, until the vegetables are tender and golden, about 3 minutes. Return the meat to the pan, add the vinegar, and deglaze the pan, using the wooden spoon or a spatula to dislodge the crispy browned bits from the pan bottom. Add the diced tomatoes, tomato sauce, orange zest (to taste), bay leaves, thyme, oregano, basil, and 1 teaspoon each salt and pepper. Stir to mix well and bring to a gentle boil, stirring occasionally. Turn down the heat to low and simmer uncovered, stirring every now and again, until the meat is very tender and the sauce has thickened and reduced, about 30 minutes. (You can instead cover the pan and simmer the sauce over low heat for up to 2 hours.) Taste and adjust the seasoning with salt and pepper if needed. You will have about 8 cups sugo. Transfer half of it to an airtight container, let cool, then cover and refrigerate for up to 4 days or freeze for up to 2 months. Leave the remaining sugo in the pan and cover to keep warm.

To cook the pasta, bring a large pot two-thirds full of salted water to a boil. Add the pasta, stir well, and cook until al dente, 6 to 8 minutes or according to the package directions. Drain the pasta, reserving a little of the cooking water.

Just before the pasta is ready, reheat the sauce over medium heat. Add the drained pasta to the sauce and toss to coat evenly, loosening the sauce as needed with the reserved pasta water. Transfer to a warmed platter or individual bowls, sprinkle with plenty of Parmesan, and serve.

SEARED DUCK BREASTS

with citrus sauce, candied kumquats, and farro

CHEF ROLAND PASSOT

One of the best-known duck dishes is duck à l'orange. But to be 100 percent honest, I don't think I have ever eaten it! In the Middle Ages, cooks hit upon the idea of using the acidity of citrus to preserve meats, and in time the practice evolved into a fairly sweet duck dish that eventually became more popular in Britain and the United States than in its native France. Fortunately, San Francisco chef Roland Passot of La Folie was able to provide this modern interpretation of the classic. Here in California, we're blessed with an ample array of citrus, and this updated recipe makes use of four different kinds. The candied kumquats take this dish over the top and can be made in advance, but the dish is stellar even without them. If you do opt to make them, you will have more than you need for this recipe, but they are also great on cakes, salads, or even roasted pork. This dish is delicious served with the glazed turnips that accompany the duck breasts on page 171.

Candied Kumquats
½ lb kumquats
1 cup water
¾ cup sugar

4 duck breasts
Kosher salt
1½ cups pearled or semi-pearled farro
3 cups water
2 shallots, quartered lengthwise and thinly sliced crosswise
3 tablespoons honey
1 teaspoon freshly ground black pepper
⅔ cup champagne vinegar
¾ cup orange-flavored liqueur, such as Grand Marnier or Cointreau
Finely grated zest of 1 orange
Finely grated zest of 1 lemon
Finely grated zest of 1 lime
¾ cup fresh orange juice
2 tablespoons fresh lemon juice
2 tablespoons fresh lime juice
½ cup basic duck stock (page 44) or chicken stock

Makes 4 to 6 servings

WINE: The triple citrus in this dish is a great opportunity to try a Gewürztraminer. The wine is aromatic and full bodied, acting as an extension to the flavorful sauce.

To make the candied kumquats, trim off both ends of each kumquat, then slice the fruit crosswise into ⅛-inch-thick rounds and remove any seeds. In a small saucepan over medium-high heat, bring the water and sugar to a boil, stirring until the sugar dissolves. Add the sliced kumquats, stir, lower the heat to medium, and simmer for 2 minutes. Transfer the kumquats and their liquid to a heatproof container (such as a 1-pint canning jar), let cool to room temperature, and then cap and set aside until needed. (The kumquats will keep in the refrigerator for up to 2 weeks.)

While the duck breasts are still cold from the refrigerator, using a sharp knife and working with one duck breast at a time, score the skin on each breast on the diagonal, spacing the cuts about ½ inch apart and being careful not to cut through to the meat. Rotate the duck breast 90 degrees and score the same way in the opposite direction to make a crosshatch pattern. Season the duck breasts on both sides with salt and set aside for 20 minutes to come to room temperature.

Meanwhile, begin cooking the farro. In a saucepan, combine the farro, water, and 1 teaspoon salt and bring to a boil over high heat. Cover, turn down the heat to low, and simmer until the farro is chewy but tender, about 20 minutes for pearled farro and 30 minutes for semi-pearled farro. Remove from the heat, drain off any liquid, cover, and set aside. Keep warm.

While the farro cooks, cook the duck breasts. Place the duck breasts, skin side down, in a cold large cast-iron or other heavy frying pan. Turn on the heat to low and let the breasts cook undisturbed until they render their fat and release from the pan bottom, about 8 minutes. Raise the heat to medium and continue to cook until the skin is crispy, 5 to 6 minutes longer. Turn the breasts skin side up and continue to cook until they are rare, 3 to 4 minutes longer. An instant-read thermometers inserted in the thickest part of a breast should register 125° to 130°F. Transfer the

continued . . .

breasts to a large plate and season the skin side with salt. Let rest for about 10 minutes while you make the sauce. Pour the fat in the pan into a small heatproof bowl.

To make the sauce, return the frying pan to medium heat and warm 2 tablespoons of the reserved fat. Add the shallots and cook, stirring, until translucent and browned, about 3 minutes. Add the honey and pepper and stir with a wooden spoon for about 30 seconds, scraping up any browned bits from the pan bottom. Add the vinegar and deglaze the pan, using a wooden spoon to dislodge the crispy browned bits from the pan bottom and simmering until the liquid is reduced by about half, about 3 minutes. Add the orange liqueur; the orange, lemon, and lime zests; and the orange, lemon, and lime juices and stir well. Raise the heat to medium-high and bring to a simmer, then lower the heat to medium and cook, stirring, until the mixture is reduced and syrupy, about 10 minutes. Add the stock and continue to reduce until the sauce coats the back of the spoon, 2 to 3 minutes longer. At this point, you can leave the sauce as is or strain it through a fine-mesh sieve to remove the solids.

To serve, divide the farro among 4 to 6 individual plates. Thinly slice the duck breasts crosswise, then divide the slices evenly among the plates, placing them on top of the farro. Using a slotted spoon, add about half of the candied kumquats to the sauce (reserve the remainder for another use). Spoon the sauce over the duck and around the plate and serve at once.

RED CURRY DUCK

with pineapple, thai basil, and lime leaves

A traditional dish of central Thailand, red curry is flavored and colored by crushed red chiles, garlic, salt, lemongrass, and coriander root. Thai spices have a way of sneaking up on you when you least expect it. The single spiciest dish I've ever had in my life was a papaya salad from a street-food stall in Bangkok. The first bite was warm, but the crunchy cold papaya was refreshing in the sticky heat. With each bite, the spice built and built, and I think I only got ten bites in before I turned the color of this curry. It took an order of plain rice, a milkshake, and perhaps ten glasses of water before my temperature came down. This curry has only a gentle warming spice sensation, enough to feel it but not to knock you off your seat. The addition of pineapple pairs well with duck and lends a nice sweetness to the dish.

4 duck legs
Kosher salt
1 tablespoon avocado or canola oil, plus more if needed
½ yellow onion, thinly sliced
1 tablespoon peeled and shredded fresh ginger
1 tablespoon minced lemongrass, pale yellow part only (optional)
1 Thai or serrano chile, seeded and thinly sliced
2 garlic cloves, minced
2 tablespoons Thai red curry paste
1 tablespoon light brown sugar
1 can (14 oz) coconut milk
½ cup water
2 tablespoons fish sauce
3 fresh makrut lime leaves
1 cup fresh pineapple chunks, in bite-size pieces
Juice of ½ lime, plus lime wedges for serving
2 tablespoons chopped fresh Thai basil leaves, plus more for garnish
2 tablespoons chopped fresh cilantro, plus more for garnish
Thinly sliced green onions, green part only, for garnish
Steamed jasmine rice, for serving

Makes 4 servings

Preheat the oven to 325°F. Pat the duck legs dry with paper towels and lightly salt all over. In a Dutch oven or other heavy pot, warm the oil. Add 2 duck legs, skin side down, and sear until golden brown, 4 to 5 minutes. Turn and sear on the other side until browned, 3 to 4 minutes longer. Transfer the duck legs to a plate and repeat with the other 2 legs, adding more oil if needed.

Pour off all but 1 tablespoon of the fat from the pot and return the pot to medium-low heat. Add the onion and cook, stirring, until softened, about 7 minutes. Add the ginger, lemongrass (if using), chile, and garlic and cook, stirring, until fragrant, about 1 minute. Stir in the curry paste and sugar until well mixed. Add the coconut milk, water, and fish sauce and stir until blended with all the ingredients. Return the duck legs to the pot, submerging them in the liquid, and add the lime leaves. Raise the heat to medium-high and bring the mixture to a boil, then cover and transfer to the oven.

Cook until the duck is very tender when pierced with a knife, about 1½ hours. About 30 minutes before the duck is finished cooking, stir in the pineapple. Remove from the oven and, using tongs, transfer the duck legs to a warmed serving dish or platter and cover to keep warm. Using a large metal spoon, skim off the fat from the surface of the cooking liquid.

Return the pot to the stove top over medium heat and bring to a simmer. Stir in the lime juice, basil, and cilantro. Taste and adjust the seasoning with salt if needed. Pour the sauce over the duck, then garnish with the green onions, basil, and cilantro. Serve with the rice and the lime wedges.

WINE: There's a little sweetness from the pineapple but lots of salt and citrus as well. An aromatic white with medium acidity, like Torrontés, would complement this dish.

ROASTED DUCK PIZZA

with creamed onion, delicata squash, greens, and persimmon

CHEF DINO BUGICA

Chef Dino Bugica spent many years in Italy, where he learned the art of butchery and fine Italian cooking. His Diavola restaurant in Geyserville, which uses fresh local ingredients in its dishes, is a Sonoma County gem. When I was delivering duck to his kitchen one day (which has to be one of the more adorable back entrances to a restaurant), we started talking about needing a pizza recipe for this book. I told him if he could get me a list of ingredients, we could do the rest—et voilà, this pizza was born! I am a big fan of white sauce pizzas, and this one hits that note just right. While I applaud homemade dough, I also appreciate the fresh refrigerated or frozen dough sold in many markets. Or you can even ask your local pizza place for the dough. This is a great recipe for using up leftover roast duck legs.

2 roasted duck legs (page 36)
1 delicata squash
2 tablespoons rendered duck fat (page 32), melted, or neutral oil
Kosher salt and freshly ground black pepper
1 large white onion, diced
1 cup heavy cream
1 fresh rosemary sprig
⅓ cup dry red wine
1 tablespoon honey
2 cups stemmed and chopped dandelion greens, collard greens, or dinosaur kale, in bite-size pieces
About 1½ lb pizza dough, homemade or purchased
1 Fuyu persimmon, crown removed, halved, and thinly sliced, or Asian pear, halved, cored, and thinly sliced
2 cups shredded Gouda cheese
All-purpose flour or semolina, for dusting

Makes 2 pizzas; about 4 servings

WINE: Sangiovese! The acidity of the grape lifts the richness in the sauce and cheese, bringing it all together.

Preheat the oven to 400°F and roast the duck legs as directed. Pull the meat from the bones, discarding the skin and bones, then shred the meat. Set aside. Increase the heat to 425°F.

Trim both ends off the squash, then cut the squash in half lengthwise and scoop out and discard the seeds. Cut the halves crosswise into ¼-inch-thick slices. Transfer to a sheet pan, drizzle with 1 tablespoon of the duck fat, season with salt and pepper, and toss to coat evenly. Spread the slices into a single layer. Roast the squash until soft and golden brown, about 30 minutes. Transfer to a bowl.

In a cast-iron or other heavy frying pan over medium heat, warm the remaining 1 tablespoon duck fat. Add the onion and cook, stirring, until translucent and golden, about 10 minutes. Turn down the heat to low, add the cream and rosemary, and simmer, stirring, until the sauce has thickened, about 15 minutes. Remove and discard the rosemary sprig and transfer the sauce to a bowl.

In a saucepan over medium-high heat, warm the red wine until hot, then whisk in the honey until melted. Add the dandelion greens and cook, stirring, until wilted, 3 to 5 minutes. Remove from the heat.

Position a rack in the lower third of the oven and raise the oven temperature to 550°F (or as high as your oven will go). Place a pizza stone on the rack to heat for at least 30 minutes (if you don't have a pizza stone, you can bake the pizza on a sheet pan, but don't preheat the pan).

Divide the pizza dough in half and let the halves stand, covered with a kitchen towel, at room temperature while the stone and oven heat. Put half of the dough on a lightly floured work surface and press it into a round about 1 inch thick. Then gently pull the round from opposite sides to stretch it. Continue to stretch the dough by holding it by an edge and moving it around in a circle to let gravity help you stretch it out. If the dough is resistant, let it rest for 5 minutes, then continue to stretch the dough until it is 10 to 12 inches in diameter. (You can use a rolling pin for this step, but it tends to flatten out the dough too much.)

continued . . .

If using a pizza stone, dust a pizza peel or an inverted sheet pan with flour and transfer the dough round to the peel. If using a sheet pan instead of a stone, lightly dust the sheet pan with flour and transfer the dough round to it.

Spread half of the creamed onion in an even layer on top of the dough round. Evenly layer half each of the duck, roasted squash, and braised greens over the onion. Top with half of the persimmon slices and then with half of the cheese.

If using a peel or inverted sheet pan, make sure the pizza moves easily (if not, add more flour), then slide the pizza onto the hot stone. You may need to rotate the pizza 180 degrees during baking so that it cooks evenly; tongs are a great way to do this. If baking on a sheet pan, place it on the oven rack and rotate the pan during baking if needed for even cooking. Bake the pizza until golden brown and crusty, 12 to 15 minutes.

Using the pizza peel and tongs, slide the pizza onto the peel (or sheet pan), then slide the pizza onto a large cutting board. If baked on a sheet pan, use a wide metal spatula to transfer it to the cutting board. Let the pizza sit for about 3 minutes, then cut into wedges and serve right away. Repeat to make the second pizza with the remaining dough and toppings.

DUCK SAUSAGE SANDWICHES

with caramelized spring onions, porcini, and cherry puree

CHEF MICHAEL CIMARUSTI

Providence restaurant in Los Angeles is known for its seafood dishes. Chef Michael Cimarusti sources the highest-quality sustainable seafood around, and it's earned him two Michelin stars. We're honored to be one of the two other protein sources on his menu that are not seafood. This recipe uses the same ingredients Michael uses in one of his gorgeous duck presentations, but refashions them to make a dish more achievable by the home cook. The result? One of the most delicious sandwiches I have ever had in my life. From top to bottom, every part of this sandwich plays off and complements all the other parts. Whatever you do, do not skip the jus—it's just too good. Michael suggests "a crusty, naturally leavened bread toasted well with rendered duck fat for making the sandwich." Who am I to argue with that?

1 bunch spring onions or green onions
2 tablespoons extra-virgin olive oil
Kosher salt
½ lb porcini or trumpet mushrooms, brushed clean and cut lengthwise into ¼-inch-thick slices
1 tablespoon unsalted butter
1 garlic clove
1 fresh thyme sprig
½ lemon

Duck Dipping Jus

3 duck necks
2 small shallots, thinly sliced
1 teaspoon fine sea salt
1 teaspoon freshly ground black pepper
1 fresh thyme sprig
1 bay leaf
2 garlic cloves
1 cup dry red wine
1 cup basic duck stock (page 44)

Cherry Puree

1 tablespoon rendered duck fat (page 32) or olive oil
1 cup pitted sweet cherries
2 tablespoons dry red wine
½ teaspoon fine sea salt
¼ teaspoon yellow mustard seeds

To prepare the onions, cut off the root end and the top 2½ inches of the green from each onion, then cut each onion in half lengthwise. In a large sauté pan over medium heat, warm 1 tablespoon of the oil. Add the onion halves and a pinch of salt and cook, stirring often, until the onions are completely soft, about 10 minutes. Transfer to a plate and set aside until assembling the sandwiches.

To prepare the mushrooms, in a saucepan over medium heat, warm the remaining 1 tablespoon oil. Add the mushrooms and sauté until golden brown, about 10 minutes. Turn down the heat to low and add the butter. When the butter has melted, add the garlic clove, thyme, and a pinch of kosher salt, then squeeze the juice from the lemon half over the mixture. Cover and set aside until assembling the sandwiches.

To make the dipping jus, heat a saucepan over high heat. When the pan is hot, add the duck necks and cook, turning as needed, until golden on all sides, 20 to 30 minutes. When the bones are a nice color, add the shallots, salt, pepper, thyme, bay leaf, and garlic and stir to mix. Then pour in the wine and deglaze the pan, scraping up any browned bits from the pan bottom. Add the stock (the neck bones should be submerged), turn down the heat to low, and simmer until the liquid is reduced by about half, about 30 minutes. Scoop out and discard the neck bones, then pour the liquid through a fine-mesh sieve set over a bowl. Discard the solids. Set aside until assembling the sandwiches.

While the duck jus is reducing, make the cherry puree. In a saucepan over medium heat, warm the duck fat. Add the cherries and cook, stirring occasionally, until they start to break down, about 5 minutes. Add the wine and deglaze the pan, scraping up the browned bits on the pan bottom with a wooden spoon. Add the salt and mustard seeds and continue to cook until the wine is reduced by about half. Remove from the heat and let cool briefly, then transfer to a blender and blend until a smooth puree forms or puree in the pan with an immersion blender. Set aside until assembling the sandwiches.

To make the sausage, in a bowl, combine the ground duck, salt, and pepper and mix just until the seasonings are evenly distributed. Divide the meat mixture into 4 equal portions and shape each portion into a patty the shape of your roll and about ½ inch thick.

Heat a large cast-iron or other heavy frying pan over high heat. When the pan is hot, add the patties and let cook until starting to brown on the underside, about 3 minutes. Flip the patties, turn down the heat to medium, and add just enough water to cover the bottom of the pan. Cover the pan and steam the patties until they are cooked through, about 10 minutes. Remove from the heat.

To assemble the sandwiches, preheat the oven to 350°F. Place the roll halves cut side up on a sheet pan. Spread a little duck fat on each cut side and place in the oven until lightly toasted, 5 to 7 minutes. Remove from the oven.

Spread 1 tablespoon of the jus evenly on the cut side of each bottom half of the roll. On the top half, spread the cherry puree, dividing it evenly. Arrange a sausage patty on each bottom half. Top with the onions and mushrooms (discarding the garlic and thyme), dividing evenly. Close with the top half and serve, passing any additional jus alongside for dipping.

Duck Sausage
1 lb ground duck meat
½ teaspoon fine sea salt
½ teaspoon freshly ground black pepper

4 large, crusty, naturally leavened rolls, such as ciabatta, split
Rendered duck fat (page 32), for spreading

Makes 4 servings

WINE: A bright Pinot Noir, specifically one with notes of cherry, is the perfect pairing.

GRILLED PEPPER-CORIANDER CRUSTED DUCK BREASTS

with pickled cherries and glazed turnips

CHEF AMY DENCLER

There isn't a Bay Area restaurant more iconic than Alice Waters's Chez Panisse. The fifty-year-old Berkeley favorite has been an inspiration to countless chefs and diners both for what comes out of the kitchen and for its sourcing of local ingredients. We've been delighted to have been on the Chez Panisse menu off and on for our entire thirty-year history. Chef Amy Dencler told me that this was one of Alice's favorite dishes during the pandemic, which was at its height while this cookbook was coming together. I don't know if she was pulling my leg, but I can say it's become one of my favorite preparations.

Pickled Cherries
1 lb Bing cherries, stemmed
2 cups water
½ cup white wine
⅓ cup white wine vinegar or champagne vinegar
1 tablespoon sugar
4 fresh thyme sprigs
3 allspice berries
1 teaspoon coriander seeds
1 teaspoon black peppercorns
1 teaspoon fine sea salt

Pepper- and Coriander-Crusted Duck Breasts
2 duck breasts
2 tablespoons extra-virgin olive oil
2 garlic cloves, pounded to a paste with a mortar and pestle
2 teaspoons chopped fresh flat-leaf parsley leaves
1 teaspoon chopped fresh thyme leaves
Finely grated zest of 1 lemon
1 teaspoon fresh lemon juice
Fine sea salt
1 teaspoon black peppercorns, crushed with a mortar and pestle
2 teaspoons coriander seeds, crushed with a mortar and pestle

Glazed Turnips
2 lb Tokyo turnips or other small turnips with tops
Fine sea salt
Extra-virgin olive oil, for drizzling

Makes 4 servings

To make the pickled cherries, using a thin wooden skewer, prick each cherry through the flesh to the pit (this will help them to absorb the brine). Put the cherries into a bowl. In a saucepan over medium heat, combine the water, wine, vinegar, sugar, thyme, allspice, coriander, peppercorns, and salt and bring to a simmer, stirring until the sugar and salt dissolve, about 2 minutes. Taste and adjust the seasoning with sugar and salt if needed. Remove the brine from the heat and let cool to room temperature. Pour the brine over the cherries. Cover and let sit at room temperature for at least 2 hours or up to 2 days before serving. To store, transfer the cherries submerged in the brine to an airtight container in the refrigerator for up to 2 months. You will have more cherries than you need for this recipe. If you like, serve any leftover cherries alongside cheese and charcuterie (see page 64).

To make the duck breasts, while they are still cold from the refrigerator, remove the tenders and reserve for another use. Trim away any large bits of fat along the edge of each breast, leaving a good amount of skin to extend beyond the flesh. Using a sharp knife and working with one duck breast at a time, score the skin on each breast on the diagonal, spacing the cuts about ¼ inch apart and being careful not to cut through to the meat. Rotate the duck breast 90 degrees and score the same way in the opposite direction to make a crosshatch pattern.

In a bowl, whisk together the oil, garlic, parsley, thyme, and lemon zest and juice. Coat the breasts all over with the marinade, then season on both sides with salt. Generously coat the skin with the pepper and coriander, pressing them firmly against the skin so they adhere. Transfer to a plate and refrigerate uncovered for at least 1 hour or up to 4 hours. Let come to room temperature for 30 minutes before grilling.

To prep the turnips, trim off the turnip tops, leaving a short tuft of the stems attached. Strip the turnip leaves from the stems and reserve the leaves. Peel the turnips and cut in half through the stem end. If the turnips are big, cut into quarters or sixths. Set aside.

continued . . .

WINE: With the earthy, spice, and red fruit notes, a Mourvèdre, especially one from Bandol, is a fantastic accompaniment to the pepper and coriander.

Prepare a charcoal or gas grill for direct cooking over medium to medium-high (350° to 375°F) heat. Grill the duck breasts, skin side down, moving the duck as needed to avoid flare-ups from the dripping fat, until the skin is nicely browned, about 10 minutes. Turn and grill on the meat side until the duck is cooked to medium-rare, 3 to 4 minutes longer. An instant-read thermometer inserted into the thickest part of a breast should register 130°F. Transfer to a cutting board and let rest for 5 to 10 minutes.

While the duck is resting, cook the turnips. Add the slices to a large frying pan and season with salt, drizzle with oil, and add enough water to cover the bottom of the pan. Place over medium heat, bring to a simmer, and cook until the water has reduced and the turnips are glazed with the oil and fork-tender, about 5 minutes.

Meanwhile, bring a small saucepan half full of salted water to a boil over high heat. Add the reserved turnip leaves and boil until tender, 4 to 5 minutes. Drain well, set aside to cool, and then squeeze the excess water out of the leaves. Chop the leaves and add to the glazed turnips.

To serve, thinly slice the duck breasts crosswise. Divide the duck breast slices evenly among 4 plates. Mound the turnips and greens alongside the duck, then top each portion with some pickled cherries. Serve at once.

GLAZED JOCHUNG DUCK BREASTS

with rice porridge

CHEF JUNSOO BAE

Chef Junsoo Bae's SSAL is a contemporary Korean restaurant in San Francisco. *Ssal* means "rice" in Korean, and this rice porridge is a standout in this cookbook. It is adapted from Junsoo's version, which uses a whole dry-aged duck. When I tested it, I let the breasts age in the fridge for five days, which not only developed their flavor but also meant I did not have to render their fat before sliding them under the broiler. *Jochung* is a naturally sweetened Korean brown rice syrup that gives the duck a beautiful glaze and flavor. You can use this rice syrup in other recipes in place of corn syrup for a nutty, aromatic change. Starting the porridge with day-old rice will give it that straight-out-of-the-restaurant texture. The rice dries out a bit in the refrigerator, so when it is cooked again, it keeps its structure better.

Jochung Duck Breasts

4 duck breasts
Kosher salt for sprinkling, plus ⅓ cup
3 quarts water
⅓ cup mochiko (sweet rice) flour
⅓ cup distilled white vinegar
¼ cup Korean brown rice syrup, preferably jochung

Rice Porridge

1 tablespoon rendered duck fat (page 32) or olive oil
½ cup peeled and chopped carrot
½ cup chopped yellow onion
½ cup chopped green onions, white and green parts
8 cups basic duck stock (page 44), plus more if needed
2 cups cooked short-grain white rice, preferably Koshihikari
½ cup chopped duck gizzards confit (page 33) or duck leg confit (page 35), optional
Kosher salt and freshly ground black pepper
1 tablespoon toasted sesame oil
2 tablespoons chopped fresh chives

Makes 4 to 6 servings

WINE: The rice syrup is both sweet and delicate, so an oily white, like a Grechetto from Italy, will enhance the flavors and balance them with its nice acidity.

To prepare the duck breasts, arrange them, skin side up, in a single layer on a plate or small sheet pan. Sprinkle the skin on each breast with salt. Refrigerate uncovered for 3 to 5 days to dry the skin.

To cook the duck breasts, in a 4-quart saucepan or pot, combine the water, the ⅓ cup salt, the flour, and vinegar and bring to a boil over medium-high heat, stirring to dissolve the salt and blend all the ingredients. Add a duck breast to the boiling liquid and blanch for 10 seconds. Using tongs, transfer the breast to a plate. Repeat with the remaining breasts, blanching them one at a time the same way. The duck breasts will be coated with a slurry from the blanching liquid.

Position an oven rack on the lowest rung in the oven and preheat the broiler. Place a wire rack on a sheet pan. Brush the skin side of each duck breast with the rice syrup and arrange the duck breasts, skin side up, on the rack.

Place the sheet pan under the broiler on the bottom rack and broil the breasts until they render as much fat as possible and the skin turns golden brown, 10 to 15 minutes. The longer the duck was refrigerated to dry the skin, the less time it will take to render the fat. The duck is ready when an instant- read thermometer inserted into the thickest part of a breast registers 135° to 140°F. Let the duck rest for 20 minutes before serving.

While the duck is cooking and resting, make the porridge. In a large frying pan over low heat, warm the duck fat. Add the carrot, yellow onion, and green onions and cook, stirring, until the vegetables are tender but not browned, about 15 minutes. Add the stock and rice, stir in the gizzard confit (if using), and season with salt and pepper. Raise the heat to medium and bring to a simmer, then turn down the heat to low and cook until the rice is tender, about 20 minutes. If the porridge dries out, add more stock as needed. Remove from the heat and stir in the sesame oil and chives. Taste and adjust the seasoning with salt if needed. Cover to keep warm until serving.

To serve, cut the duck breast crosswise into thin slices. Divide the porridge among shallow bowls and top with the sliced duck, dividing it evenly. Serve right away.

ROASTED MAPLE-GLAZED DUCK
with butternut squash hash

CHEF DUSTIN VALETTE

From chef Dustin Valette: "I love making this dish for the holidays or when it's just cold outside and the family gets together to cook and to share one another's company. Sit back, sip some amazing wine, and enjoy the beautiful aromas this dish creates as it roasts in the oven!" I couldn't agree more! This dish is ideal if you're having a smaller holiday celebration. It's important to use real maple syrup, not imitation.

Roasted Maple-Glazed Duck
1 whole duck
1 teaspoon extra-virgin olive oil
Kosher salt and freshly ground black pepper
1 bunch fresh thyme
¼ cup pure maple syrup

Butternut Squash Hash
½ cup dried currants
1 cup boiling water
2 tablespoons extra-virgin olive oil
1 small butternut squash, about 1½ lb, peeled, halved, seeded, and cut into ½-inch cubes
Kosher salt and freshly ground black pepper
4 tablespoons unsalted butter, cut into pieces
2 shallots, finely chopped
⅔ cup raw pepitas, lightly toasted in a dry pan

About ¼ cup (2 oz) grape must (violette) mustard or your favorite sweet-spicy mustard

Makes 4 to 6 servings

WINE: A delicious Syrah—full bodied with medium acidity and tannin—balances the slight sweetness of the maple syrup and butternut squash.

To roast the duck, preheat the oven to 425°F. Set a rack in a roasting pan. Rub the outside of the duck all over with the oil. Season the outside and the cavity of the duck with salt and pepper. Place the thyme in the cavity. Place the duck, breast side up, on the rack in the roasting pan. Tie the legs together with kitchen twine (or truss the whole duck).

Roast the duck for 15 minutes. Remove the duck from the oven and, using a pastry brush, brush the outside of the duck all over with the maple syrup. Return the duck to the oven and continue to roast until the skin is browned and crisp and an instant-read thermometer inserted into the thickest part of the duck (not touching bone) registers 145°F, about 30 minutes longer.

When the duck is nearly ready, make the butternut squash hash. In a small heatproof bowl, combine the currants with the boiling water (to cover) and set aside to plump. In a large frying pan over medium heat, warm the oil. Add the squash, season with salt and pepper, and cook, stirring occasionally, until golden brown and tender, 10 to 15 minutes. Add the butter and stir until melted. Add the shallots and cook, stirring, until tender, about 3 minutes. Drain the currants and add to the pan along with the pepitas and mix well. Remove from the heat and taste and adjust the seasoning with salt and pepper if needed. Cover to keep warm.

To carve the duck, cut away the whole leg (thigh and drumstick) in one piece, then cut between the thigh and drumstick to separate them. Cut along the side of the breastbone to separate the meat from the breastbone, then cut along the rib cage to remove the breast. Repeat to remove the whole leg and breast on the opposite side and split the thigh and drumstick. Slice the breast and thigh into medium-thick slices; each should yield 4 to 5 pieces.

To assemble each serving, on a warmed individual plate, make a "swoosh" of the mustard and place a scoop of the squash hash in the center. Arrange some of the duck around the hash and serve.

ROASTED DUCK AND RED WINE–BRAISED CABBAGE

with poached pears and apple-brandy sauce

CHEFS WALTER MANZKE AND JOE GARCIA

Chef Walter Manzke has been using our Liberty Ducks at République, his flagship Los Angeles restaurant, since its opening. In 2021, he opened Bicyclette, an ode to French bistro culture. Chef Joe Garcia joined him in the kitchen and helped develop this delectable duck leg dish. My husband and I have dear friends who are Danish, and every year on November 11, we celebrate Mortensaften—Saint Martin's Day—with them. It's now mostly just an excuse to be together with friends and family. Traditionally, goose is served, but the dinner has evolved to make duck the center of the meal, with braised cabbage served alongside. This dish from the Bicyclette team reminds me so much of those meals, often the unofficial kickoff to our holiday season.

Roasted Duck Legs
6 duck legs
1 tablespoon kosher salt
1 teaspoon ground black pepper
1 teaspoon dried thyme
1 teaspoon dried basil

Braised Cabbage
2 tablespoons unsalted butter
½ medium yellow onion, chopped
Kosher salt
4 garlic cloves, diced
1 medium head red cabbage, cored and shredded
1½ cups red wine
¾ cup basic duck stock (page 44)
1 tablespoon red wine vinegar
1 tablespoon sugar
¼ teaspoon ground cinnamon
¼ teaspoon ground cloves

Apple-Brandy Sauce
1 tablespoon black peppercorns
⅓ cup brandy or Cognac
1 shallot, sliced
1½ cups apple juice, preferably Gravenstein
2 tablespoons unsalted butter, at room temperature
2 tablespoons all-purpose flour
2 cups basic duck stock (page 44), heated
1 fresh thyme sprig
1 bay leaf
1 teaspoon sherry vinegar
1 teaspoon apple cider vinegar

To prepare the duck legs, season them all over with the salt, pepper, thyme, and basil and then roast them according to the directions on page 36.

While the legs are roasting, prepare the cabbage. In a large sauté pan with a lid, melt the butter over medium heat. Add the onion and a pinch of salt and cook, stirring occasionally, until nearly translucent, 5 to 7 minutes. Add the garlic and continue to cook, stirring, until the onion and garlic are translucent, 3 to 4 minutes longer. Add the cabbage and an additional pinch of salt and sweat the cabbage, covered, until wilted, about 2 minutes. Add the red wine, stock, wine vinegar, sugar, cinnamon, and cloves, mix well, and lower the heat to a simmer. Cover the pan and simmer, stirring occasionally, until the cabbage is completely tender, about 1 hour.

To make the sauce, in a dry frying pan over medium heat, toast the peppercorns, shaking the pan often, until fragrant, about 5 minutes. Add the brandy and reduce until the pan is nearly dry. Add the shallot and apple juice and continue to cook, stirring occasionally, until reduced to a thick glaze, about 30 minutes.

While the sauce is reducing, in a small bowl, combine the butter and flour and work them together with a fork until the flour is completely incorporated with the butter (known as a beurre manié). When the sauce is reduced to a thick glaze, add the stock, thyme sprig, bay leaf, and butter mixture, whisking well to prevent any lumps from forming, Then simmer gently, stirring occasionally, for 15 minutes longer to rid the sauce of the raw flour taste.

Strain the mixture through a fine-mesh sieve set over a small saucepan and season with the sherry and cider vinegars to ensure a good balance of sweet and acidic notes. Taste and adjust the seasoning with salt if needed.

To poach the pears, in a wide saucepan over medium-high heat, combine the white wine and water and bring to a boil. Whisk the sugar into the boiling liquid. Reduce the heat to medium-low, add the pear halves to the liquid and gently simmer until fork-tender, 10 to 15 minutes. Using a slotted spoon, transfer the pears to a plate and discard the poaching liquid. In a large sauté pan over medium heat, melt the butter. When the butter is hot, add the pear halves, cut side down, and sauté, spooning the butter over the top, until they are browned and caramelized on one side, about 5 minutes. Remove from the heat.

To serve, reheat the sauce over low heat until hot. Spoon the cabbage onto the center of 6 individual plates, dividing it evenly. Place a warm duck leg on top of each mound of cabbage and set a pear half on the side, then drizzle the sauce over the top and and serve.

Poached Pears
2 cups white wine
2 cups water
1 tablespoon sugar
3 ripe but firm pears, such as Bosc or Anjou, peeled, halved, and cored
2 tablespoons unsalted butter

Makes 6 servings

WINE: A southern Italian Aglianico, with its notes of white pepper and black cherry, will complement the bold flavors in this dish. Try to find one with age, and you'll be rewarded!

CHAPTER SIX

DESSERTS

DUCK FAT CARAMELS

SARA MORGENSTERN

Sara Morgenstern, who is a great friend of our farm, comes from a family with a rich history in candy-making and especially in these caramels. Around 1900, in Sterling, Illinois, her great-grandfather worked in his uncle Charlie's candy store. Uncle Charlie developed a caramel recipe and would send out his nephew to sell the caramels at circuses and fairs, which earned the young man the nickname "Gigs," from turning up at all the gigs in town. Since then, the family has been passing the caramel recipe down through the generations. Sara's grandfather John taught Sara and her mother, Carol, how to make the recipe, and every Christmas it has been a tradition for the parents to make the caramels while the children help wrap the individual candies. Sara reworked the recipe to use duck fat instead of butter, and the result is a luscious caramel. Don't skip the finish of Maldon salt, as it ties everything together in one perfect bite. We're honored to have a century-old tradition find its way into this cookbook.

Unsalted butter or neutral oil, for the pan
½ cup rendered duck fat (page 32)
½ cup heavy cream
1 cup sugar
¼ cup light corn syrup
3 tablespoons water
½ teaspoon coarse sea salt
Flaky sea salt, such as Maldon, for garnish (optional)

Makes about 60 caramels

WINE: Nutty and rich, a Pedro Ximenez sherry will elevate these caramels from a sweet snack to a full dessert.

Line the bottom and sides of an 8-inch square baking pan with parchment paper, allowing the parchment to overhang the sides of the pan by about 2 inches. Lightly butter the paper.

In a small saucepan over low heat, combine the duck fat and heavy cream and cook, stirring with a whisk, until the duck fat has liquefied and the cream and fat are blended, then remove from the heat (if they later separate at any point, they can be easily recombined by whisking again).

In another small saucepan with a tight-fitting lid, combine the sugar, corn syrup, and water and stir gently. Work carefully, as you want to "moisten" the sugar without splashing it up the sides of the pan. Place over medium-high heat and bring to a boil without stirring. Cover the pan for 1 minute to remove any sugar crystals that may be stuck to the pan sides.

Remove the lid and attach a candy thermometer to the side of the pan so the tip extends into the sugar mixture without touching the pan bottom. Continue to boil, swirling the pan occasionally for even cooking, until the sugar melts, turns caramel brown, and the thermometer registers 320°F, 5 to 10 minutes.

With the pan still over the heat, using a whisk, immediately stir in 2 to 3 tablespoons of the duck fat mixture, working carefully and gently, as the sugar mixture can splatter and spit. Once the first addition is fully incorporated, add another 2 to 3 tablespoons of the mixture the same way. Continue to add the duck fat mixture, 2 to 3 tablespoons at a time, until all of it is fully incorporated in the sugar mixture. The process will cause the temperature of the mixture to drop, so continue to cook until the mixture reaches 240°F, 5 to 10 minutes. Remove the pan from the heat. Add the coarse sea salt and stir gently to combine.

Pour the hot caramel into the prepared baking pan and place the pan on a wire rack to cool. After 15 to 20 minutes, sprinkle the top evenly with flaky salt, if using. Let the caramel sheet sit until it has cooled to room temperature and is set, about 1 hour.

Using the parchment paper, lift the caramel sheet out of the pan and transfer it to a cutting board. Using a large chef's knife, cut the sheet into rectangles each about ½ by 1½ inches or into 1-inch squares. Wrap each caramel in a small square of parchment or waxed paper or plastic wrap.

DUCK FAT PIE DOUGH

KIM LAIDLAW

I am notoriously bad at making any kind of dough that requires a precise hand. Whether it is pasta, pizza, or pie dough, it always ends up in a crumple on the countertop, with me sitting on the floor in a similarly crumpled, frustrated state, much like someone listening to a Taylor Swift breakup song under the shower turned on full blast. Dough is my absolute kryptonite in the kitchen. Luckily, our recipe editor Kim Laidlaw is an absolute expert. Inspired by cookbook writer Paula Wolfert, Kim developed this tender, flaky, delicate pie dough that can be used whenever you need a great pie dough. Make sure to keep the dough very cold. If it starts to warm when you're rolling it out, return it to the refrigerator to chill until it firms up slightly.

2½ cups all-purpose flour
½ teaspoon fine sea salt
1 tablespoon sugar (omit for a savory pie)
½ cup plus 2 tablespoons very cold unsalted butter, cut into cubes
6 tablespoons very cold rendered duck fat (page 32), cut into pieces
1 large egg yolk
5 tablespoons ice-cold water, plus more if needed

Makes enough for one 9-inch double-crust pie, two 9-inch single-crust pies, or 8 individual galettes or hand pies

In a food processor, combine the flour, salt, and sugar (if using) and pulse just to mix. Scatter the butter and duck fat over the flour mixture and pulse until the mixture looks like coarse bread crumbs. In a small bowl, whisk together the egg yolk and water. Pour the egg mixture over the flour mixture, then process just until the dough starts to come together in a rough mass. Add a little more water if the dough appears dry and doesn't press together.

Dump the dough onto a work surface and press it into a thick disk (or divide the dough in half and press each half into a disk). Wrap tightly in plastic wrap and refrigerate until well chilled, at least 1 hour or up to 1 day, or freeze for up to 1 month.

GRAVENSTEIN APPLE MINI GALETTES

KIM LAIDLAW

Quite simply, this wouldn't be a book about a Sonoma County product if it didn't include another Sonoma County favorite: Gravenstein apples. Gravensteins were once heavily planted around Sebastopol. As that land became more valuable for vineyards, and as the packing plants disappeared, the apples started to become less and less available. Thankfully in 2005, Slow Food Russian River was able to declare Gravensteins a heritage food, ensuring they wouldn't disappear completely. The Gravenstein, which is tart with just a touch of honey-like sweetness, is the perfect baking apple. These mini galettes are fun as single servings, but you can also roll out the dough into a single round for a full-size galette.

Line 2 large sheet pans with parchment paper. On a lightly floured work surface, using a floured rolling pin, roll out the dough into a round about ⅛ inch thick (if the dough tears, gently press it back together). Using a 6-inch round cutter (or a plate or bowl 6 inches in diameter), cut out 8 rounds, gathering up the scraps, pressing them together, and rerolling the dough as needed. Transfer the rounds to the prepared sheet pans, cover with plastic wrap, and refrigerate until chilled, at least 30 minutes.

While the dough chills, in a bowl, combine the apples, granulated and brown sugars, cinnamon, nutmeg, salt, and lemon juice and toss until the apples are evenly coated. In a large frying pan over medium-high heat, melt the butter. Add the apple mixture and cook, stirring occasionally, until the apples are crisp-tender and the liquid is syrupy, about 7 minutes. If the mixture becomes too dry (you want it to be a little syrupy), add a little water by the tablespoonful. Just before the end of cooking, taste and adjust the sweetness with more brown sugar if needed. Let cool to room temperature.

Preheat the oven to 375°F. Space the dough rounds out on a clean work surface. Set aside a sheet pan to use for baking. To shape each galette, place about ¼ cup of the apple filling on the center of a dough round, then spread the filling into an even layer, leaving a 1-inch border uncovered. Fold the 1-inch edge of the dough up and over the edge of the apple filling, gently pleating the dough as you go (if the dough cracks, gently press it back together). Gently press down on the edges of the galette to hold the dough in place. Brush the dough edges with the egg mixture. Using a wide metal spatula, transfer the galette to the reserved sheet pan and repeat with the remaining dough rounds and filling, adding the galettes to the pan.

Bake the galettes until the crust is golden brown, about 25 minutes. Let cool on the pan on a wire rack for at least 15 minutes. Serve warm or at room temperature with ice cream.

1 recipe Duck Fat Pie Dough (page 182)
6 medium tart-sweet baking apples (about 2 lb total weight), such as Gravenstein, Pink Lady, or Gala, peeled, cored, and cut into ½-inch cubes
¼ cup granulated sugar
2 tablespoons dark brown sugar, plus more if needed
½ teaspoon ground cinnamon
½ teaspoon freshly grated nutmeg
½ teaspoon fine sea salt
Juice of ½ lemon
2 tablespoons unsalted butter
1 large egg beaten with 1 teaspoon water
Vanilla ice cream or whipped cream, for serving

Makes 8 mini galettes

WINE: A good Madeira, like a special reserve or extra reserve, brings out a nutty profile. For something lighter on its feet, a Moscato d'Asti is a great way to end a meal with this special dessert.

BERRY STREUSEL TART

with crème fraîche ice cream

KIM LAIDLAW

If available, use fresh local berries to elevate this delightful streusel tart. The addition of duck fat to the streusel adds richness. If you like, use half unsalted butter and half rendered duck fat. This tart is not overly sweet and has just the right amount of crumble, which is just the way I like it!

Crème Fraiche Ice Cream
4 large egg yolks
¾ cup sugar
1¼ cups heavy cream
1¼ cups whole milk
Pinch of fine sea salt
1 cup crème fraîche
2 teaspoons pure vanilla extract

½ recipe Duck Fat Pie Dough (page 182)

Duck Fat Streusel
¾ cup all-purpose flour
¼ cup sugar
⅛ teaspoon fine sea salt
3 tablespoons unsalted butter, melted
1 tablespoon rendered duck fat (page 32), melted
1 teaspoon pure vanilla extract

Mixed Berry Filling
2 cups (11 oz) fresh blueberries
1¼ cups (6 oz) fresh blackberries, halved if large
1⅓ cups (6 oz) fresh raspberries
¼ cup sugar
3 tablespoons tapioca starch

Makes one 9-inch tart and about 1 quart ice cream; 6 servings

WINE: A Muscat de Beaumes-de-Venise is fruity and honeyed, which is a nice balance to the tart berries. Because I can't resist bubbles, pink Prosecco (a newly allowed DOC classification) would be lovely.

To make the ice cream, set a medium bowl in a larger bowl of ice water. In a small heatproof bowl, whisk together the egg yolks and ¼ cup of the sugar. In a saucepan over medium heat, combine the cream, milk, remaining ½ cup sugar, and the salt and heat, stirring to dissolve the sugar, just until steaming. While whisking constantly, pour half of the hot cream mixture into the yolk mixture. Pour the yolk-cream mixture back into the saucepan, turn down the heat to low, and cook, stirring constantly with a whisk, until slightly thickened and an instant-read thermometer registers 185°F, about 10 minutes (do not let the mixture boil). Pour the mixture into the bowl set in the ice bath and let cool completely, stirring occasionally. Add the crème fraîche and vanilla and stir to mix. Cover the bowl and refrigerate for at least 2 hours or up to overnight.

Pour the base into an ice cream maker and freeze according to the manufacturer's directions. Transfer to a freezer-safe airtight container and freeze until firm, at least 1 hour.

Lightly spray a 9-inch tart pan with a removable bottom with cooking spray. On a lightly floured work surface, using a floured rolling pin, roll out the dough into a round about ⅛ inch thick and 12 to 13 inches in diameter. If the dough tears, gently press it back together. Gently roll the dough round around the rolling pin and unroll it over the prepared tart pan, gently easing it onto the bottom and up the sides of the pan. Trim the edges of the dough, leaving a 1-inch overhang. Fold the dough back onto itself down the side of the pan and press together to create a reinforced rim. Cover and refrigerate for at least 30 minutes or freeze for up to overnight.

Preheat the oven to 375°F. Line a sheet pan with parchment paper.

To make the streusel, in a bowl, combine the flour, sugar, and salt and stir together with a fork. Add the butter, duck fat, and vanilla and stir until evenly blended and the mixture is crumbly. Use right away, or cover and refrigerate for up to overnight. (If the streusel is refrigerated, remove it from the refrigerator 30 minutes before baking so it can soften slightly.)

To make the filling, in a bowl, combine the berries, sugar, and tapioca starch and toss to mix evenly. Pour the filling into the chilled tart shell, pressing it into an even layer. Top with the streusel, spreading it in an even layer. Place the tart pan on the prepared sheet pan.

Bake the tart until the filling is bubbly and the streusel and crust are golden brown, about 1 hour. Let cool in the pan on a wire rack for at least 30 minutes before serving. Remove the pan sides and carefully transfer the tart to a serving plate. Serve warm, at room temperature, or chilled with a scoop of ice cream on top of each slice.

DUCK EGG CUSTARDS

with plum compote

CHEF TONY FERRARI

Why make a baked custard with chicken eggs when you can make it with duck eggs? Duck eggs have larger yolks, which give these custards from chef Tony Ferrari a bigger, fluffier rise. The plum compote that accompanies them was inspired by one in Nancy Silverton's *Desserts* cookbook from 1986. You can substitute apricots, peaches, or nectarines for the plums, depending on what you find at the market. You will likely have compote left over. It's good served on pancakes or waffles the next morning or alongside Country-Style Pâté (page 56) or Duck Prosciutto (page 58) and crusty bread for lunch.

Duck Egg Custard

1 whole star anise or fresh bay leaf
2 cups heavy cream
6 tablespoons sugar
¼ teaspoon fine sea salt
6 duck egg yolks

Plum Compote

1 lb Santa Rosa plums, halved and pitted
2 tablespoons sugar
1 tablespoon rendered duck fat (page 32) or unsalted butter
¼ teaspoon ground cinnamon
¼ cup dark rum

Makes 6 servings

WINE: A nutty tawny port brings an interesting note to this custard. The recipe isn't overly sweet and has a bit of spice woven throughout, making this pairing a delight.

Preheat the oven to 350°F. If using the bay leaf, tear it to expose its essential oils. In a saucepan over low heat, combine the cream, 3 tablespoons of the sugar, and the star anise or bay leaf. Bring the mixture to a gentle simmer, then whisk in the salt. Remove from the heat and set aside to steep for 10 minutes.

While the cream is steeping, in a heatproof bowl, whisk together the egg yolks and the remaining 3 tablespoons sugar until the sugar is fully dissolved, about 2 minutes.

While whisking constantly, slowly add the warm steeped cream mixture to the egg yolk mixture. (Be careful not to add the cream mixture too quickly or it will cook the eggs.) Divide the custard evenly among six 6-oz (¾-cup) heatproof jars or ramekins. Place the jars or ramekins, not touching, in a roasting pan just large enough to hold them. Pull out the oven rack, place the pan on the rack, and pour boiling water into the pan just up to the level of the custard in the jars or ramekins. Bake the custards until set, 45 minutes to 1 hour. Carefully remove from the oven and let cool completely in the water bath, then remove from the roasting pan, cover, and refrigerate until chilled, at least 2 hours or up to 1 day.

While the custards are chilling, make the plum compote. Cut each plum half lengthwise into 4 slices, then cut each slice crosswise into 4 pieces. In a saucepan over medium heat, combine the plums, sugar, duck fat, and cinnamon and cook, stirring occasionally, until the fruit has softened, 3 to 5 minutes. The riper the fruit, the faster it will cook. Add the rum and continue to cook until the alcohol has burned off, 2 to 3 minutes. Transfer the compote to a bowl and let cool to room temperature before serving

Top each custard with some plum compote and serve.

SPECULOOS DUCK FAT COOKIES

CHEF SEAN Z. PAXTON

Europeans know these traditional cookies as spice cookies, Saint Nicholas cookies, or, as they are called here, *speculoos*. In the United States, they are known as that delicious cookie served on cross-country flights. No matter what you call them, these cookies of Belgian and Dutch (the Dutch spelling is *speculaas*) origin are typically made with butter. However, Sean Z. Paxton has created a new version of this famous treat that combines the traditional warming spices (cinnamon, ginger, cardamom, clove, star anise, and white pepper) with duck fat. The result is a mouthwatering modern cookie with Old World flair.

Spice Mix

1 tablespoon ground cinnamon, preferably Ceylon
1 teaspoon ground ginger
1 teaspoon fine sea salt, preferably pink Himalayan
½ teaspoon ground cloves
½ teaspoon ground cardamom
½ teaspoon ground white pepper
½ teaspoon ground star anise

Dough

1 cup all-purpose flour
½ cup fine almond flour
½ cup sugar
½ cup rendered duck fat (page 32), cold
1 large egg
2 tablespoons blackstrap or dark molasses

Makes 24 cookies

BEER: A Belgian quadrupel will bring an almost port-like quality to the pairing, and a Flanders red ale will add tartness, with rich notes of cherry, raspberry, and strawberry.

To make the spice mix, in a small bowl, whisk together all the ingredients until fully blended.

To make the dough, in a food processor, combine the all-purpose flour, almond flour, sugar, and the spice mix and pulse several times to mix evenly. Add the duck fat, egg, and molasses and pulse just until a dough forms. Be careful not to overprocess the dough or the cookies will be tough. Transfer the dough to an airtight container and refrigerate for at least 3 hours or up to overnight to allow the flour to hydrate and the dough to rest.

Position 2 oven racks in the center of the oven and preheat the oven to 350°F. Line 2 sheet pans with parchment paper.

Transfer the chilled dough to a lightly floured work surface. Roll out the dough into a large rectangle ⅛ to ¼ inch thick. Using a 3-inch round (or other shape) cookie cutter, cut out as many cookies as possible. (Alternatively, use a knife to cut other shapes such as squares, rectangles, or triangles.) Using an offset or thin metal spatula, transfer the cookies to the prepared sheet pans, spacing them about 1 inch apart. Gather up the scraps, press them together, reroll the dough, cut out more cookies, and add them to the pans.

Bake until the edges of the cookies are beginning to brown, 12 to 14 minutes. Let cool on the pans on wire racks for 5 minutes, then transfer the cookies to the wire racks and let cool completely. The cookies will keep in an airtight container at room temperature for up to 1 week.

DUCK FAT SHORTBREAD COOKIES

CHEF ROBERT "BUTTERCUP" NIETO

At Liberty Ducks, we've known chef Robert "Buttercup" Nieto for years, and we are always—and I mean always—impressed with his desserts. A master chocolatier, he creates some pretty incredible structures out of chocolate as well as delightfully flavored bonbons, which are available through his company, Fleur Sauvage Chocolates. He keeps it simple with these shortbread cookies, swapping in duck fat for butter. The result yields a cookie that's delicious as is, or if you're feeling adventurous in the kitchen, you might add a small amount of minced fresh lavender or rosemary to the dough.

- 2 cups plus 3 tablespoons all-purpose flour
- ¼ cup whole wheat flour
- 1 teaspoon kosher salt
- ¼ teaspoon ground white pepper
- ¾ cup rendered duck fat (page 32)
- ½ cup confectioners' sugar, sifted
- Smoked Maldon salt, for sprinkling (optional)

Makes 24 cookies

Preheat the oven to 350°F. Line a sheet pan with parchment paper.

In a bowl, stir together the all-purpose and whole wheat flours, salt, and white pepper, mixing well.

In a stand mixer fitted with the paddle attachment, combine the duck fat and sugar and beat on medium speed until soft and smooth. On low speed, add the flour mixture and mix until the dough comes together. Wrap the dough in plastic wrap and refrigerate until chilled, about 40 minutes.

On a lightly floured work surface, roll out the dough ¼ inch thick. Using a 2-inch round cutter, cut out as many cookies as possible. Using an offset or thin metal spatula, transfer the cookies to the prepared sheet pan, spacing them about 1 inch apart. Gather up the scraps, press them together, reroll the dough, cut out more cookies, and add them to the pan. If desired, lightly sprinkle the cookies with smoked salt.

Bake the cookies until lightly golden brown, about 12 minutes. Let cool on the pan on a wire rack for 5 minutes, then transfer the cookies to the rack and let cool completely. The cookies will keep in an airtight container at room temperature for up to 1 week.

DRINK: This sweet can be served with a different beverage depending on the season. In spring and summer, a Sauternes, tasting of peaches or apricots drizzled in honey, is a good match. In the fall and winter, a bourbon old-fashioned, with its iconic sweetness and hint of orange, is a great pairing.

DOUBLE CHOCOLATE DUCK FAT CABERNET CAKE

CHEF ALEXA SAYAD

There's decadence and then there's *duck*-adence. With duck fat worked into both the frosting and the cake, this towering dessert is, in my opinion, a meal in itself! Created by chef Alexa Sayad from Kendall-Jackson, this cake is for true chocolate lovers, and you must lean in to the over-the-top nature of it. The good news is that you need only a small slice, so it's a great dessert to make for a big dinner party.

Cabernet Cake
Cooking spray, for the pans
2 cups granulated sugar
1½ cups all-purpose flour
1 cup Dutch process cocoa powder
2 teaspoons baking soda
1 teaspoon baking powder
1 teaspoon kosher salt
3 large eggs
1 cup buttermilk
1 cup Cabernet Sauvignon, warmed
½ cup rendered duck fat (page 32), melted

Chocolate Frosting
2 tablespoons Cabernet Sauvignon
1 teaspoon pure vanilla extract
¼ teaspoon kosher salt
1 cup unsalted butter, at cool room temperature
¼ cup rendered duck fat (page 32), cold
1 cup Dutch process cocoa powder, sifted
2 cups confectioners' sugar, sifted

Whipped cream or vanilla ice cream and/or raspberries, for serving (optional)

Makes 8 to 10 servings

WINE: This rich chocolate cake calls out for a red dessert wine or even a slightly sweet sparkling Lambrusco from Italy. If you can find one, a Recioto della Valpolicella is a smashingly good choice.

To make the cake, preheat the oven to 350°F. Spray two 8-inch round cake pans with cooking spray.

In a large bowl, sift together the granulated sugar, flour, cocoa powder, baking soda, baking powder, and salt. Add the eggs and buttermilk and whisk to mix well. Add the wine and whisk until blended. Stir in the duck fat just until well mixed.

Divide the batter evenly between the prepared cake pans. Bake the cake layers until the tops are set and a toothpick inserted into the center of each layer comes out clean, 40 to 50 minutes. Let cool in the pans on wire racks for about 10 minutes, then invert the pans onto the racks, lift off the pans, turn the cake layers right side up, and let cool completely.

To make the frosting, in a small bowl, whisk together the wine, vanilla, and salt until the salt dissolves. Set aside.

In a stand mixer fitted with the paddle attachment, beat together the butter, duck fat, and cocoa powder on medium speed until smooth and lump-free. On low speed, slowly add the confectioners' sugar in two batches, stopping between the batches to scrape down the sides of the bowl with a rubber spatula.

Replace the paddle attachment with the whisk attachment. On high speed, beat in the wine mixture until the frosting is smooth and fluffy.

To frost the cake, place a cake layer, bottom side down, on a flat cake plate and scoop about one-third of the frosting onto the layer. Then, using an offset or icing spatula, spread the frosting in a thick layer to the edges. Top with the second cake layer, bottom side up. Scoop the remaining frosting onto the top of the cake and spread it in a thick layer over the top and down the sides, covering the cake with a smooth, even layer.

To serve, cut into wedges and accompany each slice with whipped cream and a handful of berries, if desired. The cake can be made up to 2 days in advance and stored in the refrigerator; let come to room temperature before serving.

CHEF BIOS

JOHN ASH opened his acclaimed John Ash & Co. restaurant in Santa Rosa in 1980, which continues today. He has cohosted *The Good Food Hour* on KSRO radio since 1987 and has hosted two shows on the Food Network. A sought-after teacher, John has written five cookbooks, is a two-time James Beard Award winner, and received the Julia Child Cookbook of the Year award in 1996. He has appeared in a variety of culinary publications and writes regularly for the *Santa Rosa Press Democrat*. A passionate supporter of sustainable food practices, John was a founder of the Chefs Collaborative and has worked closely with the Monterey Bay Aquarium Seafood Watch program.

VALENTÍN ATAYDE moved to the United States from Mexico City when he was fifteen years old and immediately found work in the food industry. After spending time in renowned Napa Valley restaurant kitchens and taking culinary classes, Valentín decided to pursue his dream of cooking what he knows best. In 2016, he cofounded the Mercadito Catering & Food Truck, which serves food that draws on the flavors and dishes of his childhood and the cuisine of Mexico City.

JUNSOO BAE, a native of South Korea, is the chef and co-owner of SSAL, a contemporary Korean restaurant in San Francisco. After attending The Culinary Institute of America, Junsoo started his professional kitchen career at Blue Hill at Stone Barns in Westchester County, New York, and then worked at Noma in Denmark, Gramercy Tavern in New York City, and The Restaurant at Meadowood in Napa Valley. Junsoo opened SSAL in early 2019 with his wife, Hyunyoung, who previously worked at The French Laundry, Bouley, and Gramercy Tavern.

DAVID BARZELAY turned his passion for hosting elaborate dinner parties from hobby into career after he was laid off from his job as a lawyer in 2009. He began his underground dining operation in his San Francisco apartment under the name Lazy Bear, an anagram of his surname. After moving to a warehouse, he refined his vision and cuisine and built a following. In 2014, David moved Lazy Bear aboveground to its current location in the city's Mission District. The restaurant was awarded a Michelin star in its first year of eligibility, with a second star added the following year.

RUPERT BLEASE moved to France with his family at the age of 10, where he was introduced to the cultural importance of sitting down at the dinner table. That experience shaped his goal as a chef: to create simple yet well-thought-out cuisine. After studying culinary arts and pastry in Toulouse, the British-born chef went on to work at Michelin-starred restaurants in France, England, and New York. During his tenure at Le Manoir aux Quatr'Saisons in Oxford, he met his future wife, Carrie. In 2011, the couple moved to San Francisco, then opened their own place, Lord Stanley, in 2015. In 2021, the space became Turntable at Lord Stanley, a place for up-and-coming chefs to collaborate and showcase their cuisines.

TAYLOR BOETTICHER and his wife, Toponia Miller, started Fatted Calf Charcuterie in 2003, with stores in Napa and San Francisco. The coauthor of two cookbooks on meat and charcuterie, Dallas-born Taylor has been cooking professionally since the age of eighteen. After graduating from The Culinary Institute of America, he took positions in a variety of food and wine operations, eventually landing at Berkeley's Cafe Rouge, where he worked in charcuterie for nearly five years. After apprenticing under master Italian butcher Dario Cecchini in Tuscany, he was further convinced to open his own store selling high-quality charcuterie using old-world techniques.

STUART BRIOZA began his culinary career at the age of fifteen, working in restaurants around the San Francisco Bay Area. He spent several years in restaurants in Illinois and Michigan, during which he was named one of *Food & Wine* magazine's 10 Best New Chefs of America. In 2004, he returned to the Bay Area and began working at the celebrated Rubicon restaurant, then was named a Rising Star Chef by the *San Francisco Chronicle*. In 2012, Stuart and his wife and business partner, pastry chef Nicole Krasinski, opened State Bird Provisions to much acclaim. Since then, they have launched The Progress (2014) and Anchovy Bar (2021), both in San Francisco.

DINO BUGICA is an Italian-born chef who, from an early age learned the ways of the Italian kitchen from his grandmother Mary and his mother, Diane. Dino went on to spend over ten years in Italy mastering the art of butchery and learning to use locally available ingredients in time-honored Italian recipes. In 2008, he opened Diavola in the small Sonoma County community of Geyserville, where he serves authentic Italian pizza, house-cured *salumi*, and more made from locally sourced meats, fish, and produce. In 2016, Dino launched the Geyserville Gun Club Bar & Lounge, which features classic cocktails and casual food.

MICHAEL CIMARUSTI is a Los Angeles–based executive chef and restaurateur who marries his appreciation of seafood with an advocacy for sustainable fishing practices. Michael credits his culinary career in part to fishing with his grandfather and learning about the cooking of his Italian heritage from his grandmother and great-grandmother. In 2005, Michael opened his first restaurant, Providence, which was awarded two Michelin stars in 2009, and in 2019, he was the named James Beard Best Chef: West. Today, Michael, his wife and business partner, pastry chef Cristina Echiverri, and co-owner and general manager Donato Poto operate four restaurants in Los Angeles: Providence, Connie & Ted's, Best Girl, and Il Pesce Cucina.

JOSIAH CITRIN has been an important force in the Los Angeles gourmet dining scene for more than a quarter century. Chef and owner of Santa Monica's celebrated Mélisse (two Michelin stars), the grill-centric Charcoal Venice, and the fast-casual Dave's Doghouse (in two locations), Josiah attributes his passion for food to growing up in Santa Monica and Venice with a mother who was a caterer, and a French grandmother who cooked family meals. After high school, he spent three years in Paris working at the highly acclaimed Le Vivarois and La Poste, where he deepened his knowledge and respect for traditional French cooking.

CHRIS COSENTINO, a graduate of Johnson & Wales University, began his culinary career at some of the country's best-known restaurants, including Red Sage in Washington, DC, and Chez Panisse in Berkeley. He is currently the co-owner of two restaurants, Acacia House in Napa Valley and Rosalie in Houston, Texas. Known for his whole-animal cookery and mastery of handcrafted cured meats, Chris hosts a weekly podcast and is a regular judge and competitor on television food shows. He is also a sponsored cyclist, competing in mountain bike races around the county, and participates in Chefs Cycle, a three-hundred-mile annual bicycle ride that raises funds and awareness for No Kid Hungry.

AMY DENCLER, a graduate of The Culinary Institute of America, worked at a number of East Coast restaurants where she was constantly amazed by the fresh California-grown vegetables and fruits that were delivered to the kitchens in the dead of winter. In 1995, she packed up her belongings and drove across the country to California, where she worked first at Oliveto in Oakland and then, in 1996, landed a job in the upstairs café at Chez Panisse. In 2000, she moved downstairs to the restaurant kitchen. After leaving for a time to work as a private chef, she returned to the downstairs kitchen, where she has worked ever since. When owner Alice Waters offered her the position of co-chef in 2016, she immediately said yes.

TRACI DES JARDINS has been an important part of the San Francisco food community for over three decades. Her diverse group of award-winning San Francisco eateries included Jardinière, which showcased her commitment to supporting local farms and ranches; Public House, the Commissary; Arguello; and School Night. A dedicated philanthropist, she sat on the board of La Cocina, a San Francisco nonprofit incubator that aids women of color and immigrant food entrepreneurs, for ten years; has worked closely with José Andrés's nonprofit World Central Kitchen; and continually supports No Kid Hungry and Share Our Strength.

ANDY DOUBRAVA has been cooking in restaurants for most of his life, with stops in Boston, New York City, and Los Angeles. He has always been attracted to simple, rustic food crafted from seasonal ingredients and especially enjoys working with preservation, fermentation, and "the primal uncertainty of wood-fired cooking." In 2015, Andy began working in the kitchen of Santa Monica's Rustic Canyon. Just four years later, he was named its executive chef.

DUSKIE ESTES is the executive director of Farm to Pantry, a nonprofit dedicated to rescuing produce from over 350 farms and backyards in Sonoma County for families facing food insecurity. Duskie and her husband, John Stewart, own Black Pig Meat Co, where they make dry-cured bacon and snout-to-tail products. For nineteen years, they were chef-owners of Zazu Kitchen + Farm in Sonoma County. At Zazu, they were dedicated to ethical purchasing from farmers, ranchers, and makers. On their farm, they raise pigs, goats, sheep, ducks, and chickens. Duskie has appeared on the Food Network and PBS and is a founding board member of BAR-C (Bay Area Ranchers Co-op).

TONY FERRARI knew from age thirteen, when he was hired for his first kitchen job, that he wanted to be a chef. After graduating from Johnson & Wales University, he worked at a handful of popular Miami restaurants before heading off to Europe to learn as much as he could about old-world culinary traditions. Ferrari then received a Jean-Louis Palladin Foundation grant to travel to Thailand and the US West Coast to study holistic farming, cooking, and agriculture. He spent ten years in San Francisco, where he operated Hillside Supper Club and Provender Coffee. Today, he resides in his hometown of Cincinnati, where he owns Fausto Restaurant and Mom 'n 'em Coffee & Wine with his younger brother, Austin.

JEREMY FOX is the chef-owner of three Santa Monica restaurants, Birdie G's, Rustic Canyon, and Tallula's. At Birdie G's—Birdie is the name of his daughter and G is for his grandmother Gladys, who has inspired him in matters of food and more since his Cleveland, Ohio, days—Jeremy makes dishes that draw on the regional cuisines of the United States and eastern Europe, with an emphasis on comfort food made with seasonal ingredients.

KEN FRANK moved to France with his parents as a teenager, where he discovered the glories of French cuisine. In 1977, at age twenty-one, Ken received national notice as chef of Southern California's La Guillotine restaurant. He was the opening chef of Michael's in Santa Monica, considered by some the Los Angeles birthplace of California cuisine, which he left in 1979 to open La Toque in West Hollywood. In 1998, he relocated to wine country and opened La Toque in Rutherford. After a successful ten-year run, he moved the restaurant to the Westin Verasa Napa, where he oversees the kitchen and visits with his many long-time guests in the dining room.

NEAL FRASER and his business partner and wife, Amy Knoll Fraser, own and operate the Los Angeles restaurant Redbird, where they serve modern American cuisine influenced by the city's cultural diversity. The couple also run the special events and performing arts venue Vibiana and the fast-casual restaurant Fritzi Coop in the Farmers Market at The Grove. Neal and Amy donate their time and talent to local charities, including Beefsteak, an annual event benefiting the Los Angeles Food Bank that the couple cofounded. A serious cyclist, Neal rides in the annual Chefs Cycle, a three-day fundraising endurance event that supports No Kid Hungry.

JOE GARCIA's first official cooking job was at El Encanto Hotel in his hometown of Santa Barbara, where he began working while attending culinary school. In 2006, at age twenty-three, he went to France, where he secured positions at two Michelin-starred restaurants, experiences that completely changed his perspective on food. After jobs in Ohio and Dubai, he landed at Thomas Keller's Bouchon Bistro in Beverly Hills and then at The French Laundry in Saint Helena, where he worked first as a butcher and then as sous chef. In 2021, he joined chef Walter Manzke of République to open Bicyclette Bistro in Los Angeles.

TANYA HOLLAND ran the popular Brown Sugar Kitchen in Oakland, California, for nearly fifteen years, which showcased her innovative take on modern soul food. Tanya holds a bachelor's degree in Russian language and literature from the University of Virginia and a grande diplôme from École de Cuisine La Varenne in Burgundy, France. She began her restaurant career in New York City in management and wine before moving into the kitchen. In 2003, after years of expanding her culinary knowledge in France and on the East Coast, she moved to the San Francisco Bay Area, where she served as creative director at Le Théâtre bistro in Berkeley before opening Brown Sugar Kitchen in 2008. Tanya is the author of two cookbooks, served as the host and soul food expert on the Food Network series *Melting Pot*, and competed in season fifteen of Bravo's *Top Chef*.

BRANDON JEW is the chef-owner of Mister Jiu's, a contemporary Chinese restaurant housed in an 1880s San Francisco Chinatown clinker-brick building, which he opened in 2016. In the kitchen, Brandon marries the local seasonal bounty of Northern California with classic Chinese techniques and flavors. His culinary training ranges from stints in Bologna, Italy, and Shanghai, China, to working behind the stove at several well-known Bay Area restaurants. He counts his late Cantonese grandmother, Ying Ying, among his most influential mentors. Mr. Jiu's was awarded a Michelin star within six months of opening, and Brandon has received two James Beard nominations for Best Chef: West, in 2018 and 2020.

MOURAD LAHLOU immigrated to the United States from Morocco at the age of seventeen to attend university. Homesick for his country's cuisine, Mourad, drawing on watching his mother cook and trips to food markets with his grandfather, taught himself how to re-create versions of his favorite Moroccan dishes using local ingredients and his own twists on traditional techniques. Today, he is the chef and founder of two popular San Francisco restaurants serving Moroccan-inspired food, Aziza, opened in 2001, and Mourad, which debuted in 2015. In 2009, Mourad won the Food Network's *Iron Chef* competition; two years later, he released his debut cookbook, *Mourad: New Moroccan*.

KIM LAIDLAW is an award-winning cookbook editor, best-selling author, and recipe developer, and the owner of Cast Iron Media. She is the coauthor of *The Nightmare Before Christmas Cookbook* and *Five Mary's Ranch Raised Cookbook* and the author of five cookbooks for Williams Sonoma. Her clients include Williams Sonoma, Weber, Kendall-Jackson—whose cookbook, *Season*, was the 2019 IACP Book of the Year—KitchenAid, and more. She is a former instructor at the San Francisco Cooking School, graduated from the California Culinary Academy, and was a baker at La Farine French Bakery in Oakland, California.

ZONGYI LIU is the owner and executive chef of Royal Feast restaurant in Millbrae, California. A master of traditional Sichuan and Beijing cooking, he was formerly executive chef of the Grand Hotel Beijing, where he oversaw the preparation of elaborate banquets for international dignitaries. The *San Francisco Chronicle* named Royal Feast one of the Top 100 Bay Area Restaurants in 2018 soon after its debut, and Michelin has continuously bestowed its Bib Gourmand award on the restaurant.

MARK MALICKI is a longtime Sonoma County chef who worked at Truffles and Iron Horse Vineyards in Sebastopol before opening his own restaurant, Cafe Saint Rose, in Santa Rosa, then moving it to Sebastopol. Since 2011, Mark has been cooking at Casino Bar & Grill, a seventy-two-year-old

bar that operates as a watering hole and de facto town square for the tiny California coastal town of Bodega. Owner Evelyn Casini contracts out food service to Mark and to other local chefs when he's off. At Casino, Mark focuses on fresh, local ingredients and changes the menu daily. Assisted by just a dishwasher and one server, he turns out some of the most honest and pure food in Sonoma County.

WALTER MANZKE began his fine-dining career in Los Angeles at Patina alongside famed chef Joachin Splichal. From there, he worked with two culinary legends in Europe, chefs Ferran Adrià and Alain Ducasse. After returning to the States, he opened Relais & Chateaux properties in the San Francisco Bay Area, then went back to Los Angeles to head up the kitchen at Bastide and later Church & State. Since then, Walter and his wife and business partner, Margarita Manzke, have opened four critically acclaimed Los Angeles restaurants, République, Petty Cash Taqueria, Sari Sari Store, and Bicyclette Bistro, as well as sixteen Wildflour bakeries in the Philippines.

KEVIN MEEHAN's first job in the restaurant world was in a fried chicken joint when he was a teenager. With the opening of Kali restaurant in Los Angeles in 2016, Kevin's quarter-century culinary career reached its apex. After spending years in some of the most highly regarded restaurant kitchens in the city, Kevin joined forces with long-time friend and professional colleague Drew Langley to launch this neighborhood restaurant offering modern cuisine in a modern setting. When Kevin is not in the kitchen, or finding inspiration from the food books he collects, he can be found spending time with his wife and twin girls or watching English Premier League football games.

PREETI MISTRY founded Juhu Beach Club in Oakland and Navi Kitchen in Emeryville, both now closed, after a long career in the culinary world. Born in London and raised in the United States, Preeti ran the kitchens at the de Young Museum in San Francisco and the Google headquarters in Mountain View before striking out on their own. They were a contestant on season six of *Top Chef* and have been featured in numerous publications, including *Food & Wine*, *Time*, *Bon Appétit*, the *Wall Street Journal*, and *Vogue India*. They were nominated as Best Chef: West by the James Beard Foundation twice, in 2017 and 2018.

SARA MORGENSTERN, who comes from a long line of bakers and candy makers, insists on making Jen her birthday cake every year—whether Jen wants one or not. Although not professionally trained, Sara worked at various bakeries in Florida before moving to the West Coast to join the California wine scene. She is the co-owner, with Jen, of Little Trouble Wine Company and is the director of operations for the Sonoma County–based Ruth Lewandowski Wines.

TONY NAJIOLA, the great-grandson of a Sicilian vegetable farmer, was born and raised in New Orleans. At seventeen, he got his first restaurant job; at twenty-one, he moved to Manhattan; and six years later, he was named executive chef at the Village Green, a small restaurant in the West Village. In 1991, he moved to San Francisco, where he was chef at Brasserie Savoie and then executive chef at Ernie's. He later headed up the kitchen at Ravenswood Winery in Sonoma County. In 2003, he opened his own restaurant, Central Market, in the Sonoma County town of Petaluma, which has a rich agricultural history. In 2011, he realized his dream of owning a farm, where he now raises livestock and grows organic produce that he serves at the restaurant.

ROBERT NIETO is a professional pastry chef, chocolatier, and baker, and the owner of Fleur Sauvage Chocolates, where he makes artistic chocolate bonbons, candy bars, chocolate tablets, and chocolate showpieces. He has competed in several international and national pastry and chocolate competitions, including the Mondial des Arts Sucrés, the Valrhona Chocolate Chef Competition (C3), and Pastry Live, and in December 2019, he was a member of the Bah Hum Bakers, the four-person team that won the Food Network's *Holiday Wars* dessert competition. In 2016, Robert was named one of the Top 10 Pastry Chefs in America by *Dessert Professional Magazine*.

NATE NORRIS joined Zuni Café as a line cook under chef-owner Judy Rodgers in 2004, working alongside her for nine years. Nate returned to Zuni as chef de cuisine in 2018 to work with chef-owner Gilbert Pilgram in his efforts to carry on the restaurant's tradition of excellence. In the kitchen, he focuses on both crafting beautiful and comforting food and creating the best possible workspace for the learning, growth, and development of young chefs.

ROLAND PASSOT grew up in Lyon, France, and began apprenticing in restaurant kitchens at the age of fifteen. Not long after, he became an assistant to Jean-Paul Lacombe, who headed up Léon de Lyon, a Michelin-starred restaurant known for its exquisite Lyonnaise cuisine and seasonal menus. He helped the now-legendary Pierre Orsi open his namesake restaurant, which quickly became another Lyon institution. Roland moved from France to Chicago to Dallas and finally to San Francisco, where, along with his wife, Jamie, he opened La Folie in 1988, his own groundbreaking restaurant that blended French tradition with modern creativity.

SEAN Z. PAXTON is primarily a self-taught chef whose main focus has always been on creating a quality product. From an early age, he sought to learn various cooking techniques and styles in order to prepare dishes from cuisines around the globe. In time, his experience and skill led him to work in restaurants, hotels, and catering and to writing for culinary magazines. Sean's recipes have been featured in a number of cookbooks, and he has archived many of his recipes online. He also shares his passion for food with others through teaching, podcasts, radio appearances, and even a movie.

MELISSA PERELLO spent childhood summers in the Texas kitchen of her grandmother Frances, where she was influenced by two culinary icons, Julia Child and Nathalie Dupree. Those lessons stuck, and in high school, she took a job in the kitchen of the local country club. She attended The Culinary Institute of America, then worked in top-flight restaurants in San Francisco before taking a hiatus from the industry to travel, with the goal of opening her own restaurant. In 2009, she launched Frances, naming it for her grandmother. It quickly gained critical praise, earning a Michelin star in 2011. Six years later, she opened her second San Francisco restaurant, Octavia, which was awarded a Michelin star in its first year.

TU DAVID PHU comes from a family that has been producing small-batch fish sauce on Phu Quoc island in southwest Vietnam since 1895. After stints at some of the Bay Area's top restaurants, including Acquerello and Chez Panisse, he began developing his own distinctive California-influenced Vietnamese cuisine, which he started serving at pop-up dinners in 2016, instantly garnering great reviews. A year later, the *San Francisco Chronicle* named him a Rising Star Chef. He competed in season fifteen of Bravo's *Top Chef* and was a host of ABC's *Taste Buds: Chefsgiving*. Tu finds opportunities to use food for meaningful work through cooking with incarcerated men in San Quentin, working with the Oakland Asian Cultural Center, and serving as an adviser to Real Food Real Stories, which works to democratize food culture.

GILBERT PILGRAM joined chef-owner Judy Rodgers as the second chef-owner of San Francisco's Zuni Café in 2006. At the time, Gilbert was an old friend of Judy's and had been a devoted customer of the restaurant, known for its rustic French- and Italian-influenced dishes, for two decades. Before the move to Zuni, he had worked for nineteen years at Chez Panisse, first as a cook and ultimately the chef, partner, and general manager. With the passing of Judy Rodgers in 2013, Gilbert became sole owner and executive chef of Zuni and has upheld Judy's goal of perfectionism and her vision of honest, local, seasonal food.

DOMINICA RICE-CISNEROS is a second-generation Mexican American whose family originally hails from Chihuahua. Born and raised in downtown Los Angeles, Dominica has sharpened her culinary skills over a thirty-year career that includes six years at Chez Panisse, stints at restaurant Daniel and the Four Seasons Hotel in New York City, and working with esteemed chef Antonio Rivera in Mexico City. She opened Cosecha, a casual Mexican café, in downtown Oakland's historic Swan's Market in 2008, shuttering it in 2021. That same year, she opened a second Mexican food destination, Bombera. In addition to being an accomplished chef, Dominica is a devoted community activist who works to put high-quality food in the hands of every person.

DAISY RYAN is a native of California's Santa Ynez Valley and graduated from the Culinary Institute of America. She worked at such storied East Coast institutions as Gramercy Tavern, Chef's Table at Brooklyn Fare, and Per Se, before returning to the West Coast with her husband, Greg, another Per Se alum. In Los Angeles, she helped open The LINE LA hotel in Koreatown before heading to Austin, Texas, to oversee the beverage program for McGuire Moorman Hospitality. Three years later, Daisy and Greg permanently relocated to California's Central Coast, where they opened Bell's, their first independent restaurant project.

ALEXA SAYAD is a pastry chef with over a decade of cooking and culinary training, who joined the kitchen team at Kendall-Jackson Wine Estate & Gardens in July 2021. Alexa oversees the dessert offerings and strives to source as many ingredients as possible from the winery's extensive gardens. All of the desserts are carefully paired with Kendall-Jackson wines for serving at both the winery and at off-site events.

GAVIN SCHMIDT's first restaurant job was as a dishwasher in a café on Bainbridge Island, Washington. In college, he continued working in restaurant kitchens but decided he was more interested in a culinary career than a chemistry degree, so he left school and moved to San Francisco in 2002, where he worked in several high-end restaurant kitchens. In 2007, he was named executive chef of the Campton Place hotel restaurant, one of the city's top fine-dining destinations, remaining for just a few years. He then relocated to San Diego for several years, before returning to San Francisco and, in 2016, becoming chef at The Morris, an unpretentious neighborhood bistro known for its world-class cuisine.

SARAH SCOTT is the executive chef of Opus One Winery in Oakville. A resident of Napa Valley since 1979, Sarah served as executive chef at Robert Mondavi Winery for fourteen years, overseeing its extensive wine and food programs. In 2006, she launched her own company, Sarah Scott Chef, which organized food and wine events for both companies and private clients in the San Francisco Bay Area. She coauthored *The Wild Table: Seasonal Foraged Foods and Recipes* with master forager Connie Green in 2010, and in 2016, she was inducted into the San Francisco chapter of Les Dames d'Escoffier.

ANTHONY SECVIAR is chef and partner at Protégé in Palo Alto. A graduate of the California Culinary Academy, he honed his culinary skills in some of the world's most renowned kitchens, including cooking under Ferran Adrià at El Bulli in Spain and Thomas Keller at The French Laundry in Napa Valley. In 2017, together with partner and master sommelier Dennis Kelly, Anthony opened Protégé, which offers new American cuisine in a casual fine-dining setting. Within just nine months of its first day, Protégé was awarded a Michelin star. When not in the restaurant kitchen, Anthony enjoys spending time with his wife and three children and skateboarding, boating, dirt biking, and exploring the redwood forest near his home.

ALON SHAYA is an Israeli-born chef who now calls New Orleans his home. In 2017, Alon, along with his wife, Emily, formed Pomegranate Hospitality, a restaurant group seeking "to create a space where meaningful relationships are created, community engagement prospers, and cultural differences are celebrated." While cooking at Dominica restaurant, he won two James Beard Awards: Best Chef: South (2015), and Best New Restaurant (2016). He was named one of the 50 People Who Are Changing the South by *Southern Living* magazine and one of the 50 Most Influential Jews in America by *The Forward*. Alon is also an active chef fundraiser for such organizations as No Kid Hungry, Alex's Lemonade Stand, DC Central Kitchen, and Martha's Table.

TRACEY SHEPOS CENAMI first worked as a dishwasher at summer camp, an experience that hooked her on the camaraderie and artistic expression of the kitchen. After high school, Tracey attended the California Culinary Academy and then, beginning in 2001, spent eight years as executive chef at Sonoma County–based Stark Reality restaurants, where she helped open new restaurants and create a catering division. Today, at Kendall-Jackson Wine Estate & Gardens, she specializes in wine country cuisine and artisanal cheeses. Tracey is a three-time winner of the Food Network's *Guy's Grocery Games* and is a coauthor of *Season: A Year of Wine Country Food, Farming, Family & Friends*.

CRAIG STOLL is a graduate of the Culinary Institute of America and Florida International University. After working in some of San Francisco's finest restaurants, the New York–born chef was awarded a scholarship to attend the International Culinary Institute for Foreigners in Turin, Italy. It was there, through an externship at Tuscany's one-Michelin-star restaurant Da Delfina, that he developed his culinary vision. He returned to San Francisco, and in 1998, along with his wife and business partner, Annie Stoll, opened Delfina, a neighborhood restaurant located in the Mission District that serves rustic Italian food prepared with local, seasonal ingredients. They followed their restaurant with Pizzeria Delfina, first next door and then in additional locations.

BRIAN STREETER has been highlighting the celebrated wines of Cakebread Cellars with seasonal menus using the finest ingredients Northern California has to offer since 1989. For inspiration, executive chef Brian draws on the cuisines of the Mediterranean, where food and wine have been linked for centuries. In addition to managing a team that develops recipes and prepares meals for winery guests, he leads hands-on cooking classes for gourmet yet approachable recipes to pair with Cakebread Cellars wines. A graduate of the New England Culinary Institute, Brian is the coauthor of *The Cakebread Cellars Napa Valley Cookbook* and *The Cakebread Cellars American Harvest Cookbook*.

KEN TAKAYAMA was born in Saitama, Japan, and grew up in Monterey Park, California. Ken went directly from high school into the restaurant business, getting his start at Kayo, a neighborhood restaurant where he learned traditional techniques for preparing sushi, tempura, and other Japanese classics. He credits his grandmother, an artist, with being an important influence on his creative career path. Josiah Citrin, chef-owner of Mélisse, rejected Ken twice before allowing him to work as an extern. Through persistence, his desire to improve, and years of on-the-job experience, Ken was eventually hired as a sous chef and then promoted to chef de cuisine at Mélisse, where he remains today.

JOSHUA TANGO worked at Michelin-starred restaurants in London, New York, and Los Angeles before finding his home in Napa Valley. His career has always been fueled by the desire to learn from the best in the industry, in the hope of continually expanding his creativity and improving every day. In 2020, he turned his attention to a new venture—Tango With Chef—which prepares fresh, restaurant-level pastas, sauces, and other expertly made foods that are delivered directly to homes across the San Francisco Bay Area.

STAFFAN TERJE is the chef and co-owner of the stylish Perbacco in San Francisco. When asked why a Swedish-born chef would choose to open an authentic Italian restaurant, he replied, "Italian food is the food that talks to me. You don't choose who you fall in love with. It just happens." Staffan grew up on his grandfather's farm outside of Stockholm, where he developed a passion for food. Surrounded by fresh produce and a family that loved to cook and eat, his decision to enroll in hotel and restaurant school directly after high school was an easy one. After traveling and working through the mid-1980s, he found himself in the San Francisco Bay Area and wine country—hotbeds for California cuisine—where he was able to apply his classic training to the bounty of the West Coast in some of the state's finest restaurants.

ASUKA UCHIDA is the chef and co-owner of Fish & Bird, a contemporary *izakaya* in Berkeley, California. Classically trained in both Japanese and French cooking techniques, Asuka offers a modern, sophisticated interpretation of traditional dishes that reflects current culinary trends in Japan. Asuka grew up in the restaurant business, helping in her family's restaurant as a young girl. After culinary school, she worked in many restaurants, some with Michelin stars, in cities ranging from Osaka, Sydney, and New York to San Francisco. At Fish & Bird, she pairs local, seasonal ingredients with high-quality foods from Japan to prepare her regularly changing menus.

PILAR VALDES was born in the Philippines, graduated from Sarah Lawrence College in the early 2000s, and then spent the first years of her professional life working with young people through educational workshops and video storytelling. In 2010, longing for both the cooking of her childhood and for relationships forged over shared meals, she switched careers and cofounded Kickshaw Cookery, a bespoke catering company known for its thoughtfully prepared menus made from carefully sourced ingredients. Pilar also currently works as a private chef; is the coauthor, with Drew Barrymore, of the best-selling *Rebel Homemaker*; and is a regular contributor to *The Drew Barrymore Show*.

DUSTIN VALETTE dreamed of opening his own restaurant for more than twenty years. While he waited, he practiced his craft in some of the most celebrated restaurants on the West Coast, including Aqua in San Francisco, Bouchon in Napa Valley, and VOX in Henderson, Nevada. The idea of Valette restaurant had been hatched while Dustin and his brother, Aaron Garzini, were sharing a glass of wine in their father's house overlooking the Alexander Valley. At the time, Aaron was establishing himself at John Ash & Co. in Santa Rosa as a server and sommelier and Dustin was in New York fine-tuning his culinary skills. Finally, in 2015, Valette restaurant opened its doors in the brothers' hometown of Healdsburg, with a menu that showcases the food producers and wine purveyors of Sonoma County.

JUSTIN WANGLER grew up in Asheville, North Carolina, and frequently visited his stepfather's restaurant, The Market Place, which inspired him to learn how to cook. By age ten, Justin was helping prepare meals in his mother's kitchen. He attended culinary school in Asheville and then worked in several restaurant kitchens in the South before moving to California wine country to take up a position at the Culinary Institute of America. In 2005, he joined Kendall-Jackson Wine Estates & Gardens, where his focus is farm-to-table cuisine that complements the Kendall-Jackson wines.

ACKNOWLEDGMENTS

First and foremost, I want to thank my dad, Jim Reichardt. Without him, there would be no Liberty Ducks. He is also responsible for instilling in me a lifelong passion for the food industry.

Plus, from day one, Dad has not only worked with all of the chefs (and plenty more!) in this book but has also mentored them, providing them with invaluable guidance. I am forever grateful for my dad's support, for his love, and for his passion for the food systems of California.

To my husband, Mike Dmytrenko, thank you for keeping me sane throughout both this cookbook journey and this crazy thing called life. There has never been a kinder and more compassionate partner—someone who listens and provides support in every way imaginable. This book wouldn't exist without your encouragement, and I couldn't ask for a better recipe taste tester.

To cookbook editor Kim Laidlaw, thank you for holding my hand and getting me through this process. You went above and beyond to make this dream a reality, and I am now proud to call you my friend.

Liberty Ducks would not exist without our employees, most of whom have been with us for well over a decade. Thank you Fidel, Fredy, Greg, Luis, Javier, and Jorge. This company is stronger because of all of you. We can never fully express our appreciation for your hard work on the farm, in the office, and out on deliveries. To my brother, Eric, and his gal Anna Clements, we are thrilled you've joined the team, kicking off 2022—the future is bright with you two.

To the publishing team at Cameron + Company—Chris Gruener, Suzi Hutsell, and Iain Morris—thank you for believing in our story and for your desire to share it with the world.

To photographer Jessica Fix: Wow, can you believe it? Who would have thought that a couple of kids on the preschool playground would not only stay in touch for over twenty-five years but also be able to collaborate on a book? Incredible! To recipe tester Sean Z. Paxton, thank you for not only rising to the occasion but for exceeding the call. To Lenora Evans, thank you for your encouragement on shoot days and your impeccable dishwashing skills; you are a wonderful person and our family is so thankful for you. And to food stylists Kim Kissling and Becca Martin, thank you for your exceptional skills in the kitchen. The food was both stunning in the images and gosh darn delicious!

Throughout the book, there are a few wine labels other than my own. To Sam Bilbro of Idlewild Wines, Jaimee Motley of Jaimee Motley Wines, Evan Lewandowski of Ruth Lewandowski Wines, and Mike Lucia of Rootdown Wine Cellars, thanks for sharing your wines when we photographed the book and for sharing your passions with me and the world.

To Charlie Pennes at White Bark Workwear, thank you for making us look oh-so professional for the cookbook shoot in our sustainably-made aprons.

And last but certainly not least, to our restaurants and our chefs. There are over fifty contributors in this book and another two hundred with whom we have created partnerships. By working with each and every one of you directly, we've established incredible relationships. We are thankful for your support throughout our thirty years.

INDEX

E

F

T

U

V

W

Z

CAMERON + COMPANY
149 Kentucky Street, Suite 7
Petaluma, CA 94952
www.cameronbooks.com

Publisher Chris Gruener
Creative Director Iain R. Morris
Art Director Suzi Hutsell
Managing Editor Jan Hughes
Editorial Assistant Krista Keplinger

Executive Editor Kim Laidlaw
Photographer Jessica Fix
Food Stylist Kim Kissling
Assistant Food Stylist Becca Martin

Additional photography: Courtesy of Reichardt family, pages 13–14

Page 15: Article "Julia Child tours Sonoma County" with accompanying photo by Jeff Kan Lee / *The Press Democrat*, published on April 15, 1992, page B1.

Library of Congress Cataloging-in-Publication Data available.

ISBN: 978-1-951836-61-0

10 9 8 7 6 5 4 3 2 1

Printed in China